AWS Certified Machine Learning - Specialty (MLS-C01) Certification Guide

Second Edition

The ultimate guide to passing the MLS-C01 exam on your first attempt

Somanath Nanda

Weslley Moura

AWS Certified Machine Learning - Specialty (MLS-C01) Certification Guide

Second Edition

Authors: Somanath Nanda and Weslley Moura

Reviewer: Patrick Uzuwe

Publishing Product Manager: Sneha Shinde

Senior-Development Editor: Ketan Giri

Development Editor: Kalyani S.

Presentation Designer: Shantanu Zagade

Editorial Board: Vijin Boricha, Megan Carlisle, Wilson D'souza, Ketan Giri, Saurabh Kadave, Alex Mazonowicz, Abhishek Rane, Gandhali Raut, and Ankita Thakur

First Published: March 2021

Second Edition: February 2024

Production Reference: 1280224

Published by Packt Publishing Ltd.
Grosvenor House
11 St Paul's Square
Birmingham
B3 1RB

ISBN: 978-1-83508-220-1

www.packtpub.com

Contributors

About the Authors

Somanath Nanda has 14 years of experience designing and building Data and ML products. He emphasizes implementing fault-tolerant system design practices throughout the software development lifecycle. He currently holds a prominent leadership position in the finance domain, actively shaping strategic decisions and executions and expertly guiding engineering teams to achieve success.

Weslley Moura has been developing data products for the past decade. At his recent roles, he has been influencing data strategy and leading data teams into the urban logistics and blockchain industries.

About the Reviewer

Patrick Uzuwe serves as the Chief Technology Officer (CTO) at Sparkrena, a company based in Sheffield, England, United Kingdom. In this role, he specializes in assisting customers in the design and development of cloud-native machine learning products. Driven by a passion for solving challenging problems, he collaborates with partners and customers to modernize their machine learning stack, integrating seamlessly with Amazon SageMaker. Dr. Uzuwe actively works alongside both business and engineering teams to ensure the success of products.

His academic background includes a Ph.D. in Information Systems, which he earned from The University of Bolton in Manchester, United Kingdom.

Table of Contents

3

AWS Services for Data Migration and Processing   51

4

Data Preparation and Transformation   75

5

Data Understanding and Visualization   115

6

Applying Machine Learning Algorithms   133

11

Preface

The AWS Machine Learning Specialty certification exam tests your competency to perform **machine learning** (**ML**) on AWS infrastructure. This book covers the entire exam syllabus in depth using practical examples to help you with your real-world ML projects on AWS.

Starting with an introduction to ML on AWS, you will learn the fundamentals of ML and explore important AWS services for **artificial intelligence** (**AI**). You will then see how to store and process data for ML using several AWS services, such as S3 and EMR.

You will also learn how to prepare data for ML and discover different techniques for data manipulation and transformation for different types of variables. The book covers the handling of missing data and outliers and takes you through various ML tasks, such as classification, regression, clustering, forecasting, anomaly detection, text mining, and image processing, along with their specific ML algorithms, that you need to know in order to pass the exam. Finally, you will explore model evaluation, optimization, and deployment and get to grips with deploying models in a production environment and monitoring them.

By the end of the book, you will have gained knowledge of all the key fields of ML and the solutions that AWS has released for each of them, along with the tools, methods, and techniques commonly used in each domain of AWS ML. This book is not only intended to support you in the AWS Machine Learning Specialty certification exam but also to make your ML professional journey a lot easier.

Who This Book Is for

This book is designed for both students and professionals preparing for the AWS Certified Machine Learning Specialty exam or enhance their understanding of machine learning, with a specific emphasis on AWS. Familiarity with machine learning basics and AWS services is recommended to fully benefit from this book.

What This Book Covers

Chapter 1, Machine Learning Fundamentals, covers some ML definitions, different types of modeling approaches, and all the steps necessary to build an ML product.

Chapter 2, AWS Services for Data Storage, teaches you about the AWS services used to store data for ML. You will learn about the many different S3 storage classes and when to use each of them. You will also learn how to handle data encryption and how to secure your data at rest and in transit. Finally, you will learn about other types of data store services that are also worth knowing for the exam.

Chapter 3, AWS Services for Data Migration and Processing, teaches you about the AWS services used to process data for ML. You will learn how to deal with batch and real-time processing, how to directly query data on Amazon S3, and how to create big data applications on EMR.

Chapter 4, Data Preparation and Transformation, deals with categorical and numerical features and applying different techniques to transform your data, such as one-hot encoding, binary encoding, ordinal encoding, binning, and text transformations. You will also learn how to handle missing values and outliers in your data, two important topics for building good ML models.

Chapter 5, Data Understanding and Visualization, teaches you how to select the most appropriate data visualization technique according to different variable types and business needs. You will also learn about AWS services for visualizing data.

Chapter 6, Applying Machine Learning Algorithms, covers different types of ML tasks, such as classification, regression, clustering, forecasting, anomaly detection, text mining, and image processing. Each of these tasks has specific algorithms that you should know about to pass the exam. You will also learn how ensemble models work and how to deal with the curse of dimensionality.

Chapter 7, Evaluating and Optimizing Models, teaches you how to select model metrics to evaluate model results. You will also learn how to optimize your model by tuning its hyperparameters.

Chapter 8, AWS Application Services for AI/ML, covers details of the various AI/ML applications offered by AWS that you need to know about to pass the exam.

Chapter 9, Amazon SageMaker Modeling, teaches you how to spin up notebooks to work with exploratory data analysis and how to train your models on Amazon SageMaker. You will learn where and how your training data should be stored in order to make it accessible through SageMaker and explore the different data formats that you can use.

Chapter 10, Model Deployment, teaches you about several AWS model deployment options. You will review SageMaker deployment options, creating alternative pipelines with Lambda functions, working with Step Functions, configuring auto scaling, and securing SageMaker applications.

How to Use This Book

This AWS Certified Machine Learning Specialty study guide explains each concept from the exam syllabus using realistic examples and comprehensive theoretical notes. The book is your go-to resource for acing the AWS Certified Machine Learning Specialty exam with confidence.

Online Practice Resources

With this book, you will unlock unlimited access to our online exam-prep platform (*Figure 0.1*). This is your place to practice everything you learn in the book.

> **How to access the resources**
>
> To learn how to access the online resources, refer *to Chapter 11, Accessing the Online Practice Resources* at the end of this book.

Figure 0.1 – Online exam-prep platform on a desktop device

Sharpen your knowledge of MLS-C01 concepts with multiple sets of mock exams, interactive flashcards, and exam tips accessible from all modern web browsers.

Download the Color Images

We also provide a PDF file that has color images of the screenshots/diagrams used in this book. You can download it here: `https://packt.link/ky8E8`.

Conventions Used

There are a number of text conventions used throughout this book.

`Code in text`: Indicates code words in text, database table names, folder names, filenames, file extensions, pathnames, dummy URLs, user input, and Twitter handles. Here is an example: "You will use the `detect_labels` API from Amazon Rekognition in the code."

A block of code is set as follows:

```
from sagemaker.predictor import Predictor
predictor = Predictor(endpoint_name='your-endpoint-name',
sagemaker_session=sagemaker_session)
predictor.predict('input_data')
```

Any command-line input or output is written as follows:

```
sh-4.2$ cd ~/SageMaker/
sh-4.2$ git clone https://github.com/PacktPublishing/ AWS-Certified-
Machine-Learning-Specialty-MLS-C01- Certification-Guide-Second-
Edition.git
```

Bold: Indicates a new term, an important word, or words that you see onscreen. For example, words in menus or dialog boxes appear in the text like this. Here is an example: "In **CloudWatch**, each **Lambda function** will have a **log group** and, inside that log group, many **log streams**."

> **Tips or important notes**
> Appear like this.

Get in Touch

Feedback from our readers is always welcome.

General feedback: If you have questions about any aspect of this book, mention the book title in the subject of your message and email us at customercare@packt.com.

Errata: Although we have taken every care to ensure the accuracy of our content, mistakes do happen. If you have found a mistake in this book, we would be grateful if you would report this to us. Please visit www.packtpub.com/support/errata, selecting your book, clicking on the Errata Submission Form link, and entering the details. We ensure that all valid errata are promptly updated in the GitHub repository, with the relevant information available in the Readme.md file. You can access the GitHub repository: https://packt.link/QFk6t.

Piracy: If you come across any illegal copies of our works in any form on the Internet, we would be grateful if you would provide us with the location address or website name. Please contact us at copyright@packt.com with a link to the material.

If you are interested in becoming an author: If there is a topic that you have expertise in and you are interested in either writing or contributing to a book, please visit authors.packtpub.com.

Share Your Thoughts

Once you've read *AWS Certified Machine Learning - Specialty (MLS-C01) Certification Guide, Second Edition*, we'd love to hear your thoughts! Scan the QR code below to go straight to the Amazon review page for this book and share your feedback.

https://packt.link/r/1835082203

Your review is important to us and the tech community and will help us make sure we're delivering excellent quality content.

Download a Free PDF Copy of This Book

Thanks for purchasing this book!

Do you like to read on the go but are unable to carry your print books everywhere?

Is your eBook purchase not compatible with the device of your choice?

Don't worry, now with every Packt book you get a DRM-free PDF version of that book at no cost.

Read anywhere, any place, on any device. Search, copy, and paste code from your favorite technical books directly into your application.

The perks don't stop there, you can get exclusive access to discounts, newsletters, and great free content in your inbox daily.

Follow these simple steps to get the benefits:

1. Scan the QR code or visit the link below:

https://packt.link/free-ebook/9781835082201

2. Submit your proof of purchase.

3. That's it! You'll send your free PDF and other benefits to your email directly.

1

Machine Learning Fundamentals

For many decades, researchers have been trying to simulate human brain activity through the field known as **artificial intelligence**, or **AI** for short. In 1956, a group of people met at the Dartmouth Summer Research Project on Artificial Intelligence, an event that is widely accepted as the first group discussion about AI as it's known today. Researchers were trying to prove that many aspects of the learning process could be precisely described and, therefore, automated and replicated by a machine. Today, you know they were right!

Many other terms appeared in this field, such as **machine learning** (**ML**) and **deep learning** (**DL**). These sub-areas of AI have also been evolving for many decades (granted, nothing here is new to the science). However, with the natural advance of the information society and, more recently, the advent of **big data** platforms, AI applications have been reborn with much more applicability – power (because now there are more computational resources to simulate and implement them) and applicability (because now information is everywhere).

Even more recently, cloud service providers have put AI in the cloud. This helps all sizes of companies to reduce their operational costs and even lets them sample AI applications, considering that it could be too costly for a small company to maintain its own data center to scale an AI application.

An incredible journey of building cutting-edge AI applications has emerged with the popularization of big data and cloud services. In June 2020, one specific technology gained significant attention and put AI on the list of the most discussed topics across the technology industry – its name is ChatGPT.

ChatGPT is a popular AI application that uses large language models (more specifically, **generative pre-trained transformers**) trained on massive amounts of text data to understand and generate human-like language. These models are designed to process and comprehend the complexities of human language, including grammar, context, and semantics.

Large language models utilize DL techniques (for example, deep neural networks based on transformer architecture) to learn patterns and relationships within textual data. They consist of millions of parameters, making them highly complex and capable of capturing very specific language structures.

Such mixing of terms and different classes of use cases might get one stuck on understanding the practical steps of implementing AI applications. That brings you to the goal of this chapter: being able to describe what the terms AI, ML, and DL mean, as well as understanding all the nuances of an ML pipeline. Avoiding confusion about these terms and knowing what exactly an ML pipeline is will allow you to properly select your services, develop your applications, and master the AWS Machine Learning Specialty exam.

Making the Most Out of this Book – Your Certification and Beyond

This book and its accompanying online resources are designed to be a complete preparation tool for your **MLS-C01 Exam**.

The book is written in a way that you can apply everything you've learned here even after your certification. The online practice resources that come with this book (*Figure 1.1*) are designed to improve your test-taking skills. They are loaded with timed mock exams, interactive flashcards, and exam tips to help you work on your exam readiness from now till your test day.

> **Before You Proceed**
>
> To learn how to access these resources, head over to *Chapter 11, Accessing the Online Practice Resources*, at the end of the book.

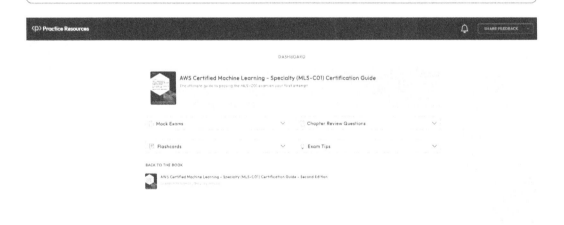

Figure 1.1 – Dashboard interface of the online practice resources

Here are some tips on how to make the most out of this book so that you can clear your certification and retain your knowledge beyond your exam:

1. Read each section thoroughly.

2. **Make ample notes**: You can use your favorite online note-taking tool or use a physical notebook. The free online resources also give you access to an online version of this book. Click the BACK TO THE BOOK link from the Dashboard to access the book in **Packt Reader**. You can highlight specific sections of the book there.

3. **Chapter Review Questions**: At the end of this chapter, you'll find a link to review questions for this chapter. These are designed to test your knowledge of the chapter. Aim to score at least **75%** before moving on to the next chapter. You'll find detailed instructions on how to make the most of these questions at the end of this chapter in the *Exam Readiness Drill - Chapter Review Questions* section. That way, you're improving your exam-taking skills after each chapter, rather than at the end.

4. **Flashcards**: After you've gone through the book and scored **75%** more in each of the chapter review questions, start reviewing the online flashcards. They will help you memorize key concepts.

5. **Mock Exams**: Solve the mock exams that come with the book till your exam day. If you get some answers wrong, go back to the book and revisit the concepts you're weak in.

6. **Exam Tips**: Review these from time to time to improve your exam readiness even further.

The main topics of this chapter are as follows:

- Comparing AI, ML, and DL
- Classifying supervised, unsupervised, and reinforcement learning
- The CRISP-DM modeling life cycle
- Data splitting
- Modeling expectations
- Introducing ML frameworks
- ML in the cloud

Comparing AI, ML, and DL

AI is a broad field that studies different ways to create systems and machines that will solve problems by simulating human intelligence. There are different levels of sophistication to create these programs and machines, which go from simple rule-based engines to complex self-learning systems. AI covers, but is not limited to, the following sub-areas:

- Robotics
- **Natural language processing (NLP)**
- Rule-based systems
- Machine learning (ML)
- Computer vision

The area this certification exam focuses on is ML.

Examining ML

ML is a sub-area of AI that aims to create systems and machines that can learn from experience, without being explicitly programmed. As the name suggests, the system can observe its underlying environment, learn, and adapt itself without human intervention. Algorithms behind ML systems usually extract and improve knowledge from the data and conditions that are available to them.

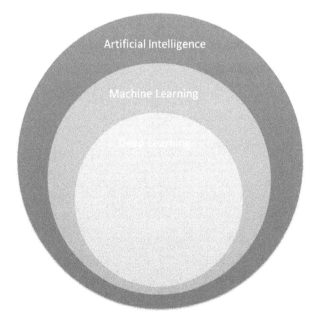

Figure 1.2 – Hierarchy of AI, ML, and DL

You should keep in mind that there are different classes of ML algorithms. For example, decision tree-based models, probabilistic-based models, and neural network models. Each of these classes might contain dozens of specific algorithms or architectures (some of them will be covered in later sections of this book).

As you might have noticed in *Figure 1.2*, you can be even more specific and break the ML field down into another very important topic for the Machine Learning Specialty exam: deep learning, or DL for short.

Examining DL

DL is a subset of ML that aims to propose algorithms that connect multiple layers to solve a particular problem. The knowledge is then passed through, layer by layer, until the optimal solution is found. The most common type of DL algorithm is deep neural networks.

At the time of writing this book, DL is a very hot topic in the field of ML. Most of the current state-of-the-art algorithms for machine translation, image captioning, and computer vision were proposed in the past few years and are a part of the DL field (GPT-4, used by the ChatGPT application, is one of these algorithms).

Now that you have an overview of types of AI, take a look at some of the ways you can classify ML.

Classifying supervised, unsupervised, and reinforcement learning

ML is a very extensive field of study; that's why it is very important to have a clear definition of its sub-divisions. From a very broad perspective, you can split ML algorithms into two main classes: supervised learning and unsupervised learning.

Introducing supervised learning

Supervised algorithms use a class or label (from the input data) as support to find and validate the optimal solution. In *Table 1.1*, there is a dataset that aims to classify fraudulent transactions from a financial company.

Day of the week	Hour	Transaction amount	Merchant type	Is fraud?
Mon	09:00	$1000	Retail	No
Tue	23:00	$5500	E-commerce	Yes
Fri	14:00	$500	Travel	No
Mon	10:00	$100	Retail	No
Tue	22:00	$100	E-commerce	No
Tue	22:00	$6000	E-commerce	Yes

Table 1.1 – Sample dataset for supervised learning

The first four columns are known as **features** or **independent variables**, and they can be used by a supervised algorithm to find fraudulent patterns. For example, by combining those four features (day of the week, EST hour, transaction amount, and merchant type) and six observations (each row is technically one observation), you can infer that e-commerce transactions with a value greater than $5,000 and processed at night are potentially fraudulent cases.

> **Important note**
>
> In a real scenario, you will have more observations in order to have statistical support to make this type of inference.

The key point is that you were able to infer a potential fraudulent pattern just because you knew, *a priori*, what is fraud and what is not fraud. This information is present in the last column of *Table 1.1* and is commonly referred to as a target variable, label, response variable, or dependent variable. If the input dataset has a target variable, you should be able to apply supervised learning.

In supervised learning, the target variable might store different types of data. For instance, it could be a binary column (yes or no), a multi-class column (class A, B, or C), or even a numerical column (any real number, such as a transaction amount). According to the data type of the target variable, you will find which type of supervised learning your problem refers to. *Table 1.2* shows how to classify supervised learning into two main groups: **classification** and **regression** algorithms:

Data type of the target variable	Sub data type of the target variable	Type of supervised learning applicable
Categorical	Binary	Binary classification
Categorical	Multi class	Multi classification
Numerical	N/A	Regression

Table 1.2 – Choosing the right type of supervised learning given the target variable

While classification algorithms predict a class (either binary or multiple classes), regression algorithms predict a real number (either continuous or discrete).

Understanding data types is important to make the right decisions on ML projects. You can split data types into two main categories: numerical and categorical data. Numerical data can then be split into continuous or discrete subclasses, while categorical data might refer to ordinal or nominal data:

- **Numerical/discrete data** refers to individual and countable items (for example, the number of students in a classroom or the number of items in an online shopping cart).

- **Numerical/continuous data** refers to an infinite number of possible measurements and they often carry decimal points (for example, temperature).

- **Categorical/nominal data** refers to labeled variables with no quantitative value (for example, name or gender).

- **Categorical/ordinal data** adds a sense of order to a labeled variable (for example, education level or employee title level).

In other words, when choosing an algorithm for your project, you should ask yourself: *do I have a target variable? Does it store categorical or numerical data?* Answering these questions will put you in a better position to choose a potential algorithm that will solve your problem.

However, what if you don't have a target variable? In that case, you are facing an unsupervised learning problem. Unsupervised problems do not provide labeled data; instead, they provide all the independent variables (or features) that will allow unsupervised algorithms to find patterns in the data. The most common type of unsupervised learning is **clustering**, which aims to group the observations of the dataset into different clusters, purely based on their features. Observations from the same cluster are expected to be similar to each other, but very different from observations from other clusters. Clustering will be covered in more detail in future chapters of this book.

Semi-supervised learning is also present in the ML literature. This type of algorithm can learn from partially labeled data (some observations contain a label and others do not).

Finally, another learning approach that has been taken by another class of ML algorithms is **reinforcement learning**. This approach rewards the system based on the good decisions that it has made autonomously; in other words, the system learns by experience.

You have been learning about approaches and classes of algorithms at a very broad level. However, it is time to get specific and introduce the term **model**.

The CRISP-DM modeling life cycle

Modeling is a very common term used in ML when you want to specify the steps taken to solve a particular problem. For example, you could create a binary classification model to predict whether the transactions from *Table 1.1* are fraudulent or not.

A model, in this context, represents all the steps to create a solution as a whole, which includes (but is not limited to) the algorithm. The **Cross-Industry Standard Process for Data Mining**, more commonly referred to as **CRISP-DM**, is one of the methodologies that provides guidance on the common steps that you should follow to create models. This methodology is widely used by the market and is covered in the AWS Machine Learning Specialty exam:

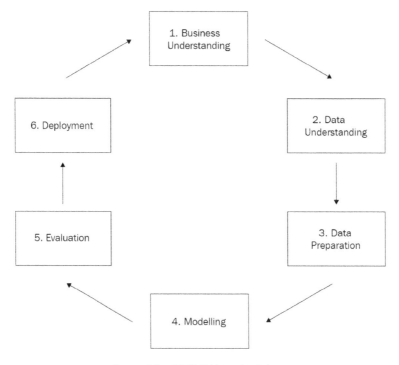

Figure 1.3 – CRISP-DM methodology

Everything starts with business understanding, which will produce the business objectives (including success criteria), situation assessment, data mining goals, and project plan (with an initial assessment of tools and techniques). During the situation assessment, you should also look into an inventory of resources, requirements, assumptions and constraints, risks, terminology, costs, and benefits. Every single assumption and success criterion matters when you are modeling.

The next step is known as data understanding, where you will collect raw data, describe it, explore it, and check its quality. This is an initial assessment of the data that will be used to create the model. Again, data scientists must be skeptical. You must be sure you understand all the nuances of the data and its source.

The data preparation phase is actually the one that usually consumes most of the time during modeling. In this phase, you need to select and filter the data, clean it according to the task that needs to be performed, come up with new attributes, integrate the data with other data sources, and format it as expected by the algorithm that will be applied. These tasks are often called **feature engineering**.

Once the data is prepared, you can finally start the modeling phase. Here is where the algorithms come in. You should start by ensuring the selection of the right technique. Remember: according to the presence or absence of a target variable (and its data type), you will have different algorithms to choose from. Each modeling technique might carry some implicit assumptions of which you have to be aware. For example, if you choose a multiple linear regression algorithm to predict house prices, you should be aware that this type of model expects a linear relationship between the variables of your data.

There are hundreds of algorithms out there and each of them might have its own assumptions. After choosing the ones that you want to test in your project, you should spend some time checking their specifics. In later chapters of this book, you will learn about some of them.

Important note

Some algorithms incorporate in their logic a sub-process known as **feature selection**. This is a step where the most important features will be selected to build your best model. Decision trees are examples of algorithms that perform feature selection automatically. You will learn about feature selection in more detail later on, since there are different ways to select the best variables for your model.

During the modeling phase, you should also design a testing approach for the model, defining which evaluation metrics will be used and how the data will be split. With that in place, you can finally build the model by setting the hyperparameters of the algorithm and feeding the model with data. This process of feeding the algorithm with data to find a good estimator is known as the **training process**. The data used to feed the model is known as **training data**. There are different ways to organize the training and **testing data**, which you will learn about in this chapter.

> **Important note**
>
> ML algorithms are built of parameters and hyperparameters. Parameters are learned from the data; for example: a decision-tree-based algorithm might learn from the training data that a particular feature should compose its root level based on information gain assessments. Hyperparameters, on the other hand, are used to control the learning process. Taking the same example about decision trees, you could specify the maximum allowed depth of the tree (regardless of the training data). Hyperparameter tuning is a very important topic in the exam and will be covered in fine-grained detail later on.

Once the model is trained, you can evaluate and review the results in order to propose the next steps. If the results are not acceptable (based on business success criteria), you should go back to earlier steps to check what else can be done to improve the model's results. It could either be the subtle tuning of the hyperparameters of the algorithm, a new data preparation step, or even the redefinition of business drivers. On the other hand, if the model quality is acceptable, you can move on to the deployment phase.

In this last phase of the CRISP-DM methodology, you have to think about the deployment plan, monitoring, and maintenance of the model. You can look at this step from two perspectives: training and inference. The **training pipeline** consists of those steps needed to train the model, which include data preparation, hyperparameter definition, data splitting, and model training itself. Somehow, you must store all the model artifacts somewhere, since they will be used by the next pipeline that needs to be developed: the **inference pipeline**.

The inference pipeline just uses model artifacts to execute the model against brand-new observations (data that has never been seen by the model during the training phase). For example, if the model was trained to identify fraudulent transactions, this is the time when new transactions will pass through the model to be classified.

In general, models are trained once (through the training pipeline) and executed many times (through the inference pipeline). However, after some time, it is expected that there will be some model degradation, also known as **model drift**. This phenomenon happens because the model is usually trained in a static training set that aims to represent the business scenario at a given point in time; however, businesses evolve, and it might be necessary to retrain the model on more recent data to capture new business aspects. That's why it is important to keep tracking model performance even after model deployment.

The CRISP-DM methodology is so important to the context of the AWS Machine Learning Specialty exam that, if you look at the four domains covered by AWS, you will realize that they were generalized from the CRISP-DM stages: data engineering, exploratory data analysis, modeling, and ML implementation and operations.

You now understand all the key stages of a modeling pipeline and you know that the algorithm itself is just part of a larger process! Next, you will see how to split your data to create and validate ML models.

Data splitting

Training and evaluating ML models are key tasks of the modeling pipeline. ML algorithms need data to find relationships among features in order to make inferences, but those inferences need to be validated before they are moved to production environments.

The dataset used to train ML models is commonly called the training set. This training data must be able to represent the real environment where the model will be used; it will be useless if that requirement is not met.

Coming back to the fraud example presented in *Table 1.1*, based on the training data, you found that e-commerce transactions with a value greater than $5,000 and processed at night are potentially fraudulent cases. With that in mind, after applying the model in a production environment, the model is supposed to flag similar cases, as learned during the training process.

Therefore, if those cases only exist in the training set, the model will flag **false positive** cases in production environments. The opposite scenario is also true: if there is a particular fraud case in production data, not reflected in the training data, the model will flag a lot of **false negative** cases. False positive and false negative ratios are just two of many quality metrics that you can use for model validation. These metrics will be covered in much more detail later on.

By this point, you should have a clear understanding of the importance of having a good training set. Now, supposing you do have a valid training set, how could you have some level of confidence that this model will perform well in production environments? The answer is by using testing and validation sets:

Figure 1.4 – Data splitting

Figure 1.4 shows the different types of data splitting that you can have during training and inference pipelines. The training data is used to create the model; the testing data is used to extract the final model quality metrics. The testing data *cannot* be used during the training process for any reason other than to extract model metrics.

The reason to avoid using the testing data during training is simple: you *cannot* let the model learn on top of the data that will be used to validate it. This technique of holding one piece of the data for testing is often called **hold-out validation**.

The box on the right side of *Figure 1.4* represents the production data. Production data usually comes in continuously and you have to execute the inference pipeline in order to extract model results from it. No training, nor any other type of recalculation, is performed on top of production data; you just have to pass it through the inference pipeline as it is.

From a technical perspective, most ML libraries implement training steps with the `.fit` method, while inference steps are implemented by the `.transform` *or* `.predict` method. Again, this is just a common pattern used by most ML libraries, but be aware that you might find different name conventions across ML libraries.

Still looking at *Figure 1.4*, there is another box, close to the training data, named **Validation data**. This is a subset of the training set often used to support the creation of the best model, before moving on to the testing phase. You will learn about validation sets in much more detail, but first, you should understand why you need them.

Overfitting and underfitting

ML models might suffer from two types of fitting issues: **overfitting** and **underfitting**. Overfitting means that your model performs very well on the training data but cannot be generalized to other datasets, such as testing and, even worse, production data. In other words, if you have an overfitted model, it only works on your training data.

When you are building ML models, you want to create solutions that are able to generalize what they have learned and infer decisions on other datasets that follow the same data distribution. A model that only works on the data that it was trained on is useless. Overfitting usually happens due to the large number of features or the lack of configuration of the hyperparameters of the algorithm.

On the other hand, underfitted models cannot fit the data during the training phase. As a result, they are so generic that they can't perform well within the training, testing, or production data. Underfitting usually happens due to the lack of good features/observations or due to the lack of time to train the model (some algorithms need more iterations to properly fit the model).

Both overfitting and underfitting need to be avoided. There are many modeling techniques to work around them. For instance, you will learn about the commonly used **cross-validation** technique and its relationship with the validation data box shown in *Figure 1.4*.

Applying cross-validation and measuring overfitting

Cross-validation is a technique where you split the training set into training and validation sets. The model is then trained on the training set and tested on the validation set. The most common cross-validation strategy is known as **k-fold cross-validation**, where *k* is the number of splits of the training set.

Using k-fold cross-validation and assuming the value of k equals 10, you are splitting the training set into 10 folds. The model will be trained and tested 10 times. On each iteration, it uses 9 splits for training and leaves one split for testing. After 10 executions, the evaluation metrics extracted from each iteration are averaged and will represent the final model performance during the training phase, as shown in *Figure 1.5*:

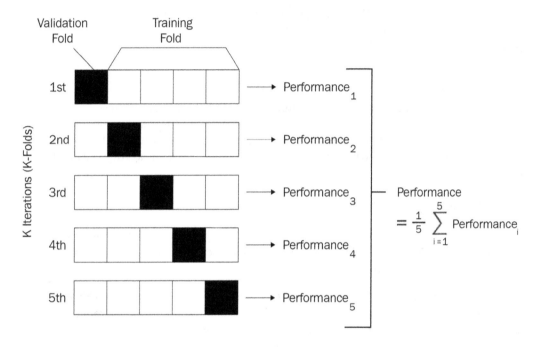

Figure 1.5 – Cross-validation in action

Another common cross-validation technique is known as **leave-one-out cross-validation (LOOCV)**. In this approach, the model is executed many times and, within each iteration, one observation is separated for testing and all the others are used for training.

There are many advantages of using cross-validation during training:

- You mitigate overfitting in the training data since the model is always trained on a particular chunk of data and tested on another chunk that hasn't been used for training.

- You avoid overfitting in the test data since there is no need to keep using the testing data to optimize the model.

- You expose the presence of overfitting or underfitting. If the model performance in the training/validation data is very different from the performance observed in the testing data, something is wrong.

It might be worth diving into the third item on that list since it is widely covered in the AWS Machine Learning Specialty exam. For instance, assume you are creating a binary classification model, using cross-validation during training, and using a testing set to extract final metrics (hold-out validation). If you get 80% accuracy in the cross-validation results and 50% accuracy in the testing set, it means that the model was overfitted to the training set, and so cannot be generalized to the testing set.

On the other hand, if you get 50% accuracy in the training set and 80% accuracy in the testing set, there is a systemic issue in the data. It is very likely that the training and testing sets do not follow the same distribution.

> **Important note**
> Accuracy is a model evaluation metric commonly used on classification models. It measures how often the model made a correct decision during its inference process. That metric was selected just for the sake of demonstration, but be aware that there are many other evaluation metrics applicable for each type of model (which will be covered at the appropriate time).

Bootstrapping methods

Cross-validation is a good strategy to validate ML models, and you should try it in your daily activities as a data scientist. However, you should also know about other resampling techniques available out there. **Bootstrapping** is one of them.

While cross-validation works *with no replacement*, a bootstrapping approach works *with replacement*. With replacement means that, while you are drawing multiple random samples from a population dataset, the same observation might be duplicated across samples.

Usually, bootstrapping is not used to validate models as you do in the traditional cross-validation approach. The reason is simple: since it works with replacement, the same observation used for training could potentially be used for testing, too. This would result in inflated model performance metrics since the estimator is likely to be correct when predicting an observation that was already seen in the training set.

Bootstrapping is often used by ML algorithms in an embedded way that requires resampling capabilities to process the data. In this context, bootstrapping is not used to *validate* the model but to *create* the model. **Random forest**, which will be covered in *Chapter 6, Applying Machine Learning Algorithms*, is one of those algorithms that use bootstrapping internally for model building.

Designing a good data splitting/sampling strategy is crucial to the success of the model or the algorithm. You should come up with different approaches to split your data, check how the model is performing on each split, and make sure those splits represent the real scenario where the model will be used.

The variance versus bias trade-off

Any ML model is supposed to contain errors. There are three types of errors that you can find in models: **bias** errors, **variance** errors, and **unexplained** errors. The last one, as expected, cannot be explained. It is often related to the context of the problem and the relationships between the variables (you can't control it).

The other two types of errors can be controlled during modeling. You can say that there is a trade-off between bias and variance errors because one will influence the other. In this case, increasing bias will decrease variance and vice versa.

Bias errors relate to assumptions taken by the model to learn the target function, the one that you want to solve. Some types of algorithms, such as linear algorithms, usually carry over that type of error because they make a lot of assumptions during model training. For example, linear models assume that the relationship present in the data is linear. Linear regression and logistic regression are types of algorithms that, in general, contain high bias. Decision trees, on the other hand, are types of algorithms that make fewer assumptions about the data and contain less bias.

Variance relates to the difference in estimations that the model performs on different training data. Models with high variance usually overfit the training set. Decision trees are examples of algorithms with high variance (they usually rely a lot on specifics of the training set, failing to generalize), and linear and logistic regression are examples of algorithms with low variance. It does not mean that decision trees are bad estimators; it just means that you need to prune (optimize) them during training.

That being said, the goal of any model is to minimize both bias and variance. However, as already mentioned, each one will impact the other in the opposite direction. For the sake of demonstration, consider a decision tree to understand how this trade-off works.

Decision trees are nonlinear algorithms and often contain low bias and high variance. In order to decrease variance, you can prune the tree and set the max_depth hyperparameter (the maximum allowed depth of the tree) to 10. That will force a more generic model, reducing variance. However, that change will also force the model to make more assumptions (since it is now more generic) and increase bias.

Shuffling your training set

Now that you know what variance and data splitting are, you can go a little deeper into the training dataset requirements. You are very likely to find questions around data shuffling in the exam. This process consists of randomizing your training dataset before you start using it to fit an algorithm.

Data shuffling will help the algorithm to reduce variance by creating a more generalizable model. For example, let's say your training represents a binary classification problem and it is sorted by the target variable (all cases belonging to class "0" appear first, then all the cases belonging to class "1").

When you fit an algorithm on this sorted data (especially some algorithms that rely on **batch processing**), it will make strong assumptions about the pattern of one of the classes, since it is very likely that it won't be able to create random batches of data with a good representation of both classes. Once the algorithm builds strong assumptions about the training data, it might be difficult for it to change them.

> **Important note**
>
> Some algorithms are able to execute the training process by fitting the data in chunks, also known as batches. This approach lets the model learn more frequently since it will make partial assumptions after processing each batch of data (instead of making decisions only after processing the entire dataset).

On the other hand, there is no need to shuffle the testing set, since it will be used only by the inference process to check model performance.

Modeling expectations

So far, you have learned about model building, validation, and management. You can now complete the foundations of ML by learning about a couple of other expectations while modeling.

The first one is **parsimony**. Parsimony describes models that offer the simplest explanation and fit the best results when compared with other models. Here's an example: while creating a linear regression model, you realize that adding 10 more features will improve your model's performance by 0.001%. In this scenario, you should consider whether this performance improvement is worth the cost of parsimony (since your model will become more complex). Sometimes it is worth it, but most of the time it is not. You need to be skeptical and think according to your business case.

Parsimony directly supports **interpretability**. The simpler your model is, the easier it is to explain it. However, there is a battle between interpretability and **predictivity**: if you focus on predictive power, you are likely to lose some interpretability. Again, you must select what is the best situation for your use case.

Introducing ML frameworks

Being aware of some ML frameworks will put you in a much better position to pass the AWS Machine Learning Specialty exam. There is no need to master these frameworks since this is not a framework-specific certification; however, knowing some common terms and solutions will help you to understand the context of the problems/questions.

scikit-learn is probably the most popular ML framework that you should be aware of. It is an open source Python package that provides implementations of ML algorithms such as decision trees, support vector machines, linear regression, and many others. It also implements classes for data preprocessing, for example, one-hot encoding, label encoders, principal component analysis, and so on. All these preprocessing methods (and many others) will be covered in later sections of this book.

The downside of scikit-learn is the fact that it needs customization to scale up through multiple machines. There is another ML library that is very popular because of the fact that it can handle multiprocessing straight away: **Spark's ML library**.

As the name suggests, it is an ML library that runs on top of **Apache Spark**, which is a unified analytical multi-processing framework used to process data on multiple machines. AWS offers a specific service that allows developers to create Spark clusters with a few clicks, known as **EMR**. Additionally, SageMaker (a fully managed ML service provided by AWS, which you will cover in a separate chapter) is well integrated with Apache Spark.

The Spark ML library is in constant development. As of the time of writing, it offers support to many ML classes of algorithms, such as classification and regression, clustering, and collaborative filtering. It also offers support for basic statistics computation, such as correlations and some hypothesis tests, as well as many data transformations, such as one-hot encoding, principal component analysis, min-max scaling, and others.

Another very popular ML framework is known as **TensorFlow**. This ML framework was created by the Google team and it is used for numerical computation and large-scale ML model development. TensorFlow implements not only traditional ML algorithms but also DL models.

TensorFlow is considered a low-level API for model development, which means that it can be very complex to develop more sophisticated models, such as **transformers** (for text mining). As an attempt to facilitate model development, other ML frameworks were built on top of TensorFlow to make it easier. One of these high-level frameworks is **Keras**. With Keras, developers can create complex DL models with just a few lines of code. More recently, Keras was incorporated into TensorFlow and it can be now called inside the TensorFlow library.

MXNet is another open source DL library. Using MXNet, you can scale up neural network-based models using multiple GPUs running on multiple machines. It also supports different programming languages, such as Python, R, Scala, and Java.

Graphical processing unit (**GPU**) support is particularly important in DL libraries such as TensorFlow and MXNet. These libraries allow developers to create and deploy neural network-based models with multiple layers. The training process of neural networks relies a lot on matrix operations, which perform much better on GPUs rather than on CPUs. That's why these DL libraries commonly offer GPU support. AWS also offers EC2 instances with GPU enabled.

These ML frameworks need a special channel to communicate with GPU units. NVIDIA, the most common supplier of GPUs nowadays, has created an API called the **Compute Unified Device Architecture (CUDA)**. CUDA is used to configure GPU units on NVIDIA devices; for example, setting up caching memory and the number of threads needed to train a neural network model. There is no need to master CUDA or GPU architecture for the AWS Machine Learning Specialty exam, but you definitely need to know what they are and how DL models take advantage of them.

Last, but not least, you should also be aware of some development frameworks widely used by the data science community, but not necessarily to create ML models. These frameworks interoperate with ML libraries to facilitate data manipulation and calculations. For example: **pandas** is a Python library that provides data processing capabilities and **NumPy** is an open source Python library that provides numerical computing.

These terms and libraries are so incorporated into data scientists' daily routines that they might come up during the exam to explain some problem domain for you. Being aware of what they are will help you to quickly understand the context of the question.

ML in the cloud

ML has gone to the cloud and developers can now use it as a service. AWS has implemented ML services at different levels of abstraction. ML application services, for example, aim to offer out-of-the-box solutions for specific problem domains. **AWS Lex** is a very clear example of an ML application as a service, where people can implement chatbots with minimum development.

AWS Rekognition is another example, which aims to identify objects, people, text, scenes, and activities in images and videos. AWS provides many other ML application services, which will be covered in the next chapter of this book.

Apart from application services, AWS also provides ML development platforms, such as **SageMaker**. Unlike out-of-the-box services such as AWS Lex and Rekognition, SageMaker is a development platform that will let you build, train, and deploy your own models with much more flexibility.

SageMaker speeds up the development and deployment process by automatically handling the necessary infrastructure for the training and inference pipelines of your models. Behind the scenes, SageMaker orchestrates other AWS services (such as EC2 instances, load balancers, auto-scaling, and so on) to create a scalable environment for ML projects. SageMaker is probably the most important service that you should master for the AWS Machine Learning Specialty exam, and it will be covered in detail in a separate section. For now, you should focus on understanding the different approaches that AWS uses to offer ML-related services.

The third option that AWS offers for deploying ML models is the most generic and flexible one: you can deploy ML models by combining different AWS services and managing them individually. This essentially does what SageMaker does for you, building your applications from scratch. For example, you could use EC2 instances, load balancers, auto-scaling, and an API gateway to create an inference pipeline for a particular model. If you prefer, you can also use AWS serverless architecture to deploy your solution, for example, using **AWS Lambda functions**.

Summary

You are now heading toward the end of this chapter, in which you have learned about several important topics regarding the foundations of ML. You started the chapter with a theoretical discussion about AI, ML, and DL, and how this entire field has grown over the past few years due to the advent of big data platforms, cloud providers, and AI applications.

You then moved on to the differences between supervised, unsupervised, and reinforcement learning, highlighting some use cases related to each of them. This is likely to be a topic in the AWS Machine Learning Specialty exam.

You learned that an ML model is built in many different stages and the algorithm itself is just one part of the modeling process. You also learned about the expected behaviors of a good model.

You did a deep dive into data splitting, where you learned about different approaches to train and validate models, and you became aware of the mythic battle between variance and bias. You completed the chapter by getting a sense of ML frameworks and services.

Coming up next, you will learn about AWS application services for ML, such as Amazon Polly, Amazon Rekognition, Amazon Transcribe, and many other AI-related AWS services. But first, look at some sample questions to give you an idea of what you can expect in the exam.

Exam Readiness Drill – Chapter Review Questions

Apart from a solid understanding of key concepts, being able to think quickly under time pressure is a skill that will help you ace your certification exam. That is why working on these skills early on in your learning journey is key.

Chapter review questions are designed to improve your test-taking skills progressively with each chapter you learn and review your understanding of key concepts in the chapter at the same time. You'll find these at the end of each chapter.

> **How To Access These Resources**
>
> To learn how to access these resources, head over to the chapter titled *Chapter 11, Accessing the Online Practice Resources*.

To open the Chapter Review Questions for this chapter, perform the following steps:

1. Click the link – `https://packt.link/MLSC01E2_CH01`.

    Alternatively, you can scan the following **QR code** (*Figure 1.6*):

Figure 1.6 – QR code that opens Chapter Review Questions for logged-in users

2. Once you log in, you'll see a page similar to the one shown in *Figure 1.7*:

Figure 1.7 – Chapter Review Questions for Chapter 1

3. Once ready, start the following practice drills, re-attempting the quiz multiple times.

Exam Readiness Drill

For the first three attempts, don't worry about the time limit.

ATTEMPT 1

The first time, aim for at least **40%**. Look at the answers you got wrong and read the relevant sections in the chapter again to fix your learning gaps.

ATTEMPT 2

The second time, aim for at least **60%**. Look at the answers you got wrong and read the relevant sections in the chapter again to fix any remaining learning gaps.

ATTEMPT 3

The third time, aim for at least **75%**. Once you score 75% or more, you start working on your timing.

> **Tip**
>
> You may take more than **three** attempts to reach 75%. That's okay. Just review the relevant sections in the chapter till you get there.

Working On Timing

Target: Your aim is to keep the score the same while trying to answer these questions as quickly as possible. Here's an example of how your next attempts should look like:

Attempt	Score	Time Taken
Attempt 5	77%	21 mins 30 seconds
Attempt 6	78%	18 mins 34 seconds
Attempt 7	76%	14 mins 44 seconds

Table 1.3 – Sample timing practice drills on the online platform

> **Note**
>
> The time limits shown in the above table are just examples. Set your own time limits with each attempt based on the time limit of the quiz on the website.

With each new attempt, your score should stay above **75%** while your "time taken" to complete should "decrease". Repeat as many attempts as you want till you feel confident dealing with the time pressure.

2

AWS Services for Data Storage

AWS provides a wide range of services to store your data safely and securely. There are various storage options available on AWS, such as block storage, file storage, and object storage. It is expensive to manage on-premises data storage due to the higher investment in hardware, admin overheads, and managing system upgrades. With AWS storage services, you just pay for what you use, and you don't have to manage the hardware. You will also learn about various storage classes offered by Amazon S3 for intelligent access to data and to reduce costs. You can expect questions in the exam on storage classes. As you continue through this chapter, you will master the **single-AZ** and **multi-AZ** instances, and **Recovery Time Objective (RTO)** and **Recovery Point Objective (RPO)** concepts of Amazon RDS.

In this chapter, you will learn about storing your data securely for further analytical purposes throughout the following sections:

- Storing data on Amazon S3
- Controlling access on S3 buckets and objects
- Protecting data on Amazon S3
- Securing S3 objects at rest and in transit
- Using other types of data stores
- **Relational Database Services (RDSes)**
- Managing failover in Amazon RDS
- Taking automatic backup, RDS snapshots, and restore and read replicas
- Writing to Amazon Aurora with multi-master capabilities
- Storing columnar data on Amazon Redshift
- Amazon DynamoDB for NoSQL databases as a service

Technical requirements

All you will need for this chapter is an AWS account and the AWS CLI configured. The steps to configure the AWS CLI for your account are explained in detail by Amazon here: `https://docs.aws.amazon.com/cli/latest/userguide/cli-chap-configure.html`.

You can download the code examples from GitHub, here: `https://github.com/PacktPublishing/AWS-Certified-Machine-Learning-Specialty-MLS-C01-Certification-Guide-Second-Edition/tree/main/Chapter02`.

Storing Data on Amazon S3

S3 is Amazon's cloud-based object storage service, and it can be accessed from anywhere via the internet. It is an ideal storage option for large datasets. It is region-based, as your data is stored in a particular region until you move the data to a different region. Your data will never leave that region until it is configured to do so. In a particular region, data is replicated in the availability zones of that region; this makes S3 regionally resilient. If any of the availability zones fail in a region, then other availability zones will serve your requests. S3 can be accessed via the AWS console UI, AWS CLI, AWS API requests, or via standard HTTP methods.

S3 has two main components: **buckets** and **objects**.

- Buckets are created in a specific AWS region. Buckets can contain objects but cannot contain other buckets.

- Objects have two main attributes. One is the **key**, and the other is the **value**. The value is the content being stored, and the key is the name. The maximum size of an object can be 5 TB. As per the Amazon S3 documentation (`https://docs.aws.amazon.com/AmazonS3/latest/dev/UsingObjects.html`), objects also have a version ID, metadata, access control information, and sub-resources.

> **Important note**
>
> As per Amazon's docs, S3 provides read-after-write consistency for PUTs of new objects, which means that if you upload a new object or create a new object and you immediately try to read the object using its key, then you get the exact data that you just uploaded. However, for overwrites and deletes, it behaves in an **eventually consistent manner**. This means that if you read an object straight after the delete or overwrite operation, then you may read an old copy or a stale version of the object. It takes some time to replicate the content of the object across three Availability Zones.

A folder structure can be maintained logically by using a prefix. Take an example where an image is uploaded into a bucket, `bucket-name-example`, with the prefix `folder-name` and the object name `my-image.jpg`. The entire structure looks like this: `/bucket-name-example/folder-name/my-image.jpg`.

The content of the object can be read by using the bucket name of `bucket-name-example` and the key of `/folder-name/my-image.jpg`.

There are several storage classes offered by Amazon for objects stored in S3:

- **Standard Storage (S3 Standard):** This is the storage class for frequently accessed objects and for quick access. S3 Standard has a millisecond first-byte latency and objects can be made publicly available.

- **Standard Infrequent Access (S3 Standard-IA):** This option is used when you need data to be returned quickly, but not for frequent access. The object size has to be a minimum of 128 KB. The minimum storage timeframe is 30 days. If the object is deleted before 30 days, you are still charged for 30 days. Standard-IA objects are resilient to the loss of Availability Zones.

- **One Zone Infrequent Access (S3 One Zone-IA):** Objects in this storage class are stored in just one Availability Zone, which makes it cheaper than **Standard-IA**. The minimum object size and storage timeframe are the same as Standard-IA. Objects from this storage class are less available and less resilient. This storage class is used when you have another copy, or if the data can be recreated. A **One Zone-IA** storage class should be used for long-lived data that is non-critical and replaceable, and where access is infrequent.

- **Amazon S3 Glacier Flexible Retrieval (formerly S3 Glacier):** This option is used for long-term archiving and backup. It can take anything from minutes to hours to retrieve objects in this storage class. The minimum storage timeframe is 90 days. For archived data that doesn't need to be accessed right away but requires the ability to retrieve extensive data sets without incurring additional charges, like in backup or disaster-recovery scenarios, S3 Glacier Flexible Retrieval (formerly known as S3 Glacier) is the perfect storage option.

- **Amazon S3 Glacier Instant Retrieval:** This storage class offers cost-effective, high-speed storage for seldom-accessed, long-term data. Compared to S3 Standard-Infrequent Access, it can cut storage expenses by up to 68% when data is accessed once per quarter. This storage class is perfect for swiftly retrieving archive data like medical images, news media assets, or user-generated content archives. You can upload data directly or use S3 Lifecycle policies to move it from other S3 storage classes.

- **Glacier Deep Archive:** The minimum storage duration of this class is 180 days. This is the least expensive storage class and has a default retrieval time of 12 hours.

- **S3 Intelligent-Tiering:** This storage class is designed to reduce operational overheads. Users pay a monitoring fee and AWS selects a storage class between Standard (a frequent-access tier) and Standard-IA (a lower-cost, infrequent-access tier) based on the access pattern of an object. This option is designed for long-lived data with unknown or unpredictable access patterns.

Through sets of rules, the transition between storage classes and deletion of the objects can be managed easily and are referred to as **S3 Lifecycle configurations**. These rules consist of actions. These can be applied to a bucket or a group of objects in that bucket defined by prefixes or tags. Actions can either be **transition actions** or **expiration actions**. Transition actions define the storage class transition of the objects following the creation of *a user-defined* number of days. Expiration actions configure the deletion of versioned objects, or the deletion of delete markers or incomplete multipart uploads. This is very useful for managing costs.

An illustration is given in *Figure 2.1*. You can find more details here: `https://docs.aws.amazon.com/AmazonS3/latest/dev/storage-class-intro.html`.

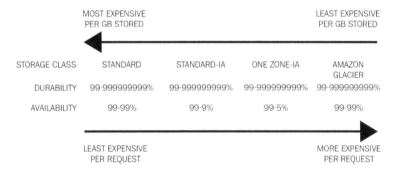

Figure 2.1 – A comparison table of S3 Storage classes

Creating buckets to hold data

Now, you will see how to create a bucket, upload an object, and read the object using the AWS CLI:

1. In the first step, check whether you have any buckets created by using the `aws s3 ls` command:

    ```
    $ pwd
    /Users/baba/AWS-Certified-Machine-Learning-Specialty-
    2020-Certification-Guide/Chapter-5/s3demo/demo-files
    $ aws s3 ls
    ```

2. This command returns nothing here. So, create a bucket now by using the `mb` argument. Let's say the bucket name is `demo-bucket-baba` in the `us-east-1` Region:

    ```
    $ aws s3 mb s3://demo-bucket-baba --region us-east-1
    make_bucket: demo-bucket-baba
    $ aws s3 ls
    2020-11-04 14:39:50 demo-bucket-baba
    ```

3. As you have created a bucket now, your next step is to copy a file to your bucket using the cp argument, as shown in the following code:

```
$ aws s3 cp sample-file.txt s3://demo-bucket-baba/
upload: ./sample-file.txt to s3://demo-bucket-baba/sample-file.txt
```

4. To validate the file upload operation via the AWS console, please log in to your AWS account and go to the AWS S3 console to see the same. The AWS S3 console lists the result as shown in *Figure 2.2*. The console may have changed by the time you are reading this book!

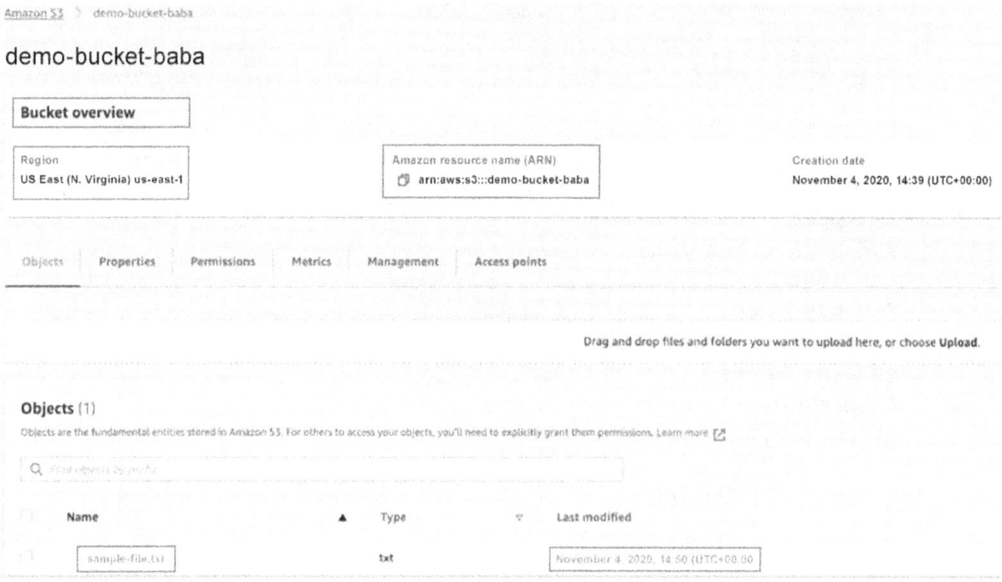

Amazon S3 > demo-bucket-baba

demo-bucket-baba

Bucket overview		
Region	Amazon resource name (ARN)	Creation date
US East (N. Virginia) us-east-1	arn:aws:s3:::demo-bucket-baba	November 4, 2020, 14:39 (UTC+00:00)

Objects   Properties   Permissions   Metrics   Management   Access points

Drag and drop files and folders you want to upload here, or choose **Upload**.

Objects (1)

Objects are the fundamental entities stored in Amazon S3. For others to access your objects, you'll need to explicitly grant them permissions. Learn more

Name	Type	Last modified
sample-file.txt	txt	November 4, 2020, 14:50 (UTC+00:00)

Figure 2.2 – AWS S3 listing your files

You can also list the files in your S3 bucket from the command line, as shown here:

```
$ aws s3 ls s3://demo-bucket-baba/
2020-11-04 14:50:02          99 sample-file.txt
```

5. If you want to upload your filesystem directories and files to the S3 bucket, then --recursive will do the job for you:

```
$ aws s3 cp . s3://demo-bucket-baba/ --recursive
upload: folder-1/a.txt to s3://demo-bucket-baba/folder-1/a.txt
upload: folder-2/sample-image.jpg to s3://demo-bucket-baba/
folder-2/sample-image.jpg
upload: ./sample-file.txt to s3://demo-bucket-baba/sample-file.
txt
$ aws s3 ls s3://demo-bucket-baba/
```

6. The contents of one bucket can be copied/moved to another bucket via the cp command and the --recursive parameter. To achieve this, you will have to create two buckets, demo-bucket-baba-copied and demo-bucket-baba-moved. The steps are as follows:

```
$ aws s3 mb s3://demo-bucket-baba-copied --region us-east-2
$ aws s3 mb s3://demo-bucket-baba-moved --region us-east-2
$ aws s3 cp s3://demo-bucket-baba s3://demo-bucket-baba-copied/
--recursive
$ aws s3 mv s3://demo-bucket-baba s3://demo-bucket-baba-moved/
--recursive
$ aws s3 ls
2020-11-04 14:39:50 demo-bucket-baba
2020-11-04 15:44:28 demo-bucket-baba-copied
2020-11-04 15:44:37 demo-bucket-baba-moved
$ aws s3 ls s3://demo-bucket-baba/
```

If all the commands are run successfully, then the original bucket should be empty at the end (as all the files have now been moved).

> **Note**
>
> In the certification exam, you will not find many questions on bucket- and object-level operations. However, it is always better to know the basic operations and the required steps.

7. The buckets must be deleted to avoid costs as soon as the hands-on work is finished. The bucket has to be empty before you run the rb command:

```
$ aws s3 rb s3://demo-bucket-baba
$ aws s3 rb s3://demo-bucket-baba-moved
remove_bucket failed: s3://demo-bucket-baba-moved An error
occurred (BucketNotEmpty) when calling the DeleteBucket
operation: The bucket you tried to delete is not empty
```

8. The `demo-bucket-baba-moved` bucket is not empty, so you couldn't remove the bucket. In such scenarios, use the `--force` parameter to delete the entire bucket and all its contents, as shown here:

    ```
    $ aws s3 rb s3://demo-bucket-baba-moved --force
    $ aws s3 rb s3://demo-bucket-baba-copied--force
    ```

    If you want to delete all the content from a specific prefix inside a bucket using the CLI, then it is easy to use the `rm` command with the `--recursive` parameter.

9. Let's take an example of a bucket, `test-bucket`, that has a prefix, `images`. This prefix contains four image files named `animal.jpg`, `draw-house.jpg`, `cat.jpg`, and `human.jpg`.

10. Now, to delete the contents inside the images, the command will be as follows: `aws s3 rm s3://test-bucket/images —recursive`

11. The bucket should now be empty.

In the next section, you are going to learn about object tags and object metadata.

Distinguishing between object tags and object metadata

Let's compare these two terms:

- **Object tag**: An object tag is a **key-value** pair. AWS S3 object tags can help you filter analytics and metrics, categorize storage, secure objects based on certain categorizations, track costs based on certain categorization of objects, and much more besides. Object tags can be used to create life cycle rules to move objects to cheaper storage tiers. You can have a maximum of 10 tags added to an object and 50 tags to a bucket. A tag key can contain 128 Unicode characters, while a tag value can contain 256 Unicode characters.

- **Object metadata**: Object metadata is descriptive data describing an object. It consists of **name-value** pairs. Object metadata is returned as HTTP headers on objects. They are of two types: one is **system metadata**, and the other is **user-defined metadata**. User-defined metadata is a custom name-value pair added to an object by the user. The name must begin with **x-amz-meta**. You can change all system metadata such as storage class, versioning, and encryption attributes on an object. Further details are available here: `https://docs.aws.amazon.com/AmazonS3/latest/dev/UsingMetadata.html`.

> **Important note**
> Metadata names are case-insensitive, whereas tag names are case-sensitive.

In the next section, you are going to learn about controlling access to buckets and objects on Amazon S3 through different policies, including the resource policy and the identity policy.

Controlling access to buckets and objects on Amazon S3

Once the object is stored in the bucket, the next major step is to manage access. S3 is private by default, and access is given to other users, groups, or resources via several methods. This means that access to the objects can be managed via **Access Control Lists (ACLs)**, **Public Access Settings**, **Identity Policies**, and **Bucket Policies**.

Let's look at some of these in detail.

S3 bucket policy

An **S3 bucket policy** is a resource policy that is attached to a bucket. Resource policies decide who can access that resource. It differs from identity policies in that identity policies can be attached or assigned to the identities inside an account, whereas resource policies can control identities from the same account or different accounts. Resource policies control anonymous principals too, which means an object can be made public through resource policies. The following example policy allows everyone in the world to read the bucket because `Principal` is rendered `*`:

```
{
  "Version":"2012-10-17"
  "Statement":[
    {
      "Sid":"AnyoneCanRead",
      "Effect":"Allow",
      "Principal":"*",
      "Action":["s3:GetObject"],
      "Resource":["arn:aws:s3:::my-bucket/*"]
    }
  ]
}
```

By default, everything in S3 is private to the owner. If you want to make a prefix public to the world, then `Resource` changes to `arn:aws:s3:::my-bucket/some-prefix/*`, and similarly, if it is intended for a specific IAM user or IAM group, then those details go in the principal part in the policy.

There can be conditions added to the bucket policy too. Let's examine a use case where the organization wants to keep a bucket public and whitelist particular IP addresses. The policy would look something like this:

```
{
  "Version":"2012-10-17"
  "Statement":[
    {
      "Sid":"ParticularIPRead",
      "Effect":"Allow",
```

```
        "Principal":"*",
        "Action":["s3:GetObject"],
        "Resource":["arn:aws:s3:::my-bucket/*"],
        "Condition":{
          "NotIpAddress":{"aws:SourceIp":"2.3.3.6/32"}
        }
      }
    ]
  }
```

More examples are available in the AWS S3 developer guide, which can be found here: `https://docs.aws.amazon.com/AmazonS3/latest/dev/example-bucket-policies.html`.

Block public access is a separate setting given to the bucket owner to avoid any kind of mistakes in bucket policy. In a real-world scenario, the bucket can be made public through bucket policy by mistake; to avoid such mistakes, or data leaks, AWS has provided this setting. It provides a further level of security, irrespective of the bucket policy. You can choose this while creating a bucket, or it can be set after creating a bucket.

Identity policies are meant for IAM users and IAM roles. Identity policies are validated when an IAM identity (user or role) requests to access a resource. All requests are denied by default. If an identity intends to access any services, resources, or actions, then access must be provided explicitly through identity policies. The example policy that follows can be attached to an IAM user and the IAM user will be allowed to have full RDS access within a specific Region (`us-east-1` in this example):

```
{
    "Version": "2012-10-17",
    "Statement": [
        {
            "Effect": "Allow",
            "Action": "rds:*",
            "Resource": ["arn:aws:rds:us-east-1:*:*"]
        },
        {

            "Effect": "Allow",
            "Action": ["rds:Describe*"],
            "Resource": ["*"]
        }
    ]
}
```

ACLs are used to grant high-level permissions, typically for granting access to other AWS accounts. ACLs are one of the **sub-resources** of a bucket or an object. A bucket or object can be made public quickly via ACLs. AWS doesn't suggest doing this, and you shouldn't expect questions about this on the test. It is good to know about this, but it is not as flexible as the **S3 bucket policy**.

Now, let's learn about the methods to protect our data in the next section.

Protecting data on Amazon S3

In this section, you will learn how to record every version of an object. Along with durability, Amazon provides several techniques to secure the data in S3. Some of those techniques involve enabling versioning and encrypting the objects.

Versioning helps you to roll back to a previous version if any problem occurs with the current object during update, delete, or put operations.

Through encryption, you can control the access of an object. You need the appropriate key to read and write an object. You will also learn **Multi-Factor Authentication (MFA)** for delete operations. Amazon also allows **Cross-Region Replication (CRR)** to maintain a copy of an object in another Region, which can be used for data backup during any disaster, for further redundancy, or for the enhancement of data access speed in different Regions.

Applying bucket versioning

Let's now understand how you can enable bucket versioning with the help of some hands-on examples. Bucket versioning can be applied while creating a bucket from the AWS S3 console:

1. To enable versioning on a bucket from the command line, a bucket must be created first and then versioning can be enabled, as shown in the following example. In this example, I have created a bucket, `version-demo-mlpractice`, and enabled versioning through the `put-bucket-versioning` command:

    ```
    $ aws s3 mb s3://version-demo-mlpractice/
    $ aws s3api put-bucket-versioning --bucket version-demo-
    mlpractice --versioning-configuration Status=Enabled
    $ aws s3api get-bucket-versioning --bucket version-demo-
    mlpractice
    {
        "Status": "Enabled"
    }
    ```

2. You have not created this bucket with any kind of encryption. So, if you run `aws s3api get-bucket-encryption --bucket version-demo-mlpractice`, then it will output an error that says the following:

    ```
    The server side encryption configuration was not found
    ```

3. **Server-Side Encryption (SSE)** can be applied from the AWS S3 console while creating a bucket. This is called bucket default encryption. You can also apply SSE via the command line using the `put-bucket-encryption` API. The command will look like this:

```
$ aws s3api put-bucket-encryption --bucket version-
demo-mlpractice --server-side-encryption-configuration
'{"Rules":[{"ApplyServerSideEncryptionByDefault":
{"SSEAlgorithm":"AES256"}}]}'
```

4. This can be verified using the following command: `aws s3api get-bucket-encryption --bucket version-demo-mlpractice`.

You will learn more about encryption in the next section.

Applying encryption to buckets

You also need to understand how enabling versioning on a bucket would help. There are use cases where a file is updated regularly, and versions will be created for the same file. To simulate this scenario, try the following example:

1. In this example, you will create a file with versions written in it. You will overwrite it and retrieve it to check the versions in that file:

```
$ echo "Version-1">version-doc.txt
$ aws s3 cp version-doc.txt s3://version-demo-mlpractice
$ aws s3 cp s3://version-demo-mlpractice/version-doc.txt
check.txt
$ cat check.txt
Version-1
$ echo "Version-2">version-doc.txt
$ aws s3 cp version-doc.txt s3://version-demo-mlpractice
$ aws s3 cp s3://version-demo-mlpractice/version-doc.txt
check.txt
$ cat check.txt
Version-2
```

2. Upon retrieval, you got the latest version of the file, in other words, `Version-2` in this case. To check each of the versions and the latest one of them, S3 provides the `list-object-versions` API, as shown here. From the JSON results, you can deduce the latest version:

```
$ aws s3api list-object-versions
--bucket version-demo-mlpractice
{
    "Versions": [
        {
            "ETag":
```

```
               "\"b6690f56ca22c410a2782512d24cdc97\"",
                   "Size": 10,
                   "StorageClass": "STANDARD",
                   "Key": "version-doc.txt",
                   "VersionId":
           "70wbLG6BMBEQhCXmwsriDgQoXafFmgGi",
                   "IsLatest": true,
                   "LastModified": "2020-11-07T15:57:05+00:00",
                   "Owner": {
                       "DisplayName": "baba",
                       "ID": "XXXXXXXXXXXX"
                   }
               },
               {
                   "ETag":
           "\"5022e6af0dd3d2ea70920438271b21a2\"",
                   "Size": 10,
                   "StorageClass": "STANDARD",
                   "Key": "version-doc.txt",
                   "VersionId": "f1iC.9L.MsP00tIb.
           sUMnfOEae240sIW",
                   "IsLatest": false,
                   "LastModified": "2020-11-07T15:56:27+00:00",
                   "Owner": {
                       "DisplayName": "baba",
                       "ID": " XXXXXXXXXXXX"
                   }
               }
           ]
       }
```

3. There may be a situation where you have to roll back to the earlier version of the current object. In the preceding example, the latest one is Version-2. You can make any desired version the latest or current version by parsing the VersionId sub-resource to the get-object API call and uploading that object again. The other way is to delete the current or latest version by passing versionId to the -version-id parameter in the delete-object API request. More details about the API are available here: https://docs.aws.amazon.com/cli/latest/reference/s3api/delete-object.html.

4. When you delete an object in a versioning-enabled bucket, it does not delete the object from the bucket. It just creates a marker called `DeleteMarker`. It looks like this:

```
$ aws s3api delete-object --bucket version-demo-mlpractice --key
version-doc.txt
{
    "DeleteMarker": true,
    "VersionId": "BKv_Cxixtm7V48MWqBO_KUkKbcOaH5JP"
}
```

5. This means that the object is not deleted. You can list it by using this command:

```
aws s3api list-object-versions --bucket version-demo-mlpractice
```

6. Now the bucket has no objects as `version-doc.txt`, and you can verify this using the `aws s3 ls` command because that marker became the current version of the object with a new ID. If you try to retrieve an object that is deleted, which means a delete marker is serving the current version of the object, then you will get a **404 error**. Hence, the permanent deletion of an object in a versioning-enabled bucket can only be achieved by deleting the object using their version IDs against each version. If a situation arises to get the object back, then the same object can be retrieved by deleting the delete marker, `VersionId`, as shown in the following example commands. A simple delete request **(without the version ID)** will not delete the delete marker and create another delete marker with a unique version ID. So, it's possible to have multiple delete markers for the same object. It is important to note at this point that it will consume your storage and you will be billed for it:

```
$ aws s3 ls s3://version-demo-mlpractice/
$ aws s3api delete-object --bucket version-demo-mlpractice --key
version-doc.txt --version-id BKv_Cxixtm7V48MWqBO_KUkKbcOaH5JP
{
    "DeleteMarker": true,
    "VersionId": "BKv_Cxixtm7V48MWqBO_KUkKbcOaH5JP"
}
```

7. Upon listing the bucket now, the older objects can be seen:

```
$ aws s3 ls s3://version-demo-mlpractice/
2020-11-07 15:57:05          10 version-doc.txt
```

As you have already covered the exam topics and practiced most of the required concepts, you should delete the objects in the bucket and then delete the bucket to save on costs. This step deletes the versions of the object and, in turn, removes the object permanently.

8. Here, the latest version is deleted by giving the version ID to it, followed by the other version ID:

```
$ aws s3api delete-object --bucket version-demo-mlpractice --key
version-doc.txt --version-id 70wbLG6BMBEQhCXmwsriDgQoXafFmgGi
$ aws s3api delete-object --bucket version-demo-mlpractice --key
version-doc.txt --version-id fliC.9L.MsP00tIb.sUMnfOEae240sIW
$ aws s3api list-object-versions --bucket version-demo-
mlpractice
```

You can clearly see the empty bucket now.

> **Important note**
>
> AWS best practices suggest adding another layer of protection through **MFA delete.** Accidental bucket deletions can be prevented, and the security of the objects in the bucket is ensured. MFA delete can be enabled or disabled via the console and CLI. As documented in AWS docs, MFA delete requires two forms of authentication together: your security credentials, and the concatenation of a valid serial number, a space, and the six-digit code displayed on an approved authentication device.

CRR helps you to separate data between different geographical Regions. A typical use case is the maintenance business-as-usual activities during a disaster. If a Region goes down, then another Region can support the users if CRR is enabled. This improves the availability of the data. Another use case is to reduce latency if the same data is used by another compute resource, such as EC2 or AWS Lambda being launched in another Region. You can also use CRR to copy objects to another AWS account that belongs to a different owner. There are a few important points that are worth noting down for the certification exam:

- In order to use CRR, versioning has to be enabled on both the source and destination bucket.

- Replication is enabled on the source bucket by adding rules. As the source, either an entire bucket, a prefix, or tags can be replicated.

- Encrypted objects can also be replicated by assigning an appropriate encryption key.

- The destination bucket can be in the same account or in another account. You can change the storage type and ownership of the object in the destination bucket.

- For CRR, an existing role can be chosen or a new IAM role can be created too.

- There can be multiple replication rules on the source bucket, with priority accorded to it. Rules with higher priority override rules with lower priority.

- When you add a replication rule, only new versions of an object that are created after the rules are enabled get replicated.

- If versions are deleted from the source bucket, then they are not deleted from the destination bucket.

- When you delete an object from the source bucket, it creates a delete marker in said source bucket. That delete marker is not replicated to the destination bucket by S3.

In the next section, you will cover the concept of securing S3 objects.

Securing S3 objects at rest and in transit

In the previous section, you learned about bucket default encryption, which is completely different from object-level encryption. Buckets are not encrypted, whereas objects are. A question may arise here: *what is the default bucket encryption?* You will learn these concepts in this section. Data during transmission can be protected by using **Secure Socket Layer (SSL)** or **Transport Layer Security (TLS)** for the transfer of HTTPS requests. The next step is to protect the data, where the authorized person can encode and decode the data.

It is possible to have different encryption settings on different objects in the same bucket. S3 supports **Client-Side Encryption (CSE)** and **Server-Side Encryption (SSE)** for objects at rest:

- **CSE**: A client uploads the object to S3 via the S3 endpoint. In CSE, the data is encrypted by the client before uploading to S3. Although the transit between the user and the S3 endpoint happens in an encrypted channel, the data in the channel is already encrypted by the client and can't be seen. In transit, encryption takes place by default through HTTPS. So, AWS S3 stores the encrypted object and cannot read the data in any format at any point in time. In CSE, the client takes care of encrypting the object's content. So, control stays with the client in terms of key management and the encryption-decryption process. This leads to a huge amount of CPU usage. S3 is only used for storage.

- **SSE**: A client uploads the object to S3 via the S3 endpoint. Even though the data in transit is through an encrypted channel that uses HTTPS, the objects themselves are not encrypted inside the channel. Once the data hits S3, then it is encrypted by the S3 service. In SSE, you trust S3 to perform encryption-decryption, object storage, and key management. There are three types of SSE techniques available for S3 objects:

  - SSE-C

  - SSE-S3

  - SSE-KMS

- **SSE with Customer-Provided Keys (SSE-C):** With SSE-C, the user is responsible for the key that is used for encryption and decryption. S3 manages the encryption and decryption process. In CSE, the client handles the encryption-decryption process, but in SSE-C, S3 handles the cryptographic operations. This potentially decreases the CPU requirements for these processes. The only overhead here is to manage the keys. Ideally, when a user is doing a PUT operation, the user has to provide a key and an object to S3. S3 encrypts the object using the key provided and attaches the hash (a cipher text) to the object. As soon as the object is stored, S3 discards the encryption key. This generated hash is one-way and cannot be used to generate a new key. When the user provides a GET operation request along with the decryption key, the hash identifies whether the specific key was used for encryption. Then, S3 decrypts and discards the key.

- **SSE with Amazon S3-Managed Keys (SSE-S3):** With SSE-S3, AWS handles both the management of the key and the process of encryption and decryption. When the user uploads an object using a PUT operation, the user just provides the unencrypted object. S3 creates a master key to be used for the encryption process. No one can change anything on this master key as this is created, rotated internally, and managed by S3 from end to end. This is a unique key for the object. It uses the AES-256 algorithm by default.

- **SSE with Customer Master Keys stored in AWS Key Management Service (SSE-KMS):** AWS Key Management Service (KMS) manages the Customer Master Key (CMK). AWS S3 collaborates with AWS KMS and generates an AWS-managed CMK. This is the default master key used for SSE-KMS. Every time an object is uploaded, S3 uses a dedicated key to encrypt that object, and that key is a **Data Encryption Key (DEK).** The DEK is generated by KMS using the CMK. S3 is provided with both a plain-text version and an encrypted version of the DEK. The plain-text version of DEK is used to encrypt the object and then discarded. The encrypted version of DEK is stored along with the encrypted object. When you are using SSE-KMS, it is not necessary to use the default CMK that is created by S3. You can create and use a customer-managed CMK, which means you can control the permission on it as well as the rotation of the key material. So, if you have a regulatory board in your organization that is concerned with the rotation of the key or the separation of roles between encryption users and decryption users, then SSE-KMS is the solution. Logging and auditing are also possible on SSE-KMS to track the API calls made against keys.

- **Default bucket encryption:** If you set AES-256 while creating a bucket, or you enable it after creating a bucket, then SSE-S3 will be used (when you don't set something at the object level while performing a PUT operation).

In the next section, you will learn about some of the data stores used with EC2 instances.

Using other types of data stores

Elastic Block Store (EBS) is used to create volumes in an Availability Zone. The volume can only be attached to an EC2 instance in the same Availability Zone. Amazon EBS provides both **Solid-State Drive (SSD)** and **Hard Disk Drive (HDD)** types of volumes. For SSD-based volumes, the dominant performance attribute is **Input-Output Per Second (IOPS)**, and for HDD it is throughput, which is generally measured as MiB/s. You can choose between different volume types, such as General Purpose SSD (gp2), Provisioned IOPS SSD (io1), or Throughput Optimized HDD (st1), depending on your requirements. Provisioned IOPS volumes are often used for high-performance workloads, such as deep learning training, where low latency and high throughput are critical. *Table 2.1* provides an overview of the different volumes and types:

Volume Types	Use cases
General Purpose SSD (gp2)	Useful for maintaining balance between price and performance. Good for most workloads, system boot volumes, dev, and test environments
Provisioned IOPS SSD (io2, io1)	Useful for mission-critical, high-throughput or low-latency workloads. For example, I/O intensive database workloads like MongoDB, Cassandra, Oracle
Throughput Optimized HDD (st1)	Useful for frequently accessed, throughput-intensive workloads. For example, big data processing, data warehouses, log processing
Cold HDD (sc1)	Useful for less frequently accessed workloads

Table 2.1 – Different volumes and their use cases

EBS is designed to be resilient within an **Availability Zone (AZ)**. If, for some reason, an AZ fails, then the volume cannot be accessed. To prevent such scenarios, **snapshots** can be created from the EBS volumes, and they are stored in S3. Once the snapshot arrives in S3, the data in the snapshot becomes Region-resilient. The first snapshot is a full copy of data on the volume and, from then onward, snapshots are incremental. Snapshots can be used to clone a volume. As the snapshot is stored in S3, a volume can be cloned in any AZ in that Region. Snapshots can be shared between Regions and volumes can be cloned from them during disaster recovery. Even after the EC2 instance is stopped/terminated, EBS volumes can retain data through an easy restoration process from backed-up snapshots.

Multiple EC2 instances can be attached via **EBS Multi-Attach** for concurrent EBS volume access. If the use case demands multiple instances to access the training dataset simultaneously (distributed training scenarios), then EBS Multi-Attach will provide the solution with improved performance and scalability.

AWS KMS manages the CMK. AWS KMS uses an AWS-managed CMK for EBS, or AWS KMS can use a customer-managed CMK. The CMK is used by EBS when an encrypted volume is created. The CMK is used to create an encrypted DEK, which is stored with the volume on the physical disk. This DEK can only be decrypted using KMS, assuming the entity has access to decrypt. When a snapshot is created from the encrypted volume, the snapshot is encrypted with the same DEK. Any volume created from this snapshot also uses that DEK.

Instance Store volumes are the block storage devices physically connected to the EC2 instance. They provide the highest performance, as the ephemeral storage attached to the instance is from the same host where the instance is launched. EBS can be attached to the instance at any time, but the instance store must be attached to the instance at the time of its launch; it cannot be attached once the instance is launched. If there is an issue on the underlying host of an EC2 instance, then the same instance will be launched on another host with a new instance store volume and the earlier instance store (ephemeral storage) and old data will be lost. The size and capabilities of the attached volumes depend on the instance types and can be found in more detail here: `https://aws.amazon.com/ec2/instance-types/`.

Elastic File System (EFS) provides a network-based filesystem that can be mounted within Linux EC2 instances and can be used by multiple instances at once. It is an implementation of **NFSv4**. It can be used in general-purpose mode, max I/O performance mode (for scientific analysis or parallel computing), bursting mode, and provisioned throughput mode. This makes it ideal for scenarios where multiple instances need to train on large datasets or share model artifacts. With EFS, you can store training datasets, pre-trained models, and other data centrally, ensuring consistency and reducing data duplication. Additionally, EFS provides high throughput and low-latency access, enabling efficient data access during training and inference processes. By leveraging EFS with SageMaker, machine learning developers can seamlessly scale their workloads, collaborate effectively, and accelerate model development and training.

As you know, in the case of instance stores, the data is volatile. As soon as the instance is lost, the data is lost from the instance store. That is not the case for EFS. EFS is separate from the EC2 instance storage. EFS is a file store and is accessed by multiple EC2 instances via mount targets inside a VPC. On-premises systems can access EFS storage via hybrid networking to the VPC, such as **VPN** or **Direct Connect**. EFS also supports two types of storage classes: Standard and Infrequent Access. Standard is used for frequently accessed data. Infrequent Access is the cost-effective storage class for long-lived, less frequently accessed data. Lifecycle policies can be used for the transition of data between storage classes. EFS offers a pay-as-you-go pricing model, where you only pay for the storage capacity you use. It eliminates the need to provision and manage separate storage volumes for each instance, reducing storage costs and simplifying storage management for your machine learning workloads.

> **Important note**
> An instance store is preferred for max I/O requirements and if the data is replaceable and temporary.

Relational Database Service (RDS)

This is one of the most commonly featured topics in AWS exams. You should have sufficient knowledge prior to the exam. In this section, you will learn about Amazon's RDS.

AWS provides several relational databases as a service to its users. Users can run their desired database on EC2 instances, too. The biggest drawback is that the instance is only available in one Availability Zone in a Region. The EC2 instance has to be administered and monitored to avoid any kind of failure. Custom scripts will be required to maintain a data backup over time. Any database major or minor version update would result in downtime. Database instances running on an EC2 instance cannot be easily scaled if the load increases on the database as replication is not an easy task.

RDS provides managed database instances that can themselves hold one or more databases. Imagine a database server running on an EC2 instance that you do not have to manage or maintain. You need only access the server and create databases in it. AWS will manage everything else, such as the security of the instance, the operating system running on the instance, the database versions, and high availability of the database server. RDS supports multiple engines, such as MySQL, Microsoft SQL Server, MariaDB, Amazon Aurora, Oracle, and PostgreSQL. You can choose any of these based on your requirements.

The foundation of Amazon RDS is a database instance, which can support multiple engines and can have multiple databases created by the user. One database instance can be accessed only by using the database DNS endpoint (the CNAME, which is an alias for the canonical name in a domain name system database) of the primary instance. RDS uses standard database engines. So, accessing the database using some sort of tool in a self-managed database server is the same as accessing Amazon RDS.

As you have now understood the requirements of Amazon RDS, let's understand the failover process in Amazon RDS. You will cover what services Amazon offers if something goes wrong with the RDS instance.

Managing failover in Amazon RDS

RDS instances can be **Single-AZ** or **Multi-AZ**. In Multi-AZ, multiple instances work together, similar to an active-passive failover design.

For a Single-AZ RDS instance, storage can be allocated for that instance to use. In a nutshell, a Single-AZ RDS instance has one attached block store (EBS storage) available in the same Availability Zone. This makes the databases and the storage of the RDS instance vulnerable to Availability Zone failure. The storage allocated to the block storage can be SSD (gp2 or io1) or magnetic. To secure the RDS instance, it is advised to use a security group and provide access based on requirements.

Multi-AZ is always the best way to design the architecture to prevent failures and keep the applications highly available. With Multi-AZ features, a standby replica is kept in sync synchronously with the primary instance. The standby instance has its own storage in the assigned Availability Zone. A standby replica cannot be accessed directly, because all RDS access is via a single database DNS endpoint (CNAME). You can't access the standby unless a failover happens. The standby provides no performance benefit, but it does constitute an improvement in terms of the availability of the RDS instance. It can only happen in the same Region, another AZ's subnet in the same Region inside the VPC. When a Multi-AZ RDS instance is online, you can take a backup from the standby replica without affecting the performance. In a Single-AZ instance, availability and performance issues can be significant during backup operation.

To understand the workings of Multi-AZ, let's take an example of a Single-AZ instance and expand it to Multi-AZ.

Imagine you have an RDS instance running in Availability Zone `AZ-A` of the `us-east-1` Region inside a VPC named `db-vpc`. This becomes a primary instance in a Single-AZ design of an RDS instance. In this case, there will be storage allocated to the instance in the `AZ-A` Availability Zone. Once you opt for Multi-AZ deployment in another Availability Zone called `AZ-B`, AWS creates a standby instance in Availability Zone `AZ-B` of the `us-east-1` Region inside the `db-vpc` VPC and allocates storage for the standby instance in `AZ-B` of the `us-east-1` Region. Along with that, RDS will enable **synchronous replication** from the primary instance to the standby replica. As you learned earlier, the only way to access our RDS instance is via the database CNAME, hence, the access request goes to the RDS primary instance. As soon as a write request comes to the endpoint, it writes to the primary instance. Then it writes the data to the hardware, which is the block storage attached to the primary instance. At the same time, the primary instance replicates the same data to the standby instance. Finally, the standby instance commits the data to its block storage.

The primary instance writes the data into the hardware and replicates the data to the standby instance in parallel, so there is a minimal time lag (almost nothing) between the data commit operations in their respective hardware. If an error occurs with the primary instance, then RDS detects this and changes the database endpoint to the standby instance. The clients accessing the database may experience a very short interruption with this. This failover occurs within 60-120 seconds. It does not provide a fault-tolerant system because there will be some impact during the failover operation.

You should now understand failover management on Amazon RDS. Let's now learn about taking automatic RDS backups and using snapshots to restore in the event of a failure, and read replicas in the next section.

Taking automatic backups, RDS snapshots, and restore and read replicas

In this section, you will see how RDS **automatic backups** and **manual snapshots** work. These features come with Amazon RDS.

Let's consider a database that is scheduled to take a backup at 5 A.M. every day. If the application fails at 11 A.M., then it is possible to restart the application from the backup taken at 11 A.M. with the loss of 6 hours' worth of data. This is called a 6-hour **Recovery Point Objective (RPO)**. The RPO is defined as the time between the most recent backup and the incident, and this determines the amount of data loss. If you want to reduce this, then you have to schedule more incremental backups, which increases the cost and backup frequency. If your business demands a lower RPO value, then the business must spend more to provide the necessary technical solutions.

Now, according to our example, an engineer was assigned the task of bringing the system back online as soon as the disaster occurred. The engineer managed to bring the database online at 2 P.M. on the same day by adding a few extra hardware components to the current system and installing some updated versions of the software. This is called a 3-hour **Recovery Time Objective (RTO).** The RTO is determined as the time between the disaster recovery and full recovery. RTO values can be reduced by having spare hardware and documenting the restoration process. If the business demands a lower RTO value, then your business must spend more money on spare hardware and an effective system setup to perform the restoration process.

In RDS, the RPO and RTO play an important role in the selection of automatic backups and manual snapshots. Both of these backup services use AWS-managed S3 buckets, which means they cannot be visible in the user's AWS S3 console. They areRegion-resilient because the backup is replicated into multiple Availability Zones in the AWS Region. In the case of a Single-AZ RDS instance, the backup happens from the single available data store, and for a Multi-AZ enabled RDS instance, the backup happens from the standby data store (the primary store remains untouched as regards the backup).

The snapshots are manual for RDS instances, and they are stored in the AWS-managed S3 bucket. The first snapshot of an RDS instance is a full copy of the data and the onward snapshots are incremental, reflecting the change in the data. In terms of the time taken for the snapshot process, it is high for the first one and, from then on, the incremental backup is quicker. When any snapshot occurs, it can impact the performance of the Single-AZ RDS instance, but not the performance of a Multi-AZ RDS instance as this happens on the standby data storage. Manual snapshots do not expire, have to be cleared automatically, and live past the termination of an RDS instance. When you delete an RDS instance, it suggests making one final snapshot on your behalf and it will contain all the databases inside your RDS instance (there is not just a single database in an RDS instance). When you restore from a manual snapshot, you restore to a single point in time, and that affects the RPO.

To automate this entire process, you can choose a time window when these snapshots can be taken. This is called an automatic backup. These time windows can be managed carefully to essentially lower the RPO value of the business. Automatic backups have a retention period of 0 to 35 days, with 0 being disabled and the maximum is 35 days. To quote AWS documentation, retained automated backups contain system snapshots and transaction logs from a database instance. They also include database instance properties such as allocated storage and a database instance class, which are required to restore it to an active instance. Databases generate transaction logs, which contain the actual change in data in a particular database. These transaction logs are also written to S3 every 5 minutes by RDS. Transaction logs can also be replayed on top of the snapshots to restore to a point in time of 5 minutes' granularity. Theoretically, the RPO can be a 5-minute point in time.

When you perform a restore, RDS creates a new RDS instance, which means a new database endpoint to access the instance. The applications using the instances have to point to the new address, which significantly affects the RTO. This means that the restoration process is not very fast, which affects the RTO. To minimize the RTO during a failure, you may consider replicating the data. With replicas, there is a high chance of replicating the corrupted data. The only way to overcome this is to have snapshots and restore an RDS instance to a particular point in time prior to the corruption. **Amazon RDS Read Replicas** are unlike the Multi-AZ replicas. In Multi-AZ RDS instances, the standby replicas cannot be used directly for anything unless a primary instance fails, whereas **Read Replicas** can be used directly, but only for read operations. Read replicas have their own database endpoints and read-heavy applications can directly point to this address. They are kept in sync **asynchronously** with the primary instance. Read Replicas can be created in the same Region as the primary instance or in a different Region. Read Replicas in other Regions are called **Cross-Region Read Replicas** and this improves the global performance of the application.

As per AWS documentation, five direct Read Replicas are allowed per database instance and this helps to scale out the read performances. Read Replicas have a very low RPO value due to asynchronous replication. They can be promoted to a read-write database instance in the case of a primary instance failure. This can be done quickly and it offers a fairly low RTO value.

In the next section, you will learn about Amazon's database engine, Amazon Aurora.

Writing to Amazon Aurora with multi-master capabilities

Amazon Aurora is the most reliable relational database engine developed by Amazon to deliver speed in a simple and cost-effective manner. Aurora uses a cluster of single primary instances and zero or more replicas. Aurora's replicas can give you the advantage of both read replicas and Multi-AZ instances in RDS. Aurora uses a shared cluster volume for storage and is available to all compute instances of the cluster (a maximum of 64 TiB). This allows the Aurora cluster to provision faster and improves availability and performance. Aurora uses SSD-based storage, which provides high IOPS and low latency. Aurora does not ask you to allocate storage, unlike other RDS instances; it is based on the storage that you use.

Aurora clusters have multiple endpoints, including the **cluster endpoint and reader endpoint.** If there are zero replicas, then the cluster endpoint is the same as the reader endpoint. If there are replicas available, then the reader endpoint is load-balanced across the reader endpoints. Cluster endpoints are used for reading/writing, while reader endpoints are intended for reading from the cluster. If you add more replicas, then AWS manages load balancing under the hood for the new replicas.

When failover occurs, the replicas are promoted to read/write mode, and this takes some time. This can be prevented in a **Multi-Master** mode of an Aurora cluster. This allows multiple instances to perform reads and writes at the same time.

Storing columnar data on Amazon Redshift

Amazon Redshift is not used for real-time transactions, but it is used for data warehouse purposes. It is designed to support huge volumes of data at a petabyte scale. It is a column-based database used for analytics, long-term processing, tending, and aggregation. **Redshift Spectrum** can be used to query data on S3 without loading data to the Redshift cluster (a Redshift cluster is required, though). It's not an OLTP, but an OLAP. **AWS QuickSight** can be integrated with Redshift for visualization, with a SQL-like interface that allows you to connect using JDBC/ODBC connections to query the data.

Redshift uses a clustered architecture in one AZ in a VPC with faster network connectivity between the nodes. It is not high availability by design as it is tightly coupled to the AZ. A Redshift cluster has a leader node, and this node is responsible for all the communication between the client and the computing nodes of the cluster, query planning, and aggregation. Compute nodes are responsible for running the queries submitted by the leader lode and for storing the data. By default, Redshift uses a public network for communicating with external services or any AWS services. With **enhanced VPC routing**, it can be controlled via customized networking settings.

By combining Redshift with SageMaker, data scientists and analysts can leverage the scalability and computational power of Redshift to preprocess and transform data before training machine learning models. They can utilize Redshift's advanced SQL capabilities to perform aggregations, joins, and filtering operations, enabling efficient feature engineering and data preparation. The processed data can then be seamlessly fed into SageMaker for model training, hyperparameter tuning, and evaluation.

Amazon DynamoDB for NoSQL Database-as-a-Service

Amazon DynamoDB is a NoSQL database-as-a-service product within AWS. It's a fully managed key/value and document database. Accessing DynamoDB is easy via its endpoint. The input and output throughputs can be managed or scaled manually or automatically. It also supports data backup, point-in-time recovery, and data encryption.

One example where Amazon DynamoDB can be used with Amazon SageMaker in a cost-efficient way is for real-time prediction applications. DynamoDB can serve as a storage backend for storing and retrieving input data for prediction models built using SageMaker. Instead of continuously running and scaling an inference endpoint, which can be costlier, you can leverage DynamoDB's low-latency access and scalability to retrieve the required input data on demand.

In this setup, the input data for predictions can be stored in DynamoDB tables, where each item represents a unique data instance. When a prediction request is received, the application can use DynamoDB's efficient querying capabilities to retrieve the required input data item(s) based on specific attributes or conditions. Once the data is retrieved, it can be passed to the SageMaker endpoint for real-time predictions.

By using DynamoDB in this way, you can dynamically scale your application's read capacity based on the incoming prediction requests, ensuring that you only pay for the read capacity you actually need. This approach offers a cost-efficient solution as it eliminates the need for running and managing a continuously running inference endpoint, which may incur high costs even during periods of low prediction demand. With DynamoDB and SageMaker working together, you can achieve scalable and cost-efficient real-time prediction applications while maintaining low latency and high availability.

You will not cover the DynamoDB table structure or key structure in this chapter as this is not required for the certification exam. However, it is good to have a basic knowledge of them. For more details, please refer to the AWS docs available here: `https://docs.aws.amazon.com/amazondynamodb/latest/developerguide/SQLtoNoSQL.html`.

Summary

In this chapter, you learned about various data storage services from Amazon, and how to secure data through various policies and use these services. If you are working on machine learning use cases, then you may encounter such scenarios where you have to choose an effective data storage service for your requirements.

In the next chapter, you will learn about the migration and processing of stored data.

Exam Readiness Drill – Chapter Review Questions

Apart from a solid understanding of key concepts, being able to think quickly under time pressure is a skill that will help you ace your certification exam. That is why working on these skills early on in your learning journey is key.

Chapter review questions are designed to improve your test-taking skills progressively with each chapter you learn and review your understanding of key concepts in the chapter at the same time. You'll find these at the end of each chapter.

> **How To Access These Resources**
>
> To learn how to access these resources, head over to the chapter titled *Chapter 11*, *Accessing the Online Practice Resources*.

To open the Chapter Review Questions for this chapter, perform the following steps:

1. Click the link – `https://packt.link/MLSC01E2_CH02`.

    Alternatively, you can scan the following **QR code** (*Figure 2.3*):

Figure 2.3 – QR code that opens Chapter Review Questions for logged-in users

2. Once you log in, you'll see a page similar to the one shown in *Figure 2.4*:

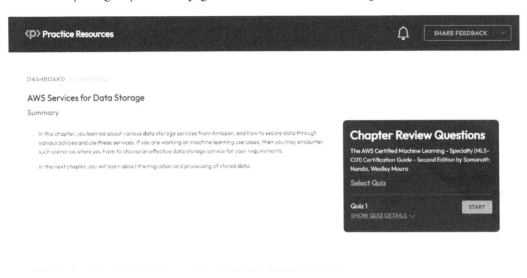

Figure 2.4 – Chapter Review Questions for Chapter 2

3. Once ready, start the following practice drills, re-attempting the quiz multiple times.

Exam Readiness Drill

For the first three attempts, don't worry about the time limit.

ATTEMPT 1

The first time, aim for at least **40%**. Look at the answers you got wrong and read the relevant sections in the chapter again to fix your learning gaps.

ATTEMPT 2

The second time, aim for at least **60%**. Look at the answers you got wrong and read the relevant sections in the chapter again to fix any remaining learning gaps.

ATTEMPT 3

The third time, aim for at least **75%**. Once you score 75% or more, you start working on your timing.

> **Tip**
> You may take more than **three** attempts to reach 75%. That's okay. Just review the relevant sections in the chapter till you get there.

Working On Timing

Target: Your aim is to keep the score the same while trying to answer these questions as quickly as possible. Here's an example of how your next attempts should look like:

Attempt	Score	Time Taken
Attempt 5	77%	21 mins 30 seconds
Attempt 6	78%	18 mins 34 seconds
Attempt 7	76%	14 mins 44 seconds

Table 2.2 – Sample timing practice drills on the online platform

> **Note**
> The time limits shown in the above table are just examples. Set your own time limits with each attempt based on the time limit of the quiz on the website.

With each new attempt, your score should stay above **75%** while your "time taken" to complete should "decrease". Repeat as many attempts as you want till you feel confident dealing with the time pressure.

3

AWS Services for Data Migration and Processing

In the previous chapter, you learned about several ways of storing data in AWS. In this chapter, you will explore the techniques for using that data and gaining some insight from the data. There are use cases where you have to process your data or load the data to a hive data warehouse to query and analyze the data. If you are on AWS and your data is in S3, then you have to create a table in hive on AWS EMR to query the data in the hive table. To provide the same functionality as a managed service, AWS has a product called Athena, where you create a data catalog and query your data on S3. If you need to transform the data, then AWS Glue is the best option to transform and restore it to S3. Imagine a use case where you need to stream data and create analytical reports on that data. For this, you can opt for AWS Kinesis Data Streams to stream data and store it in S3. Using Glue, the same data can be copied to Redshift for further analytical utilization. AWS **Database Migration Service (DMS)** provides seamless migration of heterogeneous and homogeneous databases. This chapter will cover the following topics that are required for the purpose of the certification:

- Using Glue to design ETL jobs
- Querying S3 data using Athena
- Streaming data through AWS Kinesis Data Streams and storing it using Kinesis Firehose
- Ingesting data from on-premises locations to AWS
- Migrating data to AWS and extending on-premises data centers to AWS
- Processing data on AWS

Technical requirements

You can download the data used in the examples from GitHub, available here: `https://github.com/PacktPublishing/AWS-Certified-Machine-Learning-Specialty-MLS-C01-Certification-Guide-Second-Edition/tree/main/Chapter03`.

Creating ETL jobs on AWS Glue

In a modern data pipeline, there are multiple stages, such as generating data, collecting data, storing data, performing ETL, analyzing, and visualizing. In this section, you will cover each of these at a high level and understand the **extract, transform, load (ETL)** process in depth:

- Data can be generated from several devices, including mobile devices or IoT, weblogs, social media, transactional data, and online games.

- This huge amount of generated data can be collected by using polling services, through API gateways integrated with AWS Lambda to collect the data, or via streams such as AWS Kinesis, AWS-managed Kafka, or Kinesis Firehose. If you have an on-premises database and you want to bring that data to AWS, then you would choose AWS DMS for that. You can sync your on-premises data to Amazon S3, Amazon EFS, or Amazon FSx via AWS DataSync. AWS Snowball is used to collect/transfer data into and out of AWS.

- The next step involves storing data. You learned about some of the services to do this in the previous chapter, such as S3, EBS, EFS, RDS, Redshift, and DynamoDB.

- Once you know your data storage requirements, an ETL job can be designed to extract-transform-load or extract-load-transform your structured or unstructured data into the format you desire for further analysis. For example, you can use AWS Lambda to transform the data on the fly and store the transformed data in S3, or you can run a Spark application on an EMR cluster to transform the data and store it in S3 or Redshift or RDS.

- There are many services available in AWS for performing an analysis on transformed data, for example, EMR, Athena, Redshift, Redshift Spectrum, and Kinesis Analytics.

- Once the data is analyzed, you can visualize it using AWS QuickSight to understand the patterns or trends. Data scientists or machine learning professionals would want to apply statistical analysis to understand data distribution in a better way. Business users use statistical analysis to prepare reports. You will learn and explore various ways to present and visualize data in *Chapter 5, Data Understanding and Visualization*.

What you understood from the traditional data pipeline is that ETL is all about coding and maintaining code on the servers so that everything runs smoothly. If the data format changes in any way, then the code needs to be changed, and that results in a change to the target schema. If the data source changes, then the code must be able to handle that too, and it's an overhead. *Should you write code to recognize these changes in data sources? Do you need a system to adapt to the change and discover the data for you?* The answer to these questions is yes, and to do so, you can use **AWS Glue**. Now, you will learn why AWS Glue is so popular.

Features of AWS Glue

AWS Glue is a completely managed serverless ETL service on AWS. It has the following features:

- It automatically discovers and categorizes your data by connecting to the data sources and generates a data catalog.

- Services such as Amazon Athena, Amazon Redshift, and Amazon EMR can use the data catalog to query the data.

- AWS Glue generates the ETL code, which is an extension to Spark in Python or Scala, which can be modified, too.

- It scales out automatically to match your Spark application requirements for running the ETL job and loading the data into the destination.

AWS Glue has the **Data Catalog**, and that's the secret to its success. It helps with discovering data from data sources and understanding a bit about it:

- The Data Catalog automatically discovers new data and extracts schema definitions. It detects schema changes and version tables. It detects Apache Hive-style partitions on Amazon S3.

- The Data Catalog comes with built-in classifiers for popular data types. Custom classifiers can be written using **Grok expressions**. The classifiers help to detect the schema.

- Glue crawlers can be run ad hoc or in a scheduled fashion to update the metadata in the Glue Data Catalog. Glue crawlers must be associated with an IAM role with sufficient access to read the data sources, such as Amazon RDS, Redshift, and S3.

As you now have a brief idea of what AWS Glue is used for, move on to run the following example to get your hands dirty.

Getting hands-on with AWS Glue Data Catalog components

In this example, you will create a job to copy data from S3 to Redshift by using AWS Glue. All my components were created in the `us-east-1` region. Start by creating a bucket:

1. Navigate to the AWS S3 console and create a bucket. I have named the bucket `aws-glue-example-01`.

2. Click on **Create Folder** and name it `input-data`.

3. Navigate inside the folder and click on the **Upload** button to upload the `sales-records.csv` dataset. The data is available in the following GitHub location: `https://github.com/PacktPublishing/AWS-Certified-Machine-Learning-Specialty-MLS-C01-Certification-Guide-Second-Edition/tree/main/Chapter03/AWS-Glue-Demo/input-data`.

    As you have the data uploaded in the S3 bucket, now create a VPC in which you will create your Redshift cluster.

4. Navigate to the VPC console by accessing the `https://console.aws.amazon.com/vpc/home?region=us-east-1#` URL and click on **Endpoints** on the left-hand side menu. Click on **Create Endpoint** and then fill in the fields as shown here:

    A. **Service Category**: `AWS services`

    B. **Select a service**: `com.amazonaws.us-east-1.s3` (gateway type)

    C. **VPC**: Select **the Default VPC** (use this default VPC in which your Redshift cluster will be created)

5. Leave the other fields as is and click on **Create Endpoint**.

6. Click on **Security Groups** from the VPC console. Give a name to your security group, such as `redshift-self`, and choose the default VPC drop-down menu. Provide an appropriate description, such as `Redshift Security Group`. Click on **Create security group**.

7. Click on the **Actions** dropdown and select **Edit Inbound rules**. Click on **Add rule** and complete the fields as shown here:

    A. **Type**: All traffic

    B. **Source**: Custom

    C. In the search field, select the same security group (redshift-self)

8. Click on **Save Rules**.

    Now, create your Redshift cluster.

9. Navigate to the Amazon Redshift console. Click on **Create Cluster** and complete the highlighted fields, as shown in *Figure 3.1*:

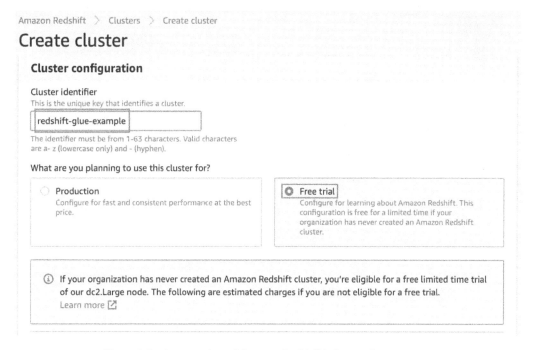

Figure 3.1 – A screenshot of Amazon Redshift's Create cluster screen

10. Scroll down and fill in the highlighted fields shown in *Figure 3.2* with your own values:

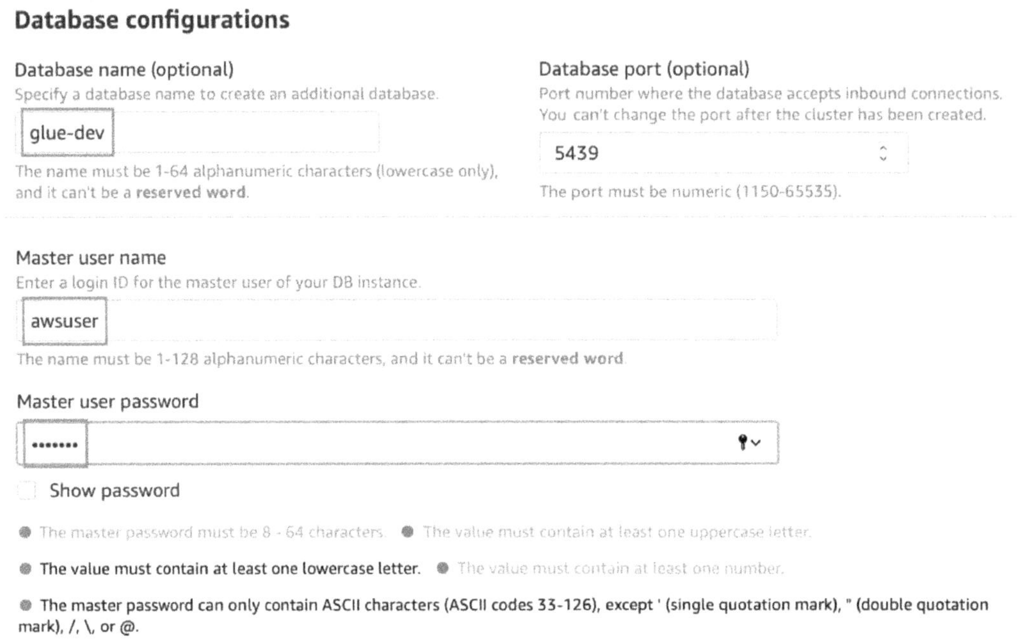

Database configurations

Database name (optional)
Specify a database name to create an additional database.

glue-dev

The name must be 1-64 alphanumeric characters (lowercase only), and it can't be a **reserved word**.

Database port (optional)
Port number where the database accepts inbound connections. You can't change the port after the cluster has been created.

5439

The port must be numeric (1150-65535).

Master user name
Enter a login ID for the master user of your DB instance.

awsuser

The name must be 1-128 alphanumeric characters, and it can't be a **reserved word**.

Master user password

••••••••

☐ Show password

● The master password must be 8 - 64 characters.   ● The value must contain at least one uppercase letter.

● **The value must contain at least one lowercase letter.**   ● The value must contain at least one number.

● **The master password can only contain ASCII characters (ASCII codes 33-126), except ' (single quotation mark), " (double quotation mark), /, \, or @.**

Figure 3.2 – A screenshot of an Amazon Redshift cluster's Database configurations section

11. Scroll down and change the **Additional configurations** settings, as shown in *Figure 3.3*:

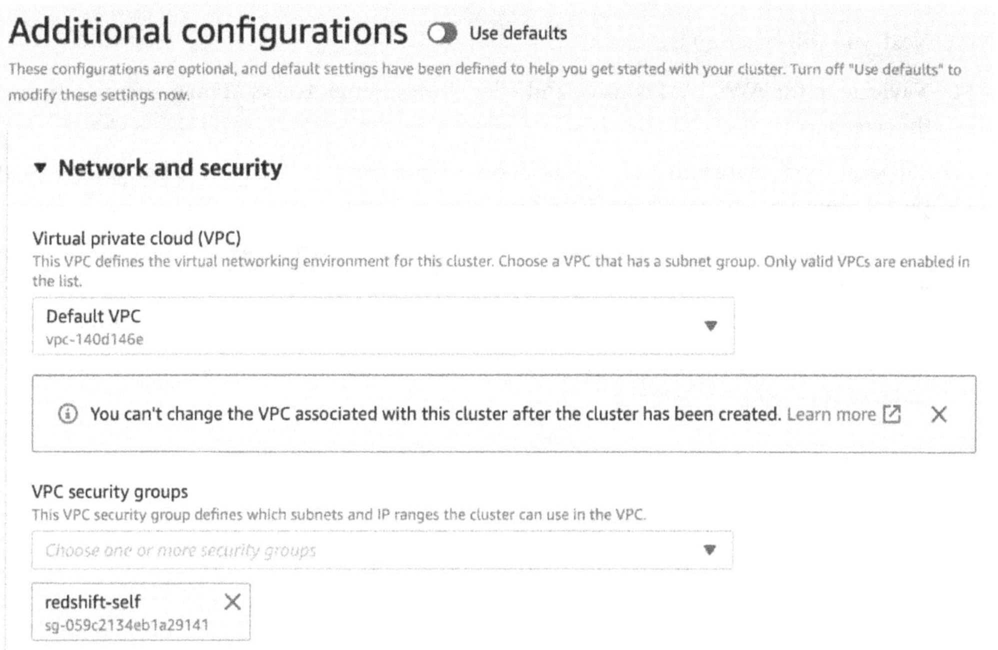

Additional configurations ◯ Use defaults

These configurations are optional, and default settings have been defined to help you get started with your cluster. Turn off "Use defaults" to modify these settings now.

▼ **Network and security**

Virtual private cloud (VPC)

This VPC defines the virtual networking environment for this cluster. Choose a VPC that has a subnet group. Only valid VPCs are enabled in the list.

Default VPC	
vpc-140d146e	▼

ⓘ You can't change the VPC associated with this cluster after the cluster has been created. Learn more ⧉   ✕

VPC security groups

This VPC security group defines which subnets and IP ranges the cluster can use in the VPC.

Choose one or more security groups	▼

redshift-self   ✕
sg-059c2134eb1a29141

Figure 3.3 – A screenshot of an Amazon Redshift cluster's Additional configurations section

12. Change the IAM permissions too, as shown in *Figure 3.4*:

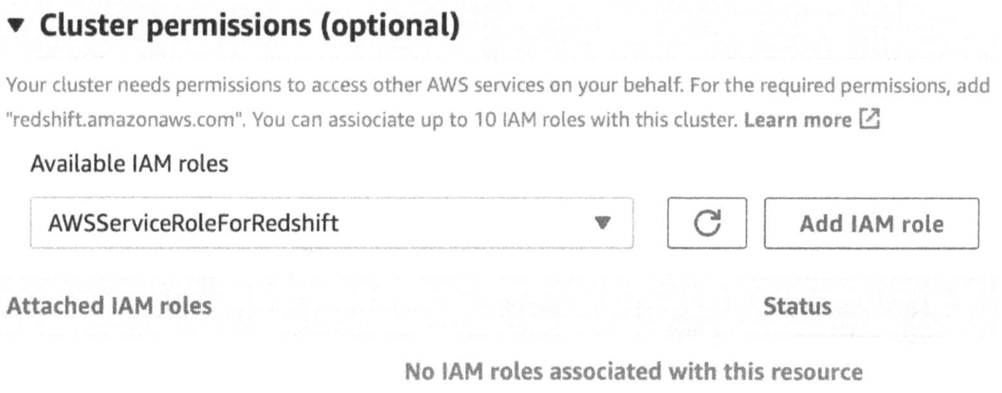

▼ Cluster permissions (optional)

Your cluster needs permissions to access other AWS services on your behalf. For the required permissions, add "redshift.amazonaws.com". You can assiociate up to 10 IAM roles with this cluster. **Learn more** ⧉

Available IAM roles

AWSServiceRoleForRedshift ▼	↻	Add IAM role

Attached IAM roles   **Status**

No IAM roles associated with this resource

Figure 3.4 – A screenshot of an Amazon Redshift cluster's Cluster permissions section

13. Scroll down and click on **Create Cluster**. It will take a minute or two to get the cluster in the available state.

Next, you will create an IAM role.

14. Navigate to the AWS IAM console and select **Roles** in the **Access Management** section on the screen.

15. Click on the **Create role** button and choose **Glue** from the services. Click on the **Next: permissions** button to navigate to the next page.

16. Search for `AmazonS3FullAccess` and select it. Then, search for `AWSGlueServiceRole` and select it. As you are writing your data to Redshift as part of this example, select **AmazonRedshiftFullAccess**. Click on **Next: Tags**, followed by the **Next: Review** button.

17. Provide a name, `Glue-IAM-Role`, and then click on the **Create role** button. The role appears as shown in *Figure 3.5*:

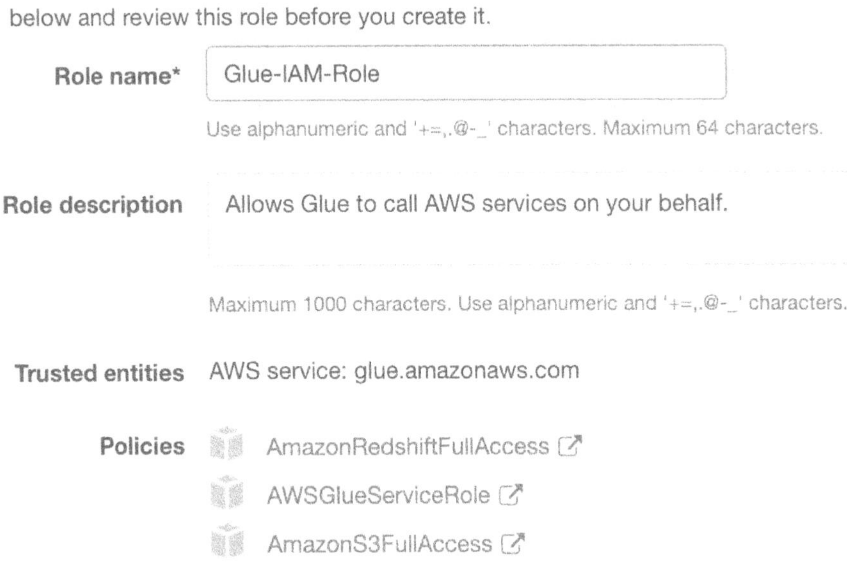

below and review this role before you create it.

Role name*	Glue-IAM-Role

Use alphanumeric and '+=,.@-_' characters. Maximum 64 characters.

Role description	Allows Glue to call AWS services on your behalf.

Maximum 1000 characters. Use alphanumeric and '+=,.@-_' characters.

Trusted entities   AWS service: glue.amazonaws.com

Policies   AmazonRedshiftFullAccess ☑

AWSGlueServiceRole ☑

AmazonS3FullAccess ☑

Figure 3.5 – A screenshot of the IAM role

Now, you have the input data source and the output data storage handy. The next step is to create the Glue crawler from the AWS Glue console.

18. Select **Connections** under **Databases**. Click on the **Add connection** button and complete the fields as shown here:

    A. **Connection name**: `glue-redshift-connection`

    B. **Connection type**: `Amazon Redshift`

19. Click on **Next** and then fill in the fields as shown here:

    A. **Cluster**: `redshift-glue-example`

    B. **Database name**: `glue-dev`

    C. **Username**: `awsuser`

    D. **Password**: `********` (enter the value chosen in *step 10*)

20. Click on **Next** and then **Finish**. To verify that it's working, click on **Test Connection**, select **Glue-IAM-Role** in the IAM role section, and then click **Test Connection**.

21. Go to Crawler and select Add Crawler. Provide a name for the crawler, S3-glue-crawler, and then click Next. On the Specify crawler source type page, leave everything as their default settings and then click Next.

22. On the **Add a data store** page, choose **Include path** option and enter `s3://aws-glue-example-01/input-data/sales-records.csv`.

23. Click **Next**.

24. Set **Add another datastore** to No. Click **Next**.

25. For **Choose an existing IAM Role**, set `Glue-IAM-Role`. Then, click **Next**.

26. Set **Frequency** to **Run on demand**. Click **Next**.

27. No database has been created, so click on **Add database**, provide a name, `s3-data`, click **Next**, and then click **Finish**.

28. Select the crawler, **S3-glue-crawler**, and then click on **Run Crawler**. Once the run is complete, you can see that there is a *1* in the **Tables Added** column. This means that a database, `s3-data`, has been created, as mentioned in the previous step, and a table has been added. Click on **Tables** and select the newly created table, **sales_records_csv**. You can see that the schema has been discovered now. You can change the data type if the inferred data type does not meet your requirements.

In this hands-on section, you learned about database tables, database connections, crawlers in S3, and the creation of a Redshift cluster. In the next hands-on section, you will learn about creating ETL jobs using Glue.

Getting hands-on with AWS Glue ETL components

In this section, you will use the Data Catalog components created earlier to build a job. You will start by creating a job:

1. Navigate to the AWS Glue console and click on **Jobs** under the **ETL** section.

2. Click on the **Add Job** button and complete the fields as shown here:

    - **Name**: `s3-glue-redshift`

    - **IAM role**: **Glue-IAM-Role** (this is the same role you created in the previous section)

    - **Type**: `Spark`

    - **Glue version**: **Spark 2.4, Python 3 with improved job start up times (Glue version 2.0)**

3. Leave the other fields as they are and then click on **Next**.

4. Select **sales_records_csv** and click on **Next**.

5. Select **Change Schema** by default and then click **Next** (at the time of writing this book, machine learning transformations are not supported for Glue 2.0).

6. Select **Create tables in your data target**. Choose **JDBC** as the data store and **glue-redshift-connection** as the connection. Provide `glue-dev` as the database name (as created in the previous section) and then click **Next**.

7. Next comes the **Output Schema Definition** page, where you can choose the desired columns to be removed from the target schema. Scroll down and click on **Save job and edit script**.

8. You can now see the pipeline being created on the left-hand side of the screen and the suggested code on the right-hand side, as shown in *Figure 3.6*. You can modify the code based on your requirements. Click on the **Run job** button. A pop-up window appears, asking you to edit any details that you wish to change.

This is optional. Then, click on the **Run job** button:

Figure 3.6 – A screenshot of the AWS Glue ETL job

9. Once the job is successful, navigate to Amazon Redshift and click on **Query editor**.

10. Set the database name as `glue-dev` and then provide the username and password to create a connection.

11. Select the `public` schema, and now you can query the table to see the records, as shown in *Figure 3.7*:

Figure 3.7 – A screenshot of Amazon Redshift's Query editor

You now understand how to create an ETL job using AWS Glue to copy the data from an S3 bucket to Amazon Redshift. You also queried data in Amazon Redshift using the query editor from the UI console. It is recommended to delete the Redshift cluster and AWS Glue job once you have completed the steps successfully. AWS creates two buckets in your account to store AWS Glue scripts and temporary results from AWS Glue. Delete these as well to save costs. You will use the data catalog created on S3 data in the next section.

In the following section, you will learn about querying S3 data using Athena.

Querying S3 data using Athena

Athena is a serverless service designed for querying data stored in S3. It is serverless because the client doesn't manage the servers that are used for computation:

- Athena uses a schema to present the results against a query on the data stored in S3. You define how (the way or the structure) you want your data to appear in the form of a schema and Athena reads the raw data from S3 to show the results as per the defined schema.

- The output can be used by other services for visualization, storage, or various analytics purposes. The source data in S3 can be in any of the following structured, semi-structured, or unstructured data formats: XML, JSON, CSV/TSV, AVRO, Parquet, or ORC (as well as others). CloudTrail, ELB logs, and VPC flow logs can also be stored in S3 and analyzed by Athena.

- This follows the schema-on-read technique. Unlike traditional techniques, tables are defined in advance in a data catalog, and the data's structure is validated against the table's schema while reading the data from the tables. SQL-like queries can be carried out on data without transforming the source data.

Now, to help you understand this, here's an example, where you will use **AWSDataCatalog** created in AWS Glue on the S3 data and query them using Athena:

1. Navigate to the AWS Athena console. Select `AWSDataCatalog` from **Data source** (if you are doing this for the first time, then a `sampledb` database will be created with a table, `elb_logs`, in the AWS Glue Data Catalog).

2. Select `s3-data` as the database.

3. Click on **Settings** in the top-right corner and fill in the details as shown in *Figure 3.8* (I have used the same bucket as in the previous example and a different folder):

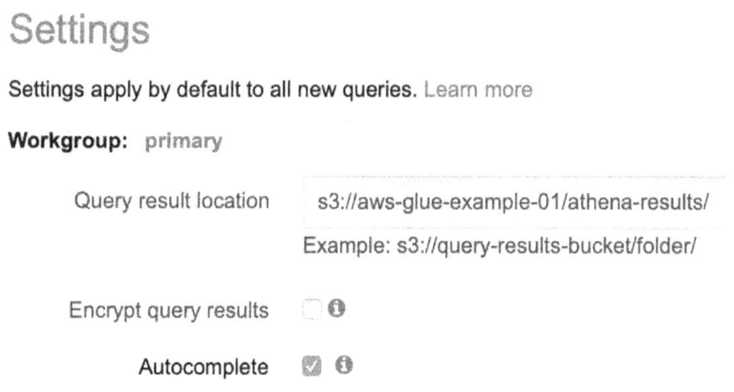

Settings

Settings apply by default to all new queries. Learn more

Workgroup: primary

Query result location	s3://aws-glue-example-01/athena-results/
	Example: s3://query-results-bucket/folder/
Encrypt query results	☐ ⓘ
Autocomplete	☑ ⓘ

Figure 3.8 – A screenshot of Amazon Athena's settings

4. The next step is to write your query in the query editor and execute it. Once your execution is complete, please delete your S3 buckets and AWS Glue data catalogs. This will save you money.

In this section, you learned how to query S3 data using Amazon Athena through the AWS Glue Data Catalog. You also learned how to create a schema and query data from S3. In the next section, you will learn about Amazon Kinesis Data Streams.

Processing real-time data using Kinesis Data Streams

Kinesis is Amazon's streaming service and can be scaled based on requirements. It has a level of persistence that retains data for 24 hours by default or optionally up to 365 days. Kinesis Data Streams is used for large-scale data ingestion, analytics, and monitoring:

- Kinesis streams can be ingested by multiple producers and multiple consumers can also read data from the streams. The following is an example to help you understand this. Suppose you have a producer ingesting data to a Kinesis stream and the default retention period is 24 hours, which means data ingested at 05:00:00 A.M. today will be available in the stream until 04:59:59 A.M. tomorrow. This data won't be available beyond that point, and ideally, it should be consumed before it expires; otherwise, it can be stored somewhere if it's critical. The retention period can be extended to a maximum of 365 days, at an extra cost.

- Kinesis can be used for real-time analytics or dashboard visualization. Producers can be imagined as a piece of code pushing data into the Kinesis stream, and it can be an EC2 instance, a Lambda function, an IoT device, on-premises servers, mobile applications or devices, and so on running the code.

- Similarly, the consumer can also be a piece of code running on an EC2 instance, Lambda function, or on-premises servers that know how to connect to a Kinesis stream, read the data, and apply some action to the data. AWS provides triggers to invoke a Lambda consumer as soon as data arrives in the Kinesis stream.

- Kinesis is scalable due to its shard architecture, which is the fundamental throughput unit of a Kinesis stream. *What is a shard?* A shard is a logical structure that partitions the data based on a partition key. A shard supports a writing capacity of *1 MB/sec* and a reading capacity of *2 MB/sec*. 1,000 `PUT` records per second are supported by a single shard. If you have created a stream with *three shards*, then *3 MB/sec write throughput* and *6 MB/sec read throughput* can be achieved, and this allows 3,000 `PUT` records. So, with more shards, you have to pay an extra amount to get higher performance.

- The data in a shard is stored via a Kinesis data record and can be a maximum of 1 MB. Kinesis data records are stored across the shard based on the partition key. They also have a sequence number. A sequence number is assigned by Kinesis as soon as a `putRecord` or `putRecords` API operation is performed so as to uniquely identify a record. The partition key is specified by the producer while adding the data to the Kinesis data stream, and the partition key is responsible for segregating and routing the record to different shards in the stream to balance the load.

- There are two ways to encrypt the data in a Kinesis stream: server-side encryption and client-side encryption. Client-side encryption makes it hard to implement and manage the keys because the client has to encrypt the data before putting it into the stream and decrypt the data after reading it from the stream. With server-side encryption enabled via **AWS KMS**, the data is automatically encrypted and decrypted as you put the data and get it from a stream.

> **Note**
>
> Amazon Kinesis shouldn't be confused with Amazon SQS. Amazon SQS supports one production group and one consumption group. If your use case demands multiple users sending data and receiving data, then Kinesis is the solution.
>
> For decoupling and asynchronous communications, SQS is the solution, because the sender and receiver do not need to be aware of one another.
>
> In SQS, there is no concept of persistence. Once the message is read, the next step is deletion. There's no concept of a retention time window for Amazon SQS. If your use case demands large-scale ingestion, then Kinesis should be used.

In the next section, you will learn about storing the streamed data for further analysis.

Storing and transforming real-time data using Kinesis Data Firehose

There are a lot of use cases that require data to be streamed and stored for future analytics purposes. To overcome such problems, you can write a Kinesis consumer to read the Kinesis stream and store the data in S3. This solution needs an instance or a machine to run the code with the required access to read from the stream and write to S3. The other possible option would be to run a Lambda function that gets triggered on the putRecord or putRecords API made to the stream and reads the data from the stream to store in the S3 bucket:

- To make this easy, Amazon provides a separate service called Kinesis Data Firehose. This can easily be plugged into a Kinesis data stream and will require essential IAM roles to write data into S3. It is a fully managed service to reduce the load of managing servers and code. It also supports loading the streamed data into Amazon Redshift, Elasticsearch, and Splunk. Kinesis Data Firehose scales automatically to match the throughput of the data.

- Data can be transformed via an AWS Lambda function before storing or delivering it to the destination. If you want to build a raw data lake with the untransformed data, then by enabling source record backup, you can store it in another S3 bucket prior to the transformation.

- With the help of AWS KMS, data can be encrypted following delivery to the S3 bucket. It has to be enabled while creating the delivery stream. Data can also be compressed in supported formats, such as gzip, ZIP, or Snappy.

In the next section, you will learn about different AWS services used for ingesting data from on-premises servers to AWS.

Different ways of ingesting data from on-premises into AWS

With the increasing demand for data-driven use cases, managing data on on-premises servers is pretty tough at the moment. Taking backups is not easy when you deal with a huge amount of data. This data in data lakes is used to build deep neural networks, create a data warehouse to extract meaningful information from it, run analytics, and generate reports.

Now, if you look at the available options to migrate data into AWS, this comes with various challenges too. For example, if you want to send data to S3, then you have to write a few lines of code to send your data to AWS. You will have to manage the code and servers to run the code. It has to be ensured that the data is commuting via the HTTPS network. You need to verify whether the data transfer was successful. This adds complexity as well as time and effort challenges to the process. To avoid such scenarios, AWS provides services to match or solve your use cases by designing a hybrid infrastructure that allows data sharing between the on-premises data centers and AWS. You will learn about these in the following sections.

AWS Storage Gateway

Storage Gateway is a hybrid storage virtual appliance. It can run in three different modes – **File Gateway**, **Tape Gateway**, and **Volume Gateway**. It can be used for the extension, migration, and backups of an on-premises data center to AWS:

- In Tape Gateway mode, Storage Gateway stores virtual tapes on S3, and when ejected and archived, the tapes are moved from S3 to Glacier. Active tapes are stored in S3 for storage and retrieval. Archived or exported tapes are stored in **Virtual Tape Shelf** (**VTS**) in Glacier. Virtual tapes can be created and can range in size from 100 GiB to 5 TiB. A total of 1 petabyte of storage can be configured locally and an unlimited number of tapes can be archived to Glacier. This is ideal for an existing backup system on tape and where there is a need to migrate backup data into AWS. You can decommission the physical tape hardware later.

- In File Gateway mode, Storage Gateway maps files onto S3 objects, which can be stored using one of the available storage classes. This helps you to extend the data center into AWS. You can load more files to your file gateway and these are stored as S3 objects. It can run on your on-premises virtual server, which connects to various devices using **Server Message Block** (**SMB**) or **Network File System** (**NFS**). File Gateway connects to AWS using an HTTPS public endpoint to store the data on S3 objects. Life cycle policies can be applied to those S3 objects. You can easily integrate your **Active Directory** (**AD**) with File Gateway to control access to the files on the file share.

- In Volume Gateway mode, the storage gateway presents block storage. There are two ways of using this; one is **Gateway Cached** and the other is **Gateway Stored**:

- **Gateway Stored** is a volume storage gateway running locally on-premises. It has local storage and an upload buffer. A total of 32 volumes can be created, and each volume can be up to 16 TB in size for a total capacity of 512 TB. Primary data is stored on-premises and backup data is asynchronously replicated to AWS in the background. Volumes are made available via **Internet Small Computer Systems Interface (iSCSI)** for network-based servers to access. It connects to a Storage Gateway endpoint via an HTTPS public endpoint and creates EBS snapshots from backup data. These snapshots can be used to create standard EBS volumes. This option is ideal for migration to AWS, disaster recovery, or business continuity. The local system will still use the local volume, but the EBS snapshots are in AWS, which can be used instead of backups. It's not the best option for data center extensions because you require a huge amount of local storage.

- **Gateway Cached** is a volume storage gateway running locally on-premises. It has cache storage and an upload buffer. The difference is that the data that is added to Storage Gateway is not local but uploaded to AWS. Primary data is stored in AWS. Frequently accessed data is cached locally. This is an ideal option for extending an on-premises data center to AWS. It connects to a Storage Gateway endpoint via an HTTPS public endpoint and creates S3-backed volume (AWS-managed bucket) snapshots that are stored as standard EBS snapshots.

Snowball, Snowball Edge, and Snowmobile

These belong to the same product category or family for the physical transfer of data between business operating locations and AWS. To move a large amount of data into and out of AWS, you can use any of the three:

- **Snowball**: This physical device can be ordered from AWS by logging a job. AWS delivers a device for you to load your data onto before sending it back. Data in Snowball is encrypted using KMS. It comes with two capacity ranges: 50 TB and 80 TB. It is economical to order one or more Snowball devices for data between 10 TB and 10 PB. The device can be sent to different premises. It does not have any compute capability; it only comes with storage capability.

- **Snowball Edge**: This is like Snowball, but it comes with both storage and compute capability. It has a larger capacity than Snowball. It offers fastened networking, such as 10 Gbps over RJ45, 10/25 Gb over SFP28, and 40/100 Gb+ over QSFP+ copper. This is ideal for the secure and quick transfer of terabytes to petabytes of data into AWS.

- **Snowmobile**: This is a portable data center within a shipping container on a truck. It allows you to move exabytes of data from on-premises to AWS. If your data size exceeds 10 PB, then Snowmobile is preferred. Essentially, upon requesting to use the Snowmobile service, a truck is driven to your location and you plug your data center into the truck and transfer the data. If you have multiple sites, choosing Snowmobile for data transfer is not an ideal option.

AWS DataSync

AWS DataSync is designed to move data from on-premises storage to AWS, or vice versa:

- It is an ideal product from AWS for data processing transfers, archival or cost-effective storage, disaster recovery, business continuity, and data migrations.

- It has a special data validation feature that verifies the original data with the data in AWS, as soon as the data arrives in AWS. In other words, it checks the integrity of the data.

- To understand this product in depth, consider an example of an on-premises data center that has SAN/NAS storage. When you run the AWS DataSync agent on a VMWare platform, this agent is capable of communicating with the NAS/SAN storage via an NFS/SMB protocol. Once it is on, it communicates with the AWS DataSync endpoint, and from there, it can connect with several different types of locations, including various S3 storage classes or VPC-based resources, such as **Elastic File System** (**EFS**) and FSx for Windows Server.

- It allows you to schedule data transfers during specific periods. By configuring the built-in bandwidth throttle, you can limit the amount of network bandwidth that DataSync uses.

AWS Database Migration Service

There are several situations when an organization might decide to migrate their databases from one to another, such as the need for better performance, enhanced security, or advanced features or to avoid licensing costs from vendors. If an organization wants to expand its business to a different geolocation, it will need to carry out database migration, disaster recovery improvements, and database sync in a cost-effective manner. AWS DMS allows you to leverage the benefits of scalability, flexibility, and cost-efficiency when migrating databases from an `on-premises/EC2 instance/Amazon RDS` to Amazon RDS or Amazon Aurora.

In scenarios where multiple databases need to be consolidated into a single database or data needs to be integrated across multiple databases, AWS DMS can be a valuable tool. AWS DMS is designed to move data from a source to a target provided one of the endpoints is on AWS:

- DMS supports both homogenous and heterogeneous database migrations, allowing you to migrate between different database engines, such as Oracle, MySQL, PostgreSQL, and Microsoft SQL Server.

- DMS simplifies the database migration process by handling schema conversion, data replication, and ongoing synchronization between the source and target databases.

- DMS supports both full-load and ongoing **Change Data Capture** (**CDC**) replication methods. Full-load migration copies the entire source database to the target, while CDC captures and replicates only the changes made after the initial load. For example, for a database migration with minimal downtime, DMS performs an initial full-load migration, followed by CDC replication to keep the target database up to date with changes in the source database.

- DMS provides a user-friendly console and API for the easy configuration, monitoring, and management of database migrations. It offers detailed logging and error handling to help diagnose and resolve migration issues. For example, during a migration from Oracle to Amazon Aurora, DMS can automatically convert Oracle-specific data types and modify table structures to align with the Aurora database schema.

- DMS supports continuous data replication, allowing you to keep the source and target databases in sync even after the initial migration. This is particularly useful in scenarios requiring ongoing data synchronization or database replication. An example is if a company maintains an active-active database setup for high availability, where DMS replicates data changes between multiple database instances located in different regions for real-time synchronization.

- DMS offers built-in validation and testing capabilities to ensure the integrity and consistency of the migrated data. It performs data validation checks and generates reports to verify the success of the migration process. For example, after migrating a large database from Microsoft SQL Server to Amazon RDS for PostgreSQL, DMS validates the migrated data by comparing row counts, data types, and other metrics to ensure data accuracy.

- DMS supports both one-time migrations and continuous replication for database consolidation and integration scenarios. It enables organizations to consolidate data from multiple databases into a single target database or distribute data across multiple databases as needed. For example, say a company with several subsidiary databases wants to consolidate all the data into a centralized database for unified reporting and analysis. DMS facilitates the migration and ongoing synchronization of data from multiple sources to the target database.

Processing stored data on AWS

There are several services for processing the data stored in AWS. You will learn about AWS Batch and AWS **Elastic MapReduce** (**EMR**) in this section. EMR is a product from AWS that primarily runs `MapReduce` jobs and Spark applications in a managed way. AWS Batch is used for long-running, compute-heavy workloads.

AWS EMR

EMR is a managed implementation of Apache Hadoop provided as a service by AWS. It includes other components of the Hadoop ecosystem, such as Spark, HBase, Flink, Presto, Hive, and Pig. You will not need to learn about these in detail for the certification exam, but here's some information about EMR:

- EMR clusters can be launched from the AWS console or via the AWS CLI with a specific number of nodes. The cluster can be a long-term cluster or an ad hoc cluster. In a long-running traditional cluster, you have to configure the machines and manage them yourself. If you have jobs that need to be executed faster, then you need to manually add a cluster. In the case of EMR, these admin overheads disappear. You can request any number of nodes from EMR and it manages and launches the nodes for you. If you have autoscaling enabled on the cluster, EMR regulates nodes according to the requirement. That means, EMR launches new nodes in the cluster when the load is high and decommissions the nodes once the load is reduced.

- EMR uses EC2 instances in the background and runs in one Availability Zone in a VPC. This enables faster network speeds between the nodes. AWS Glue uses EMR clusters in the background, where users do not need to worry about having an operational understanding of AWS EMR.

- From a use case standpoint, EMR can be used to process or transform the data stored in S3 and output data to be stored in S3. EMR uses nodes (EC2 instances) as the computing units for data processing. EMR nodes come in different variants, including master nodes, core nodes, and task nodes.

- The EMR master node acts as a Hadoop NameNode and manages the cluster and its health. It is responsible for distributing the job workload among the other core nodes and task nodes. If you have SSH enabled, then you can connect to the master node instance and access the cluster.

- An EMR cluster can have one or more core nodes. If you relate it to the Hadoop ecosystem, then core nodes are similar to Hadoop data nodes for HDFS and they are responsible for running the tasks within them.

- Task nodes are optional and they don't have HDFS storage. They are responsible for running tasks. If a task node fails for some reason, then this does not impact HDFS storage, but a core node failure causes HDFS storage interruptions.

- EMR has a filesystem called EMRFS. It is backed by S3, which makes it regionally resilient. If a core node fails, the data is still safe in S3. HDFS is efficient in terms of I/O and faster than EMRFS.

In the following section, you will learn about AWS Batch, which is a managed batch-processing compute service that can be used for long-running services.

AWS Batch

This is a managed batch-processing product. If you are using AWS Batch, then jobs can be run without end user interaction or can be scheduled to run:

- Imagine an event-driven application that launches a Lambda function to process the data stored in S3. If the processing time goes beyond 15 minutes, then Lambda stops the execution and fails. For such scenarios, AWS Batch is a better solution, where computation-heavy workloads can be scheduled or driven through API events.

- AWS Batch is a good fit for use cases where a longer processing time is required or more computation resources are needed.

- AWS Batch jobs can be a script or an executable. One job can depend on another job. A job needs to be defined, such as who can run the job (with IAM permissions), where the job can be run (resources to be used), mount points, and other metadata.

- Jobs are submitted to queues, where they wait for compute environment capacity. These queues are associated with one or more compute environments.

- Compute environments do the actual work of executing the jobs. These can be ECS or EC2 instances, or any computing resources. You can define their sizes and capacities too.

- Environments receive jobs from the queues based on their priority and execute them. They can be managed or unmanaged compute environments.

- AWS Batch can store the metadata in DynamoDB for further use and can also store the output in an S3 bucket.

> **Note**
> If you get a question in the exam on an event-style workload that requires flexible compute, a higher disk space, no time limit (more than 15 minutes), or an effective resource limit, then the answer is likely to be AWS Batch.

Summary

In this chapter, you learned about different ways of processing data in AWS. You also learned the capabilities in terms of extending your data centers to AWS, migrating data to AWS, and the ingestion process. You learned about the various ways of using data to process it and make it ready for analysis. You understood the magic of using a data catalog, which helps you to query your data via AWS Glue and Athena.

In the next chapter, you will learn about various machine learning algorithms and their usage.

Exam Readiness Drill – Chapter Review Questions

Apart from a solid understanding of key concepts, being able to think quickly under time pressure is a skill that will help you ace your certification exam. That is why working on these skills early on in your learning journey is key.

Chapter review questions are designed to improve your test-taking skills progressively with each chapter you learn and review your understanding of key concepts in the chapter at the same time. You'll find these at the end of each chapter.

> **How To Access These Resources**
>
> To learn how to access these resources, head over to the chapter titled *Chapter 11, Accessing the Online Practice Resources.*

To open the Chapter Review Questions for this chapter, perform the following steps:

1. Click the link – `https://packt.link/MLSC01E2_CH03`.

    Alternatively, you can scan the following **QR code** (*Figure 3.9*):

Figure 3.9 – QR code that opens Chapter Review Questions for logged-in users

2. Once you log in, you'll see a page similar to the one shown in *Figure 3.10*:

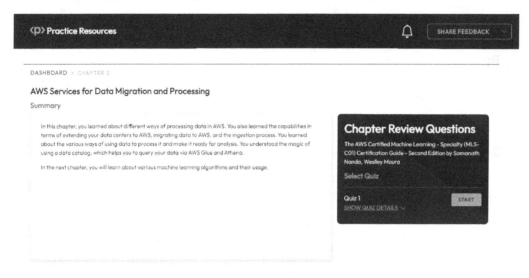

Figure 3.10 – Chapter Review Questions for Chapter 3

3. Once ready, start the following practice drills, re-attempting the quiz multiple times.

Exam Readiness Drill

For the first three attempts, don't worry about the time limit.

ATTEMPT 1

The first time, aim for at least **40%**. Look at the answers you got wrong and read the relevant sections in the chapter again to fix your learning gaps.

ATTEMPT 2

The second time, aim for at least **60%**. Look at the answers you got wrong and read the relevant sections in the chapter again to fix any remaining learning gaps.

ATTEMPT 3

The third time, aim for at least **75%**. Once you score 75% or more, you start working on your timing.

> **Tip**
> You may take more than **three** attempts to reach 75%. That's okay. Just review the relevant sections in the chapter till you get there.

Working On Timing

Target: Your aim is to keep the score the same while trying to answer these questions as quickly as possible. Here's an example of how your next attempts should look like:

Attempt	Score	Time Taken
Attempt 5	77%	21 mins 30 seconds
Attempt 6	78%	18 mins 34 seconds
Attempt 7	76%	14 mins 44 seconds

Table 3.1 – Sample timing practice drills on the online platform

> **Note**
> The time limits shown in the above table are just examples. Set your own time limits with each attempt based on the time limit of the quiz on the website.

With each new attempt, your score should stay above **75%** while your "time taken" to complete should "decrease". Repeat as many attempts as you want till you feel confident dealing with the time pressure.

4

Data Preparation and Transformation

You have probably heard that data scientists spend most of their time working on data-preparation-related activities. It is now time to explain why that happens and what types of activities they work on.

In this chapter, you will learn how to deal with categorical and numerical features, as well as how to apply different techniques to transform your data, such as one-hot encoding, binary encoders, ordinal encoding, binning, and text transformations. You will also learn how to handle missing values and outliers in your data, which are two important tasks you can implement to build good **machine learning (ML)** models.

In this chapter, you will cover the following topics:

- Identifying types of features
- Dealing with categorical features
- Dealing with numerical features
- Understanding data distributions
- Handling missing values
- Dealing with outliers
- Dealing with unbalanced datasets
- Dealing with text data

This chapter is a little longer than the others and will require more patience. Knowing about these topics in detail will put you in a good position for the AWS Machine Learning Specialty exam.

Identifying types of features

You *cannot* start modeling without knowing what a feature is and what type of information it can store. You have already read about the different processes that deal with features. For example, you know that feature engineering is related to the task of building and preparing features for your models; you also know that feature selection is related to the task of choosing the best set of features to feed a particular algorithm. These two tasks have one behavior in common: they may vary according to the types of features they are processing.

It is very important to understand this behavior (feature type versus applicable transformations) because it will help you eliminate invalid answers during your exam (and, most importantly, you will become a better data scientist).

By *types of features*, you refer to the data type that a particular feature is supposed to store. *Figure 4.1* shows how you could potentially describe the different types of features of a model.

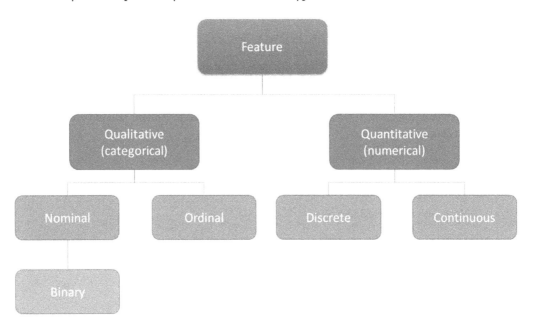

Figure 4.1 – Feature types

In *Chapter 1, Machine Learning Fundamentals*, you were introduced to the feature classification shown in *Figure 4.1*. Now, look at some real examples, so that you can eliminate any remaining questions you may have:

Feature type	Feature sub-type	Definition	Example
Categorical	Nominal	Labelled variables with no quantitative value	Cloud provider: AWS, MS, Google
Categorical	Ordinal	Adds the sense of order to the labelled variable	Job title: junior data scientist, senior data scientist, chief data scientist
Categorical	Binary	A variable with only two allowed values	Fraud classification: fraud, not fraud
Numerical	Discrete	Individual and countable items	Number of students: 100
Numerical	Continuous	Infinite number of possible measurements and they often carry decimal points	Total amount: $150.35

Table 4.1 – Real examples of feature values

Although looking at the values of the variable may help you find its type, you should never rely only on this approach. The nature of the variable is also very important for making such decisions. For example, someone could encode the cloud provider variable shown in *Table 4.1* as follows: 1 (AWS), 2 (MS), 3 (Google). In that case, the variable is still a nominal feature, even if it is now represented by discrete numbers.

If you are building an ML model and you don't tell your algorithm that this variable is not a discrete number but is instead a nominal variable, the algorithm will treat it as a number and the model won't be interpretable anymore.

> **Important note**
> Before feeding any ML algorithm with data, make sure your feature types have been properly identified.

In theory, if you are happy with your features and have properly classified each of them, you should be ready to go into the modeling phase of the CRISP-DM methodology, shouldn't you? Well, maybe not. There are many reasons you may want to spend a little more time on data preparation, even after you have correctly classified your features:

- Some ML libraries, such as `scikit-learn`, may not accept string values on your categorical features.

- The data distribution of your variable may not be the most optimal distribution for your algorithm.

- Your ML algorithm may be impacted by the scale of your data.

- Some observations of your variable may be missing information and you will have to fix it. These are also known as missing values.

- You may find outlier values of your variable that can potentially add bias to your model.

- Your variable may be storing different types of information and you may only be interested in a few of them (for example, a date variable can store the day of the week or the week of the month).

- You might want to find a mathematical representation for a text variable.

- Believe me, this list has no real end!

In the following sections, you will understand how to address all these points, starting with categorical features.

Dealing with categorical features

Data transformation methods for categorical features will vary according to the sub-type of your variable. In the upcoming sections, you will understand how to transform nominal and ordinal features.

Transforming nominal features

You may have to create numerical representations of your categorical features before applying ML algorithms to them. Some libraries may have embedded logic to handle that transformation for you, but most of them do not.

The first transformation you will learn is known as label encoding. A label encoder is suitable for categorical/nominal variables, and it will just associate a number with each distinct label of your variables. *Table 4.2* shows how a label encoder works:

Country	Label encoding
India	1
Canada	2
Brazil	3
Australia	4
India	1

Table 4.2 – Label encoder in action

A label encoder will always ensure that a unique number is associated with each distinct label. In the preceding table, although "India" appears twice, the same number was assigned to it.

You now have a numerical representation of each country, but this does not mean you can use that numerical representation in your models! In this particular case, you are transforming a nominal feature, *which does not have an order*.

According to *Table 4.2*, if you pass the encoded version of the *country* variable to a model, it will make assumptions such as "Brazil (3) is greater than Canada (2)," which does not make any sense.

One possible solution for that scenario is applying another type of transformation on top of "*country*": **one-hot encoding**. This transformation will represent all the categories from the original feature as individual features (also known as dummy **variables**), which will store the presence or absence of each category. *Table 4.3* is transforming the same information from *Table 4.2*, but this time it's applying one-hot encoding:

Country	India	Canada	Brazil	Australia
India	1	0	0	0
Canada	0	1	0	0
Brazil	0	0	1	0
Australia	0	0	0	1
India	1	0	0	0

Table 4.3 – One-hot encoding in action

You can now use the one-hot encoded version of the *country* variable as a feature of an ML model. However, your work as a skeptical data scientist is never done, and your critical thinking ability will be tested in the AWS Machine Learning Specialty exam.

Suppose you have 150 distinct countries in your dataset. How many dummy variables would you come up with? 150, right? Here, you just ran into a potential issue: apart from adding complexity to your model (which is not a desired characteristic of any model at all), dummy variables also add **sparsity** to your data.

A sparse dataset has a lot of variables filled with zeros. Often, it is hard to fit this type of data structure into memory (you can easily run out of memory), and it is very time-consuming for ML algorithms to process sparse structures.

You can work around the sparsity problem by grouping your original data and reducing the number of categories, and you can even use custom libraries that compress your sparse data and make it easier to manipulate (such as `scipy.sparse.csr_matrix`, from Python).

Therefore, during the exam, remember that one-hot encoding is definitely the right way to go when you need to transform categorical/nominal data to feed ML models; however, take the number of unique categories of your original feature into account and think about whether it makes sense to create dummy variables for all of them (it might not make sense if you have a very large number of unique categories).

Applying binary encoding

For those types of variables with a higher number of unique categories, a potential approach to creating a numerical representation for them is applying binary encoding. In this approach, the goal is transforming a categorical variable into multiple binary columns, but minimizing the number of new columns.

This process consists of three basic steps:

1. The categorical data is converted into numerical data after being passed through an ordinal encoder.
2. The resulting number is then converted into a binary value.
3. The binary value is split into different columns.

Table 4.4 shows how to convert the data from *Table 4.2* into a binary variable.

Country	Label encoder	Binary	Col1	Col2	Col3
India	1	001	0	0	1
Canada	2	010	0	1	0
Brazil	3	011	0	1	1
Australia	4	100	1	0	0
India	1	001	0	0	1

Table 4.4 – Binary encoding in action

As you can see, there are now three columns (Col1, Col2, and Col3) instead of four columns from the one-hot encoding transformation in *Table 4.3*.

Transforming ordinal features

Ordinal features have a very specific characteristic: *they have an order*. Because they have this quality, it does *not* make sense to apply one-hot encoding to them; if you do so, the underlying algorithm that is used to train your model will not be able to differentiate the implicit order of the data points associated with this feature.

The most common transformation for this type of variable is known as **ordinal encoding**. An ordinal encoder will associate a number with each distinct label of your variable, just like a label encoder does, but this time, it will respect the order of each category. The following table shows how an ordinal encoder works:

Education	Ordinal encoding
Trainee	1
Junior data analyst	2
Senior data analyst	3
Chief data scientist	4

Table 4.5 – Ordinal encoding in action

You can now pass the encoded variable to ML models and they will be able to handle this variable properly, with no need to apply one-hot encoding transformations. This time, comparisons such as "senior data analyst is greater than junior data analyst" make total sense.

Avoiding confusion in our train and test datasets

Do not forget the following statement: encoders are fitted on training data and transformed on test and production data. This is how your ML pipeline should work.

Suppose you have created a one-hot encoder that fits the data from *Table 4.2* and returns data according to *Table 4.3*. In this example, assume this is your training data. Once you have completed your training process, you may want to apply the same one-hot encoding transformation to your testing data to check the model's results.

In the scenario that was just described (which is a very common situation in modeling pipelines), you *cannot* retrain your encoder on top of the testing data! You should just reuse the previous encoder object that you have created on top of the training data. Technically, you shouldn't use the `fit` method again but the `transform` method instead.

You may already know the reasons why you should follow this rule, but just as a reminder: the testing data was created to extract the performance metrics of your model, so you should not use it to extract any other knowledge. If you do so, your performance metrics will be biased by the testing data, and you cannot infer that the same performance (shown in the test data) is likely to happen in production (when new data will come in).

Alright, all good so far. However, what if your testing set has a new category that was not present in the training set? How are you supposed to transform this data?

Going back to the one-hot encoding example in *Figure 4.3* (input data) and *Table 4.3* (output data), this encoder knows how to transform the following countries: Australia, Brazil, Canada, and India. If you had a different country in the testing set, the encoder would not know how to transform it, and that's why you need to define how it will behave in scenarios where there are exceptions.

Most ML libraries provide specific parameters for these situations. In the previous example, you could configure the encoder to either raise an error or set all zeros on our dummy variables, as shown in *Table 4.6*.

Country	India	Canada	Brazil	Australia
India	1	0	0	0
Canada	0	1	0	0
Brazil	0	0	1	0
Australia	0	0	0	1
India	1	0	0	0
Portugal	**0**	**0**	**0**	**0**

Table 4.6 – Handling unknown values on one-hot encoding transformations

As you can see, Portugal was not present in the training set (*Table 4.2*), so during the transformation, it will keep the same list of known countries and say that Portugal *is not* among them (all zeros).

As the very good skeptical data scientist you are becoming, should you be concerned about the fact that you have a particular category that has not been used during training? Well, maybe. This type of analysis really depends on your problem domain.

Handling unknown values is very common and something that you should expect to do in your ML pipeline. However, you should also ask yourself, due to the fact that you did not use that particular category during your training process, whether your model can be extrapolated and generalized.

Remember, your testing data must follow the same data distribution as your training data, and you are very likely to find all (or at least most) of the categories (of a categorical feature) either in the training or testing sets. Furthermore, if you are facing overfitting issues (doing well in the training, but poorly in the testing set) and, at the same time, you realize that your categorical encoders are transforming a lot of unknown values in the test set, guess what? It's likely that your training and testing samples are not following the same distribution, invalidating your model entirely.

As you can see, slowly, you are getting there. You are learning about bias and investigation strategies in fine-grained detail – that is so exciting! Now, move on and look at performing transformations on numerical features. Yes, each type of data matters and drives your decisions.

Dealing with numerical features

In terms of numerical features (discrete and continuous), you can think of transformations that rely on the training data and others that rely purely on the (individual) observation being transformed.

Those who rely on the training data will use the training set to learn the necessary parameters during `fit`, and then use them to transform any test or new data. The logic is pretty much the same as what you just learned for categorical features; however, this time, the encoder will learn different parameters.

On the other hand, those that rely purely on (individual) observations do not depend on training or testing sets. They will simply perform a mathematical computation on top of an individual value. For example, you could apply an exponential transformation to a particular variable by squaring its value. There is no dependency on learned parameters from anywhere – just get the value and square it.

At this point, you might be thinking about dozens of available transformations for numerical features! Indeed, there are so many options, and you will not learn all of them here. However, you are not supposed to know all of them for the AWS Machine Learning Specialty exam. You will learn the most important ones (for the exam), but you should not limit your modeling skills: take a moment to think about the unlimited options you have by creating custom transformations according to your use case.

Data normalization

Applying data **normalization** means changing the scale of the data. For example, your feature may store employee salaries that range between 20,000 and 200,000 dollars/year and you want to put this data in the range of 0 and 1; where 20,000 (the minimum observed value) will be transformed as 0; and 200,000 (the maximum observed value) will be transformed as 1.

This type of technique is especially important when you want to fit your training data on top of certain types of algorithms that are impacted by the scale/magnitude of the underlying data. For instance, you can think about those algorithms that use the dot product of the input variables (such as neural networks or linear regression) and those algorithms that rely on distance measures (such as k-**nearest neighbors (KNN)** or **k-means**).

On the other hand, applying data normalization will not result in performance improvements for rule-based algorithms, such as decision trees, since they will be able to check the predictive power of the features (either via entropy or information gain analysis), regardless of the scale of the data.

> **Important note**
> You will learn about these algorithms, along with the appropriate details, in the later chapters of this book. For instance, you can look at entropy and information gain as two types of metrics used by decision trees to check feature importance. Knowing the predictive power of each feature helps the algorithm define the optimal root, intermediaries, and leaf nodes of the tree.

Take a moment and use the following example to understand why data normalization will help those types of algorithms. You already know that the goal of a clustering algorithm is to find groups or clusters in your data, and one of the most used clustering algorithms is known as k-means.

Figure 4.2 shows how different scales of the variable could change the hyper plan's projection of k-means clustering:

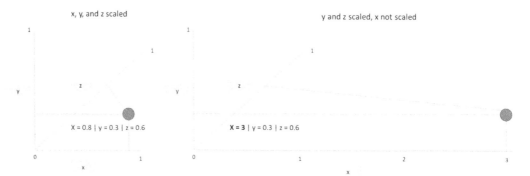

Figure 4.2 – Plotting data of different scales in a hyper plan

On the left-hand side of *Figure 4.2*, you can see a single data point plotted in a hyper plan that has three dimensions (x, y, and z). All three dimensions (also known as features) were normalized to the scale of 0 and 1. On the right-hand side, you can see the same data point, but this time, the x dimension was *not* normalized. You can clearly see that the hyper plan has changed.

In a real scenario, you would have far more dimensions and data points. The difference in the scale of the data would change the centroids of each cluster and could potentially change the assigned clusters of some points. This same problem will happen on other algorithms that rely on distance calculation, such as KNN.

Other algorithms, such as neural networks and linear regression, will compute weighted sums using your input data. Usually, these types of algorithms will perform operations such as *W1*X1 + W2*X2 + Wi*Xi*, where *Xi* and *Wi* refer to a particular feature value and its weight, respectively. Again, you will learn details of neural networks and linear models later, but can you see the data scaling problem by just looking at the calculations that were just described? It can easily come up with very large values if *X* (feature) and *W* (weight) are large numbers. That will make the algorithm's optimizations much more complex. In neural networks, this problem is known as gradient exploding.

You now have a very good understanding of the reasons you should apply data normalization (and when you should not). Data normalization is often implemented in ML libraries as **Min Max Scaler**. If you find this term in the exam, then remember that it is the same as data normalization.

Additionally, data normalization does not necessarily need to transform your feature into a range between 0 and 1. In reality, you can transform the feature into any range you want. *Figure 4.3* shows how normalization is formally defined.

$$X_{normalized} = \frac{X - X_{min}}{X_{max} - X_{min}}$$

Figure 4.3 – Normalization formula

Here, *Xmin* and *Xmax* are the lower and upper values of the range; *X* is the value of the feature. Apart from data normalization, there is another very important technique regarding numerical transformations that you *must* be aware of, not only for the exam but also for your data science career. You'll look at this in the next section.

Data standardization

Data standardization is another scaling method that transforms the distribution of the data, so that the mean will become 0 and the standard deviation will become 1. *Figure 4.4* formally describes this scaling technique, where X represents the value to be transformed, μ refers to the mean of X, and σ is the standard deviation of X:

$$X' = \frac{X - \mu}{\sigma}$$

Figure 4.4 – Standardization formula

Unlike normalization, data standardization will *not* result in a predefined range of values. Instead, it will transform your data into a standard Gaussian distribution, where your transformed values will represent the number of standard deviations of each value to the mean of the distribution.

> **Important note**
>
> The Gaussian distribution, also known as the normal distribution, is one of the most used distributions in statistical models. This is a continuous distribution with two main controlled parameters: μ (mean) and σ (standard deviation). Normal distributions are symmetric around the mean. In other words, most of the values will be close to the mean of the distribution.

Data standardization is often referred to as the zscore and is widely used to identify outliers on your variable, which you will see later in this chapter. For the sake of demonstration, *Table 4.7* simulates the data standardization of a small dataset. The input value is shown in the Age column, while the scaled value is shown in the Zscore column:

Age	Mean	Standard deviation	Zscore
5	31,83	25,47	-1,05
20	31,83	25,47	-0,46
24	31,83	25,47	-0,31
32	31,83	25,47	0,01
30	31,83	25,47	-0,07
80	31,83	25,47	1,89

Table 4.7 – Data standardization in action

Make sure you are confident when applying normalization and standardization by hand in the AWS Machine Learning Specialty exam. They might provide a list of values, as well as mean and standard deviation, and ask you for the scaled value of each element in the list.

Applying binning and discretization

Binning is a technique where you can group a set of values into a bucket or bin – for example, grouping people between 0 and 14 years old into a bucket named "children," another group of people between 15 and 18 years old into a bucket named "teenager," and so on.

Discretization is the process of transforming a continuous variable into discrete or nominal attributes. These continuous values can be discretized by multiple strategies, such as **equal-width** and **equal-frequency**.

An equal-width strategy will split your data across multiple bins of the same width. Equal-frequency will split your data across multiple bins with the same number of frequencies.

Look at the following example. Suppose you have the following list containing 16 numbers: 10, 11, 12, 13, 14, 15, 16, 17, 18, 19, 20, 21, 22, 23, 24, 90. As you can see, this list ranges between 10 and 90. Assuming you want to create four bins using an equal-width strategy, you could come up with the following bins:

- Bin >= 10 <= 30 > 10, 11, 12, 13, 14, 15, 16, 17, 18, 19, 20, 21, 22, 23, 24

- Bin > 30 <= 50 >

- Bin > 50 <= 70 >

- Bin > 71 <= 90 > 90

In this case, the width of each bin is the same (20 units), but the observations are not equally distributed. Now, the next example simulates an equal-frequency strategy:

- Bin >= 10 <= 13 > 10, 11, 12, 13

- Bin > 13 <= 17 > 14, 15, 16, 17

- Bin > 17 <= 21 > 18, 19, 20, 21

- Bin > 21 <= 90 > 22, 23, 24, 90

In this case, all the bins have the same frequency of observations, although they have been built with different bin widths to make that possible.

Once you have computed your bins, you should be wondering what's next, right? Here, you have some options:

- You can name your bins and use them as a nominal feature on your model! Of course, as a nominal variable, you should think about applying one-hot encoding before feeding an ML model with this data.

- You might want to order your bins and use them as an ordinal feature.

- Maybe you want to remove some noise from your feature by averaging the minimum and maximum values of each bin and using that value as your transformed feature.

Take a look at *Table 4.8* to understand these approaches using our equal-frequency example:

Ordinal value	Bin	Transforming to a nominal feature	Transforming to an ordinal feature	Removing noise
10	Bin >= 10 <= 13	Bin A	1	11,5
11	Bin >= 10 <= 13	Bin A	1	11,5
12	Bin >= 10 <= 13	Bin A	1	11,5
13	Bin >= 10 <= 13	Bin A	1	11,5
14	Bin > 13 <= 17	Bin B	2	15,5
15	Bin > 13 <= 17	Bin B	2	15,5
16	Bin > 13 <= 17	Bin B	2	15,5
17	Bin > 13 <= 17	Bin B	2	15,5
18	Bin > 17 <= 21	Bin C	3	19,5
19	Bin > 17 <= 21	Bin C	3	19,5
20	Bin > 17 <= 21	Bin C	3	19,5
21	Bin > 17 <= 21	Bin C	3	19,5
22	Bin > 21 <= 90	Bin D	4	55,5
23	Bin > 21 <= 90	Bin D	4	55,5
24	Bin > 21 <= 90	Bin D	4	55,5
90	Bin > 21 <= 90	Bin D	4	55,5

Table 4.8 – Different approaches to working with bins and discretization

Again, playing with different binning strategies will give you different results and you should analyze/test the best approach for your dataset. There is no standard answer here – it is all about data exploration!

Applying other types of numerical transformations

Normalization and standardization rely on your training data to fit their parameters: minimum and maximum values, in the case of normalization, and mean and standard deviation in the case of standard scaling. This also means you must fit those parameters using *only* your training data and never the testing data.

However, there are other types of numerical transformations that do not require parameters from training data to be applied. These types of transformations rely purely on mathematical computations. For example, one of these transformations is known as logarithmic transformation. This is a very common type of transformation in ML models and is especially beneficial for skewed features. If you don't know what a skewed distribution is, take a look at *Figure 4.5*.

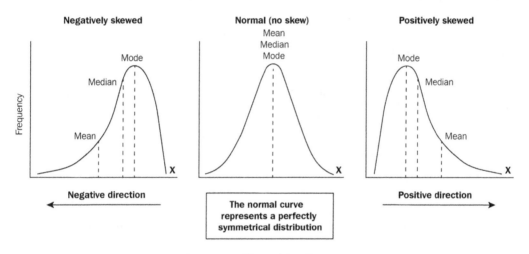

Figure 4.5 – Skewed distributions

In the middle, you have a normal distribution (or Gaussian distribution). On the left- and right-hand sides, you have skewed distributions. In terms of skewed features, there will be some values far away from the mean in one single direction (either left or right). Such behavior will push both the median and mean values of this distribution in the same direction, that of the long tail you can see in *Figure 4.5*.

One very clear example of data that used to be skewed is the annual salaries of a particular group of professionals in a given region, such as senior data scientists working in Florida, US. This type of variable usually has most of its values close to the others (because people used to earn an average salary) and just has a few very high values (because a small group of people makes much more money than others).

Hopefully, you can now easily understand why the mean and median values will move to the tail direction, right? The big salaries will push them in that direction.

Alright, but why will a logarithmic transformation be beneficial for this type of feature? The answer to this question can be explained by the math behind it:

$$\log(x^n) = n\log(x)$$

Figure 4.6 – Logarithmic properties

Computing the log of a number is the inverse of the exponential function. Log transformation will then reduce the scale of your number according to a given base (such as base 2, base 10, or base e, in the case of a natural logarithm). Looking at the salary distribution from the previous example, you would bring all those numbers down so that the higher the number, the higher the reduction; however, you would do this in a log scale and not in a linear fashion. Such behavior will remove the outliers of this distribution (making it closer to a normal distribution), which is beneficial for many ML algorithms, such as linear regression. *Table 4.9* shows you some of the differences when transforming a number in a linear scale versus a log scale:

Ordinal value	Linear scale (normalization)	Log scale (base 10)
10	0.0001	1
1,000	0.01	3
10,000	0.1	4
100,000	1	5

Table 4.9 – Differences between linear transformation and log transformation

As you can see, the linear transformation kept the original magnitude of the data (you can still see outliers, but in another scale), while the log transformation removed those differences of magnitude and still kept the order of the values.

Would you be able to think about another type of mathematical transformation that follows the same behavior of *log* (making the distribution closer to Gaussian)? OK, here you have another: square root. Take the square root of those numbers shown in *Table 4.9* and see yourself!

Now, pay attention to this: both log and square root belong to a set of transformations known as power transformations, and there is a very popular method, which is likely to be mentioned on your AWS exam, that can perform a range of power transformations like those you have seen. This method was proposed by George Box and David Cox and its name is **Box-Cox**.

> **Important note**
>
> During your exam, if you see questions about the Box-Cox transformation, remember that it is a method that can perform many power transformations (according to a lambda parameter), and its end goal is to make the original distribution closer to a normal distribution.

Just to conclude this discussion regarding why mathematical transformations can really make a difference to ML models, here is an example of **exponential transformations.**

Suppose you have a set of data points, such as those on the left-hand side of *Figure 4.7*. Your goal is to draw a line that will perfectly split blue and red points. Just by looking at the original data (again, on the left-hand side), you know that your best guess for performing this linear task would be the one you can see in the same figure. However, the science (not magic) happens on the right-hand side of the figure! By squaring those numbers and plotting them in another hyper plan, you can perfectly separate each group of points.

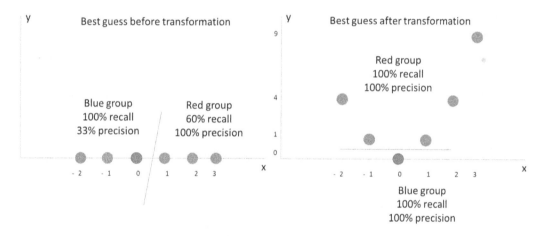

Figure 4.7 – Exponential transformation in action

You might be thinking that there are infinite ways in which you can deal with your data. Although this is true, you should always take the business scenario you are working on into account and plan the work accordingly. Remember that model improvements or exploration is always possible, but you have to define your goals (remember the CRISP-DM methodology) and move on.

By the way, data transformation is important, but it is just one piece of your work as a data scientist. Your modeling journey still needs to move to other important topics, such as missing values and outliers handling. However, before that, you may have noticed that you were introduced to Gaussian distributions during this section, so why not go deeper into it?

Understanding data distributions

Although the Gaussian distribution is probably the most common distribution for statistical and machine learning models, you should be aware that it is not the only one. There are other types of data distributions, such as the Bernoulli, binomial, and Poisson distributions.

The Bernoulli distribution is a very simple one, as there are only two types of possible events: success or failure. The success event has a probability p of happening, while the failure one has a probability of 1-p.

Some examples that follow a Bernoulli distribution are rolling a six-sided die or flipping a coin. In both cases, you must define the event of success and the event of failure. For example, assume the following success and failure events when rolling a die:

- Success: Getting a number 6
- Failure: Getting any other number

You can then say that there is a p probability of success ($1/6 = 0.16 = 16\%$) and a 1-p probability of failure ($1 - 0.16 = 0.84 = 84\%$).

The binomial distribution generalizes the Bernoulli distribution. The Bernoulli distribution has only one repetition of an event, while the binomial distribution allows the event to be repeated many times, and you must count the number of successes. Continue with the prior example, that is, counting the number of times you got a 6 out of our 10 dice rolls. Due to the nature of this example, binomial distribution has two parameters, n and p, where n is the number of repetitions and p is the probability of success in every repetition.

Finally, a Poisson distribution allows you to find a number of events in a period of time, given the number of times an event occurs in an interval. It has three parameters: lambda, e, and k, where lambda is the average number of events per interval, e is the Euler number, and k is the number of times an event occurs in an interval.

With all those distributions, including the Gaussian one, it is possible to compute the expected mean value and variance based on their parameters. This information is usually used in hypothesis tests to check whether some sample data follows a given distribution, by comparing the mean and variance **of the sample** against the **expected** mean and variance of the distribution.

You are now more familiar with data distributions, not only Gaussian distributions. You will keep learning about data distributions throughout this book. For now, it is time to move on to missing values and outlier detection.

Handling missing values

As the name suggests, missing values refer to the absence of data. Such absences are usually represented by tokens, which may or may not be implemented in a standard way.

Although using tokens is standard, the way those tokens are displayed may vary across different platforms. For example, relational databases represent missing data with *NULL*, core Python code will use *None*, and some Python libraries will represent missing numbers as **Not a Number (NaN)**.

> **Important note**
>
> For numerical fields, don't replace those standard missing tokens with *zeros*. By default, zero is not a missing value, but another number.

However, in real business scenarios, you may or may not find those standard tokens. For example, a software engineering team might have designed the system to automatically fill missing data with specific tokens, such as "unknown" for strings or "-1" for numbers. In that case, you would have to search by those two tokens to find missing data. People can set anything.

In the previous example, the software engineering team was still kind enough to give you standard tokens. However, there are many cases where legacy systems do not add any data quality layer in front of the user, and you may find an address field filled with, "I don't want to share," or a phone number field filled with, "Don't call me." This is clearly missing data, but not as standard as the previous example.

There are many more nuances that you will learn regarding missing data, all of which you will learn in this section, but be advised: before you start making decisions about missing values, you should prepare a good data exploration and make sure you find those values. You can either compute data frequencies or use missing plots, but please do something. Never assume that your missing data is represented only by those handy standard tokens.

Why should you care about this type of data? Well, first, because most algorithms (apart from decision trees implemented on very specific ML libraries) will raise errors when they find a missing value. Second (and maybe most important), by grouping all the missing data in the same bucket, you are assuming that they are all the same, but in reality, you don't know that.

Such a decision will not only add bias to your model – it will reduce its interpretability, as you will be unable to explain the missing data. Once you know why you want to treat the missing values, then you can analyze your options.

Theoretically, you can classify missing values into two main groups: **MCAR** or **MNAR**. MCAR stands for **Missing Completely at Random** and states that there is no pattern associated with the missing data. On the other hand, MNAR stands for **Missing Not at Random** and means that the underlying process used to generate the data is strictly connected to the missing values.

Look at the following example about MNAR missing values. Suppose you are collecting user feedback about a particular product in an online survey. Your process of asking questions is dynamic and depends on user answers. When a user specifies an age lower than 18 years old, you never ask his/her marital status. In this case, missing values of marital status are connected to the age of the user (MNAR).

Knowing the class of missing values that you are dealing with will help you understand whether you have any control over the underlying process that generates the data. Sometimes, you can come back to the source process and, somehow, complete your missing data.

> **Important note**
>
> Although, in real scenarios, you usually need to treat missing data via exclusion or imputation, never forget that you can always try to look at the source process and check if you can retrieve (or, at least, better understand) the missing data. You may face this option in the exam.

If you don't have an opportunity to recover your missing data from anywhere, then you should move on to other approaches, such as **listwise deletion** and **imputation**.

Listwise deletion refers to the process of discarding some data, which is the downside of this choice. This may happen at the row level or the column level. For example, suppose you have a DataFrame containing four columns and one of them has 90% of its data missing. In such cases, what usually makes more sense is dropping the entire feature (column), since you don't have that information for the majority of your observations (rows).

From a row perspective, you may have a DataFrame with a small number of observations (rows) containing missing data in one of its features (columns). In such scenarios, instead of removing the entire feature, what makes more sense is removing only those few observations.

The benefit of using this method is the simplicity of dropping a row or a column. Again, the downside is losing information. If you don't want to lose information while handling your missing data, then you should go for an imputation strategy.

Imputation is also known as replacement, where you will replace missing values by substituting a value. The most common approach to imputation is replacing the missing value with the mean of the feature. Please take note of this approach because it is likely to appear in your exam:

Age
35
30
25
80
75

Table 4.10 – Replacing missing values with the mean or median

Table 4.10 shows a very simple dataset with one single feature and five observations, where the third observation has a missing value. If you decide to replace that missing data with the mean value of the feature, you will come up with 49. Sometimes, when there are outliers in the data, the median might be more appropriate (in this case, the median would be 35):

Age	Job status
35	Employee
30	Employee
	Retired
25	Employee
80	Retired
75	Retired

Table 4.11 – Replacing missing values with the mean or median of the group

If you want to go deeper, you could find the mean or median value according to a given group of features. For example, *Table 4.11* expanded the previous dataset from *Table 4.10* by adding the *Job status* column. Now, there is some evidence that the initial approach of changing the missing value by using the overall median (35 years old) was likely to be wrong (since that person is retired).

What you can do now is replace the missing value with the mean or median of the other observations that belong to the same job status. Using this new approach, you can change the missing information to 77.5. Considering that the person is retired, 77.5 makes more sense than 35 years old.

> **Important note**
> In the case of categorical variables, you can replace the missing data with the value that has the highest occurrence in your dataset. The same logic of grouping the dataset according to specific features is still applicable.

You can also use more sophisticated methods of imputation, including constructing an ML model to predict the value of your missing data. The downside of these imputation approaches (either by averaging or predicting the value) is that you are making inferences about the data that are not necessarily right and will add bias to the dataset.

To sum this up, the trade-off while dealing with missing data is having a balance between losing data or adding bias to the dataset. Unfortunately, there is no scientific recipe that you can follow, whatever your problem is. To decide on what you are going to do, you must look at your success criteria, explore your data, run experiments, and then make your decisions.

You will now move to another headache for many ML algorithms: outliers.

Dealing with outliers

You are not on this studying journey just to pass the AWS Machine Learning Specialty exam but also to become a better data scientist. There are many different ways to look at the outlier problem purely from a mathematical perspective; however, the datasets used in real life are derived from the underlying business process, so you must include a business perspective during an outlier analysis.

An outlier is an atypical data point in a set of data. For example, *Figure 4.8* shows some data points that have been plotted in a two-dimension plan; that is, x and y. The red point is an outlier since it is an atypical value in this series of data.

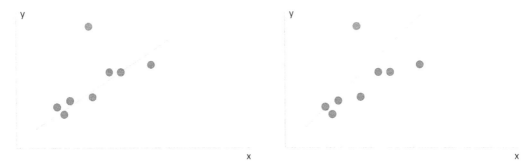

Figure 4.8 – Identifying an outlier

It is important to treat outlier values because some statistical methods are impacted by them. Still, in *Figure 4.8*, you can see this behavior in action. On the left-hand side, there has been drawn a line that best fits those data points, ignoring the red point. On the right-hand side, the same line was drawn, but including the red point.

You can visually conclude that, by ignoring the outlier point, you will come up with a better solution on the plan of the left-hand side of the preceding chart since it was able to pass closer to most of the values. You can also prove this by computing an associated error for each line (which you will learn later in this book).

It is worth reminding that you have also seen the outlier issue in action in another situation in this book: specifically, in *Table 4.10*, while dealing with missing values. In that example, the median was used to work around the problem. Feel free to go back and read it again, but what should be very clear at this point is that median values are less impacted by outliers than average (mean) values.

You now know what outliers are and why you should treat them. You should always consider your business perspective while dealing with outliers, but there are mathematical methods to find them. Now, you are ready to move on and look at some methods for outlier detection.

You have already learned about the most common method: zscore. In *Table 4.7*, you saw a table containing a set of ages. Refer to it again to refresh your memory. In the last column of that table, it was computed the zscore of each age, according to the equation shown in *Figure 4.4*.

There is no well-defined range for those zscore values; however, in a normal distribution *without* outliers, they will mostly range between -3 and 3. Remember: zscore will give you the number of standard deviations from the mean of the distribution. *Table 4.10* shows some of the properties of a normal distribution:

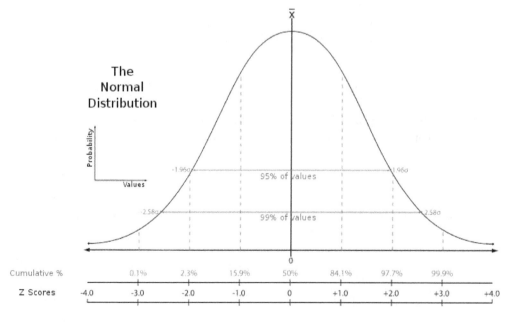

Figure 4.9 – Normal distribution properties. Image adapted from
https://pt.wikipedia.org/wiki/Ficheiro:The_Normal_Distribution.svg

According to the normal distribution properties, 95% of values will belong to the range of -2 and 2 standard deviations from the mean, while 99% of the values will belong to the range of -3 and 3. Coming back to the outlier detection context, you can set thresholds on top of those zscore values to specify whether a data point is an outlier or not!

There is no standard threshold that you can use to classify outliers. Ideally, you should look at your data and see what makes more sense for you… usually (this is not a rule), you will use some number between 2 and 3 standard deviations from the mean to flag outliers, since less than 5% of your data will be selected by this rule (again, this is just a reference threshold, so that you can select some data from further scructizing). You may remember that there are outliers *below* and *above* the mean value of the distribution, as shown in *Table 4.12*, where the outliers were flagged with an **absolute** zscore greater than 3 (the value column is hidden for the sake of this demonstration).

Value	Zscore	Is outlier?
...	1.3	NO
...	0.8	NO
...	**3.1**	**YES**
...	-2.9	NO
...	**-3.5**	**YES**
...	1.0	NO
...	1.1	NO

Table 4.12 – Flagging outliers according to the zscore value

Two outliers were found in *Table 4.12*: row number three and row number five. Another way to find outliers in the data is by applying the box plot logic. When you look at a numerical variable, it is possible to extract many descriptive statistics from it, not only the mean, median, minimum, and maximum values, as you have seen previously. Another property that's present in data distributions is known as quantiles.

Quantiles are cut-off points that are established at regular intervals from the cumulative distribution function of a random variable. Those regular intervals, also known as *q-quantiles*, will be nearly the same size and will receive special names in some situations:

- The 4-quantiles are called quartiles.
- The 10-quantiles are called deciles.
- The 100-quantiles are called percentiles.

For example, the 20th percentile (of a 100-quantile regular interval) specifies that 20% of the data is below that point. In a box plot, you can use regular intervals of 4-quantiles (also known as *quartiles*) to expose the distribution of the data (Q1 and Q3), as shown in *Figure 4.10*.

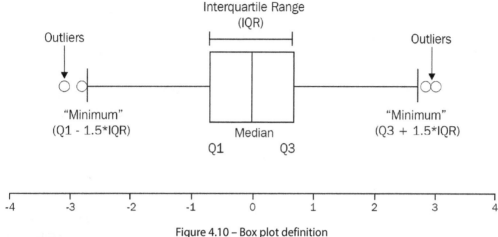

Figure 4.10 – Box plot definition

Q1 is also known as the lower quartile or 25th quartile, and this means that 25% of the data is below that point in the distribution. Q3 is also known as the upper quartile or 75th quartile, and this means that 75% of the data is below that point in the distribution.

Computing the difference between Q1 and Q3 will give you the **interquartile range (IQR)** value, which you can then use to compute the limits of the box plot, shown by the "minimum" and "maximum" labels in the preceding diagram.

After all, you can finally infer that anything below the "minimum" value or above the "maximum" value of the box plot will be flagged as an outlier.

You have now learned about two different ways you can flag outliers on your data: zscore and box plot. You can decide whether you are going to remove these points from your dataset, transform them, or create another variable to specify that they exist (as shown in *Table 4.11*).

Moving further on this journey of data preparation and transformation, you will face other types of problems in real life. Next, you will learn that several use cases contain something known as **rare events**, which makes ML algorithms focus on the wrong side of the problem and propose bad solutions. Luckily, you will learn how to either tune hyperparameters or prepare the data to facilitate algorithm convergence while fitting rare events.

Dealing with unbalanced datasets

At this point, you might have realized why data preparation is probably the longest part of the data scientist's work. You have learned about data transformation, missing data values, and outliers, but the list of problems goes on. Don't worry – you are on the right journey to master this topic!

Another well-known problem with ML models, specifically with classification problems, is unbalanced classes. In a classification model, you can say that a dataset is unbalanced when most of its observations belong to one (or some) of the classes (target variable).

This is very common in fraud identification systems: for example, where most of the events belong to a regular operation, while a very small number of events belong to a fraudulent operation. In this case, you can also say that fraud is a rare event.

There is no strong rule for defining whether a dataset is unbalanced or not, it really depends on the context of your business domain. Most challenge problems will contain more than 99% of the observations in the majority class.

The problem with unbalanced datasets is very simple: ML algorithms will try to find the best fit in the training data to maximize their accuracy. In a dataset where 99% of the cases belong to one single class, without any tuning, the algorithm is likely to prioritize the assertiveness of the majority class. In the worst-case scenario, it will classify all the observations as the majority class and ignore the minority one, which is usually our interest when modeling rare events.

To deal with unbalanced datasets, you have two major directions to follow: tuning the algorithm to handle the issue or resampling the data to make it more balanced.

By tuning the algorithm, you have to specify the weight of each class under classification. This class weight configuration belongs to the algorithm, not to the training data, so it is a hyperparameter setting. It is important to keep in mind that not all algorithms will have that type of configuration, and that not all ML frameworks will expose it, either. As a quick reference, the `DecisionTreeClassifier` class, from the scikit-learn ML library, is a good example that does implement the class weight hyperparameter.

Another way to work around unbalanced problems is changing the training dataset by applying **undersampling** or **oversampling**. If you decide to apply undersampling, all you have to do is remove some observations from the majority class until you get a more balanced dataset. Of course, the downside of this approach is that you may lose important information about the majority class that you are removing observations from.

The most common approach for undersampling is known as random undersampling, which is a naïve resampling approach where you randomly remove some observations from the training set.

On the other hand, you can decide to go for oversampling, where you will create new observations/samples of the minority class. The simplest approach is the naïve one, where you randomly select observations from the training set (with replacement) for duplication. The downside of this method is the potential issue of overfitting, since you will be duplicating/highlighting the observed pattern of the minority class.

To either underfit or overfit your model, you should always test the fitted model on your testing set.

> **Important note**
>
> The testing set cannot be under/oversampled: only the training set should pass through these resampling techniques.

You can also oversample the training set by applying synthetic sampling techniques. Random oversample does not add any new information to the training set: it just duplicates the existing ones. By creating synthetic samples, you are deriving those new observations from the existing ones (instead of simply copying them). This is a type of data augmentation technique known as the **Synthetic Minority Oversampling Technique (SMOTE).**

Technically, what SMOTE does is plot a line in the feature space of the minority class and extract points that are close to that line.

> **Important note**
>
> You may find questions in your exam where the term SMOTE has been used. If that happens, keep in mind the context where this term is applied: oversampling.

Alright – in the next section, you will learn how to prepare text data for ML models.

Dealing with text data

You have already learned how to transform categorical features into numerical representations, either using label encoders, ordinal encoders, or one-hot encoding. However, what if you have fields containing long pieces of text in your dataset? How are you supposed to provide a mathematical representation for them in order to properly feed ML algorithms? This is a common issue in **Natural Language Processing (NLP),** a subfield of AI.

NLP models aim to extract knowledge from texts; for example, translating text between languages, identifying entities in a corpus of text (also known as **Name Entity Recognition**, or **NER** for short), classifying sentiments from a user review, and many other applications.

> **Important note**
>
> In *Chapter 8, AWS Application Services for AI/ML*, you will learn about some AWS application services that apply NLP to their solutions, such as Amazon Translate and Amazon Comprehend. During the exam, you might be asked to think about the fastest or easiest way (with the least development effort) to build certain types of NLP applications. The fastest or easiest way is usually to use those out-of-the-box AWS services, since they offer pre-trained models for some use cases (especially machine translation, sentiment analysis, topic modeling, document classification, and entity recognition).
>
> In a few chapters' time, you will also learn about some built-in AWS algorithms for NLP applications, such as BlazingText, **Latent Dirichlet Allocation** (**LDA**), **Neural Topic Modeling** (**NTM**), and the **Sequence-to-Sequence** algorithm. Those algorithms also let you create the same NLP solutions that are created by those out-of-the-box services; however, you have to use them on SageMaker and write your own solution. In other words, they offer more flexibility but demand more development effort.
>
> Keep that in mind for your exam!

Although AWS offers many out-of-the-box services and built-in algorithms that allow you to create NLP applications, you will not look at those AWS product features now (you will do in *Chapter 6, Applying Machine Learning Algorithms*, and *Chapter 8, AWS Application Services for AI/ML*). You will finish this chapter by looking at some data preparation techniques that are extremely important for preparing your data for NLP.

Bag of words

The first one you will learn is known as bag of words (BoW). This is a very common and simple technique, applied to text data, that creates matrix representations to describe the number of words within the text. BoW consists of two main steps: creating a vocabulary and creating a representation of the presence of those known words from the vocabulary in the text. These steps can be seen in *Figure 4.11*.

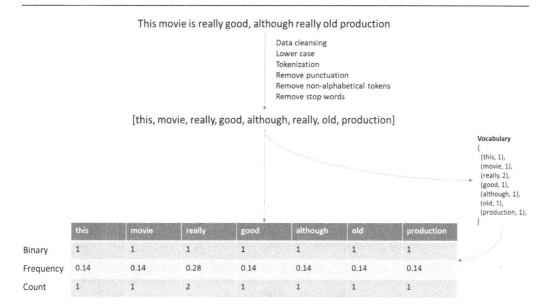

Figure 4.11 – BoW in action

First things first, you usually can't use raw text to prepare a BoW representation. There is a data cleansing step where you lowercase the text; split each work into tokens; remove punctuation, non-alphabetical, and stop words; and, whenever necessary, apply any other custom cleansing techniques you may want.

Once you have cleansed your raw text, you can add each word to a global vocabulary. Technically, this is usually a dictionary of tuples, in the form {(word, number of occurrences)} – for example, {(apple, 10), (watermelon, 20)}. As I mentioned previously, this is a global dictionary, and you should consider all the texts you are analyzing.

Now, with the cleansed text and updated vocabulary, you can build your text representation in the form of a matrix, where each column represents one word from the global vocabulary and each row represents a text you have analyzed. The way you represent those texts on each row may vary according to different strategies, such as binary, frequency, and count. Next, you will learn these strategies a little more.

In *Figure 4.11*, a single piece of text is being processed with the three different strategies for BoW. That's why you can see three rows on that table, instead of just one (in a real scenario, you have to choose one of them for implementation).

In the first row, it was used a binary strategy, which will assign 1 if the word exists in the global vocabulary and 0 if not. Because the vocabulary was built on a single text, all the words from that text belong to the vocabulary (the reason you can only see 1s in the binary strategy).

In the second row, it was used a frequency strategy, which will check the number of occurrences of each word within the text and divide it by the total number of words within the text. For example, the word "this" appears just once (1) and there are seven other words in the text (7), so 1/7 is equal to 0.14.

Finally, in the third row, it was used a count strategy, which is a simple count of occurrences of each word within the text.

> **Important note**
>
> This note is really important – you are likely to find it in your exam. You may have noticed that the BoW matrix contains unique words in the *columns* and each text representation is in the *rows*. If you have 100 long pieces of text with only 50 unique words across them, your BoW matrix will have 50 columns and 100 rows. During your exam, you are likely to receive a list of pieces of text and be asked to prepare the BoW matrix.

There is one more extremely important concept you should know about BoW, which is the n-gram configuration. The term n-gram is used to describe the way you would like to look at your vocabulary, either via single words (uni-gram), groups of two words (bi-gram), groups of three words (tri-gram), or even groups of *n* words (n-gram). So far, you have seen BoW representations using a uni-gram approach, but more sophisticated representations of BoW may use bi-grams, tri-grams, or n-grams.

The main logic itself does not change, but you need to know how to represent n-grams in BoW. Still using the example from *Figure 4.11*, a bi-gram approach would combine those words in the following way: [this movie, movie really, really good, good although, although old, old production]. Make sure you understand this before taking the exam.

> **Important note**
>
> The power and simplicity of BoW come from the fact that you can easily come up with a training set to train your algorithms. If you look at *Figure 4.11*, can you see that having more data and just adding a classification column to that table, such as good or bad review, would allow us to train a binary classification model to predict sentiments?

Alright – you might have noticed that many of the awesome techniques that you have been introduced to come with some downsides. The problem with BoW is the challenge of maintaining its vocabulary. You can easily see that, in a huge corpus of texts, the vocabulary size tends to become bigger and bigger and the matrices' representations tend to be sparse (yes – the sparsity issue again).

One possible way to solve the vocabulary size issue is by using word hashing (also known in ML as the **hashing trick**). Hash functions map data of arbitrary sizes to data of a fixed size. This means you can use the hash trick to represent each text with a fixed number of features (regardless of the vocabulary's size). Technically, this hashing space allows collisions (different texts represented by the same features), so this is something to take into account when you are implementing feature hashing.

TF-IDF

Another problem that comes with BoW, especially when you use the frequency strategy to build the feature space, is that more frequent words will strongly boost their scores due to the high number of occurrences within the document. It turns out that, often, those words with high occurrences are not the key words of the document, but just other words that *also* appear many times in several other documents.

Term Frequency-Inverse Document Frequency (TF-IDF) helps penalize these types of words, by checking how frequent they are in other documents and using that information to rescale the frequency of the words within the document.

At the end of the process, TF-IDF tends to give more importance to words that are unique to the document (document-specific words). Next, let's look at a concrete example so that you can understand it in depth.

Consider that you have a text corpus containing 100 words and the word "Amazon" appears three times. The Term Frequency (TF) of this word would be 3/100, which is equal to 0.03. Now, suppose you have other 1,000 documents and that the word "Amazon" appears in 50 of these. In this case, the Inverse Document Frequency (IDF) would be given by the log as 1,000/50, which is equal to 1.30. The TF-IDF score of the word "Amazon," in that specific document under analysis, will be the product of TF * IDF, which is 0.03 * 1.30 (*0.039*).

Suppose that instead of 50 documents, the word "Amazon" had also appeared on another 750 documents – in other words, much more frequently than in the prior scenario. In this case, the TF part of this equation will not change – it is still 0.03. However, the IDF piece will change a little, since this time it will be log 1,000/750, which is equal to *0.0036*. As you can see, now the word "Amazon" has much less importance than in the previous example.

Word embedding

Unlike traditional approaches, such as BoW and TD-IDF, modern methods of text representation will take care of the context of the information, as well as the presence or frequency of words. One very popular and powerful approach that follows this concept is known as **word embedding.** Word embeddings create a dense vector of a fixed length that can store information about the context and meaning of the document.

Each word is represented by a data point in a multidimensional hyper plan, which is known as embedding space. This embedding space will have n dimensions, where each of these dimensions refers to a particular position of this dense vector.

Although it may sound confusing, the concept is actually pretty simple. Suppose you have a list of four words, and you want to plot them in an embedding space of five dimensions. The words are king, queen, live, and castle. *Table 4.13* shows how to do this.

	Dim 1	Dim 2	Dim 3	Dim 4	Dim 5
King	0.22	0.76	0.77	0.44	0.33
Queen	0.98	0.09	0.67	0.89	0.56
Live	0.13	0.99	0.88	0.01	0.55
Castle	0.01	0.89	0.34	0.02	0.90

Table 4.13 – An embedding space representation

Forget the hypothetical numbers in *Table 4.13* and focus on the data structure; you will see that each word is now represented by n dimensions in the embedding space. This process of transforming words into vectors can be performed by many different methods, but the most popular ones are word2vec and GloVe.

Once you have each word represented as a vector of a fixed length, you can apply many other techniques to do whatever you need. One very common task is plotting those "words" (actually, their dimensions) in a hyper plan and visually checking how close they are to each other!

Technically, you don't use this to plot them as-is, since human brains cannot interpret more than three dimensions. Furthermore, you usually apply a dimensionality reduction technique (such as principal component analysis, which you will learn about later) to reduce the number of dimensions to two, and finally plot the words in a Cartesian plan. That's why you might have seen pictures like the one at the bottom of *Table 4.15*. Have you ever asked yourself how it is possible to plot words on a graph?

	Dim 1	Dim 2	Dim 3	Dim 4	Dim 5
King	0.22	0.76	0.77	0.44	0.33
Queen	0.98	0.09	0.67	0.89	0.56
Live	0.13	0.99	0.88	0.01	0.55
Castle	0.01	0.89	0.34	0.02	0.90

	PC 1	PC2
King	0.9	0.3
Queen	0.8	0.5
Live	0.33	0.7
Castle	0.28	0.7

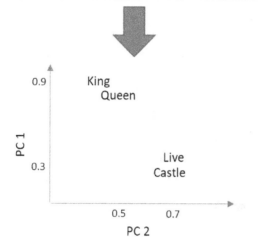

Figure 4.12 – Plotting words

Next, you will learn how the five dimensions shown in *Figure 4.12* were built. Again, there are different methods to do this, but you will learn the most popular, which uses a co-occurrence matrix with a fixed context window.

First, you have to come up with some logic to represent each word, keeping in mind that you also have to take their context into consideration. To solve the context requirement, you need to define a **fixed context window**, which is going to be responsible for specifying how many words will be grouped together for context learning. For instance, assume this fixed context window as 2.

Next, you will create a co-occurrence matrix, which will count the number of occurrences of each pair of words, according to the pre-defined context window. Consider the following text: "I will pass this exam, you will see. I will pass it."

The context window of the first word "pass" would be the ones in *bold*: "*I will* pass *this exam*, you will see. I will pass it." Considering this logic, have a look at how many times each pair of words appears in the context window (*Figure 4.13*).

	I	Will	Pass	This	Exam	You	See	It
I	0	3	...	...	...	...	...	...
Will	3	0	...	...	...	...	...	...
Pass	...	...	0	...	...	...	...	...
This	...	...	...	0	...	...	...	...
Exam	...	...	...	...	0	...	...	...
You	...	...	...	...	...	0	...	...
See	...	...	...	...	...	...	0	...
It	...	...	...	...	...	...	...	0

Figure 4.13 – Co-occurrence matrix

As you can see, the pair of words "I will" appears three times when a context window of size 2 is used:

1. *I will* pass this exam, you will see. I will pass it.
2. I will pass this exam, you *will* see. *I* will pass it.
3. I will pass this exam, you will see. *I will* pass it.

Looking at *Figure 4.13*, the same logic should be applied to all other pairs of words, replacing "…" with the associated number of occurrences. You now have a numerical representation for each word!

> **Important note**
>
> You should be aware that there are many alternatives to co-occurrence matrices with a fixed context window, such as using TD-IDF vectorization or even simpler counters of words per document. The most important message here is that, somehow, you must come up with a numerical representation for each word.

The last step is finally finding those dimensions shown in *Table 4.13*. You can do this by creating a multilayer model, usually based on neural networks, where the hidden layer will represent your embedding space. *Figure 4.14* shows a simplified example where you could potentially compress those words shown in *Figure 4.13* into an embedding space of five dimensions:

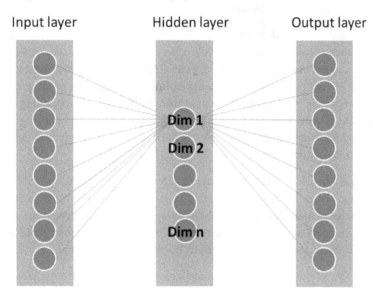

Figure 4.14 – Building embedding spaces with neural networks

You will learn about neural networks in more detail later in this book. For now, understanding where the embedding vector comes from is already an awesome achievement!

Another important thing you should keep in mind while modeling natural language problems is that you can reuse a pre-trained embedding space in your models. Some companies have created modern neural network architectures, trained on billions of documents, which have become the state of the art in this field. For your reference, take a look at Bidirectional Encoder Representations from Transformers (BERT), which was proposed by Google and has been widely used by the data science community and industry.

You have now reached the end of this long – but very important – chapter about data preparation and transformation. Take this opportunity to do a quick recap of the awesome things you have learned.

Summary

First, you were introduced to the different types of features that you might have to work with. Identifying the type of variable you'll be working with is very important for defining the types of transformations and techniques that can be applied to each case.

Then, you learned how to deal with categorical features. You saw that, sometimes, categorical variables do have an order (such as the ordinal ones), while other times, they don't (such as the nominal ones). You learned that one-hot encoding (or dummy variables) is probably the most common type of transformation for nominal features; however, depending on the number of unique categories, after applying one-hot encoding, your data might suffer from sparsity issues. Regarding ordinal features, you shouldn't create dummy variables on top of them, since you would be losing the information about the order that has been incorporated into the variable. In those cases, ordinal encoding is the most appropriate transformation.

You continued your journey by looking at numerical features, where you learned how to deal with continuous and discrete data. You walked through the most important types of transformations, such as normalization, standardization, binning, and discretization. You saw that some types of transformation rely on the underlying data to find their parameters, so it is very important to avoid using the testing set to learn anything from the data (it must strictly be used only for testing).

You have also seen that you can even apply pure math to transform your data; for example, you learned that power transformations can be used to reduce the skewness of your feature and make it more similar to a normal distribution.

After that, you looked at missing data and got a sense of how important this task is. When you are modeling, you *can't* look at the missing values as a simple computational problem, where you just have to replace x with y. This is a much bigger problem, and you need to start solving it by exploring your data and then checking whether your missing data was generated at random or not.

When you are making the decision to remove or replace missing data, you must be aware that you are either losing information or adding bias to the dataset, respectively. Remember to review all the important notes of this chapter, since they are likely to be relevant to your exam.

You also learned about outlier detection. You looked at different ways to find outliers, such as the zscore and box plot approaches. Most importantly, you learned that you can either flag or smooth them.

At the beginning, you were advised that this chapter would be a long but worthwhile journey about data preparation. You have also learned how to deal with rare events, since this is one of the most challenging problems in ML. Now you are aware that, sometimes, your data might be unbalanced, and you must either trick your algorithm (by changing the class weights) or resample your data (applying undersampling or oversampling).

Finally, you learned how to deal with text data for NLP. You should now be able to manually compute BoW and TF-IDF matrices! You went even deeper and learned how word embedding works. During this subsection, you learned that you can either create your own embedding space (using many different methods) or reuse a pre-trained one, such as BERT.

You are done! In the next chapter, you will dive into data visualization techniques.

Exam Readiness Drill – Chapter Review Questions

Apart from a solid understanding of key concepts, being able to think quickly under time pressure is a skill that will help you ace your certification exam. That is why working on these skills early on in your learning journey is key.

Chapter review questions are designed to improve your test-taking skills progressively with each chapter you learn and review your understanding of key concepts in the chapter at the same time. You'll find these at the end of each chapter.

> **How To Access These Resources**
>
> To learn how to access these resources, head over to the chapter titled *Chapter 11, Accessing the Online Practice Resources*.

To open the Chapter Review Questions for this chapter, perform the following steps:

1. Click the link – `https://packt.link/MLSC01E2_CH04`.

    Alternatively, you can scan the following **QR code** (*Figure 4.15*):

Figure 4.15 – QR code that opens Chapter Review Questions for logged-in users

2. Once you log in, you'll see a page similar to the one shown in *Figure 4.16*:

Figure 4.16 – Chapter Review Questions for Chapter 4

3. Once ready, start the following practice drills, re-attempting the quiz multiple times.

Exam Readiness Drill

For the first three attempts, don't worry about the time limit.

ATTEMPT 1

The first time, aim for at least **40%**. Look at the answers you got wrong and read the relevant sections in the chapter again to fix your learning gaps.

ATTEMPT 2

The second time, aim for at least **60%**. Look at the answers you got wrong and read the relevant sections in the chapter again to fix any remaining learning gaps.

ATTEMPT 3

The third time, aim for at least **75%**. Once you score 75% or more, you start working on your timing.

> **Tip**
> You may take more than **three** attempts to reach 75%. That's okay. Just review the relevant sections in the chapter till you get there.

Working On Timing

Target: Your aim is to keep the score the same while trying to answer these questions as quickly as possible. Here's an example of how your next attempts should look like:

Attempt	Score	Time Taken
Attempt 5	77%	21 mins 30 seconds
Attempt 6	78%	18 mins 34 seconds
Attempt 7	76%	14 mins 44 seconds

Table 4.14 – Sample timing practice drills on the online platform

> **Note**
> The time limits shown in the above table are just examples. Set your own time limits with each attempt based on the time limit of the quiz on the website.

With each new attempt, your score should stay above **75%** while your "time taken" to complete should "decrease". Repeat as many attempts as you want till you feel confident dealing with the time pressure.

5

Data Understanding and Visualization

Data visualization is an art! No matter how much effort you and your team put into data preparation and preliminary analysis for modeling, if you don't know how to show your findings effectively, your audience may not understand the point you are trying to make.

Often, such situations may be even worse when you are dealing with decision-makers. For example, if you choose the wrong set of charts to tell a particular story, people can misinterpret your analysis and make bad decisions.

Understanding the different types of data visualizations, and knowing how they fit with each type of analysis, will put you in a very good position in terms of engaging your audience and transmitting the information you want.

In this chapter, you will learn about some data visualization techniques. You will be covering the following topics:

- Visualizing relationships in your data
- Visualizing comparisons in your data
- Visualizing compositions in your data
- Visualizing distributions in your data
- Building key performance indicators
- Introducing QuickSight

You already know why you need to master these topics. Get started!

Visualizing relationships in your data

When you need to show relationships in your data, you are usually talking about plotting two or more variables in a chart to visualize their level of dependency. A **scatter plot** is probably the most common type of chart to show the relationship between two variables. *Figure 5.1* shows a scatter plot for two variables, X and Y.

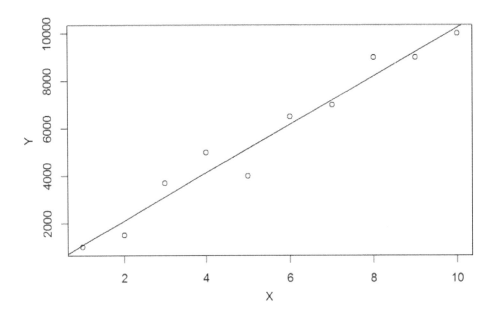

Figure 5.1 – Plotting relationships with a scatter plot

Figure 5.1 shows a clear relationship between *X* and *Y*. As *X* increases, *Y* also increases. In this particular case, you can say that there is a linear relationship between both variables. Keep in mind that scatter plots may also catch other types of relationships, not only linear ones. For example, it would also be possible to find an exponential relationship between the two variables.

Another nice chart to make comparisons with is the **bubble chart**. Just like a scatter plot, it will also show the relationship between variables; however, here, you can use a third dimension, which will be represented by the size of the point.

Figure 5.2 is a bubble chart that explains an investment schema, where the *x* axis is the annual rate, *y* is the investment period, and the size of the bubble indicates the amount allocated to each investment option.

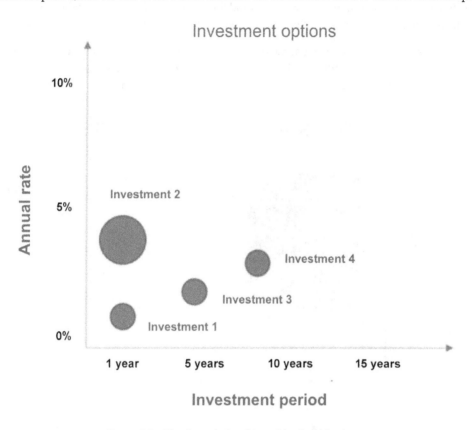

Figure 5.2 – Plotting relationships with a bubble chart

Looking at *Figure 5.2*, you can see two types of relationships. The first one is the relationship between the annual rate and investment period: the longer the investment period, the higher your annual rate. The second one is the relationship between the amount invested and the annual rate: the higher the amount invested, the higher your annual rate. As you can see, this is a very effective way to present this type of analysis. Next, you will learn how to compare variables.

Visualizing comparisons in your data

Comparisons are very common in data analysis and there are different ways to present them. Starting with the **bar chart**, you must have seen many reports that have used this type of visualization.

Bar charts can be used to compare one variable among different classes – for example, a car's price across different models or population size per country. In *Figure 5.3*, the bar chart is used to analyze the percentage of positive tests for COVID-19 in a range of regions of India as of April 7th, 2020.

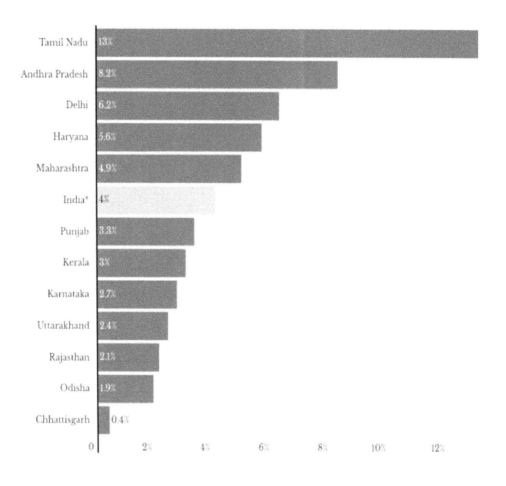

Figure 5.3 – Plotting comparisons with a bar chart (source: State Health Department of India)

Sometimes, you can also use **stacked column charts** to add another dimension to the data that is being analyzed. For example, *Figure 5.4* uses a stacked bar chart to show how many people were on board the Titanic by sex. Additionally, it breaks down the number of people who survived (positive class) and those who did not (negative class), also by sex.

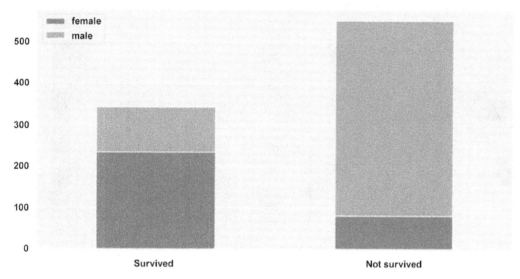

Figure 5.4 – Using a stacked bar chart to analyze the Titanic disaster dataset

As you can see, most of the women survived the disaster, while most of the men did not. The stacked bars help us visualize the difference between the fates of the sexes. Finally, you should know that you can also show percentages on those stacked bars, not just absolute numbers.

Column charts are also useful if you need to compare one or two variables across different periods. For example, in *Figure 5.5*, you can see the annual Canadian electronic vehicle sales by province.

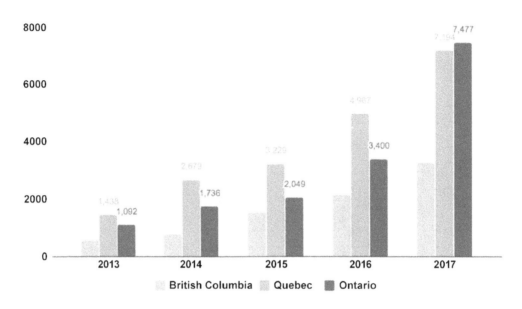

Figure 5.5 – Plotting comparisons with a column chart (source: `https://electrek.co/`)

Another very effective way to make comparisons across different periods is by using **line charts**. *Figure 5.6* shows a pretty interesting example of how you can compare different algorithms' performance, in a particular project, across different release dates.

> **Important note**
> Line charts are usually very helpful to indicate whether there is any trend in the data over the period of time under analysis. A very common use case for line charts is forecasting, where you usually have to analyze trends and seasonality in time series data.

For example, in *Figure 5.6* you can see that the **Classification and Regression Trees (CART)** model used to be the poorest performant model compared to other algorithms, such as **AdaBoost (ADA), gradient boosting (GB), random forest (RF), and logistic regression (LOGIT).**

However, in July, the CART model was optimized, and it turned out to be the third-best model across all other models. The whole story about the best model for each period can easily be seen in *Figure 5.6*.

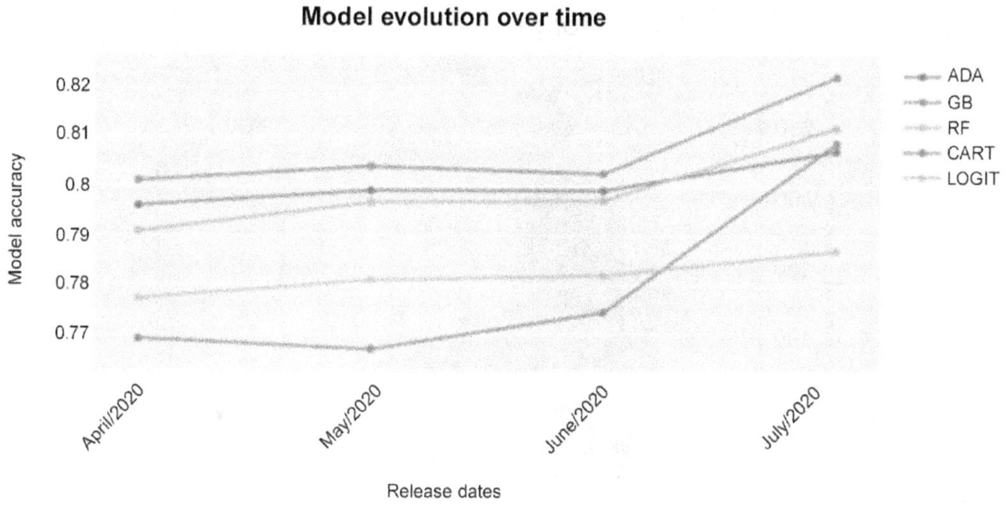

Figure 5.6 – Plotting comparisons with a line chart

Finally, you can also show comparisons of your data using tables. Tables are more useful when you have multiple dimensions (usually placed in the rows of the table) and one or multiple metrics to make comparisons against (usually placed in the columns of the table).

In the next section, you will learn about another set of charts that aims to show the distribution of your variables. This set of charts is particularly important for modeling tasks, since you must know the distribution of a feature to think about potential data transformations for it.

Visualizing distributions in your data

Exploring the distribution of your feature is very important to understand some key characteristics of it, such as its skewness, mean, median, and quantiles. You can easily visualize skewness by plotting a histogram. This type of chart groups your data into bins or buckets and performs counts on top of them. For example, *Figure 5.7* shows a histogram for the *age* variable:

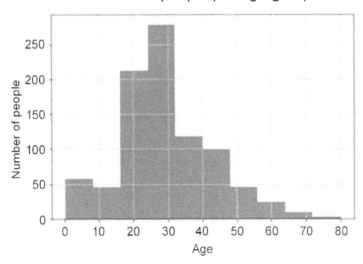

Figure 5.7 – Plotting distributions with a histogram

Looking at the histogram, you could conclude that most of the people are between 20 and 50 years old. You can also see a few people more than 60 years old. Another example of a histogram is shown in *Figure 5.8*, which plots the distribution of payments from a particular event that has different ticket prices. It aims to analyze how much money people are paying per ticket.

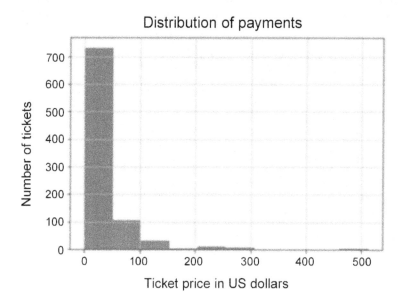

Figure 5.8 – Checking skewness with a histogram

Here, you can see that most of the people are paying a maximum of 100 dollars per ticket. That is the reason why you can see a skewed distribution to the right-hand side (the tail side).

If you want to see other characteristics of the distribution, such as its median, quantiles, and outliers, then you should use box plots. In *Figure 5.9*, there is another performance comparison of different algorithms in a given dataset.

These algorithms were executed many times, in a cross-validation process, which resulted in multiple outputs for the same algorithm; for example, one accuracy metric for each execution of the algorithm on each fold.

Since there are multiple accuracy metrics for each algorithm, you can use a box plot to check how each of those algorithms performed during the cross-validation process.

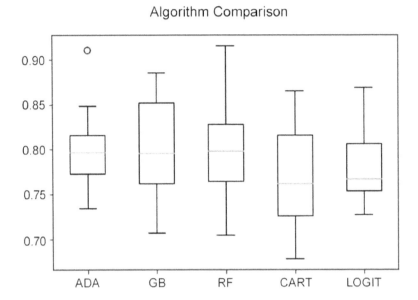

Figure 5.9 – Plotting distributions with a box plot

Here, you can see that box plots can present some information about the distribution of the data, such as its median, lower quartile, upper quartile, and outliers. For a complete understanding of each element of a box plot, take a look at *Figure 5.10*.

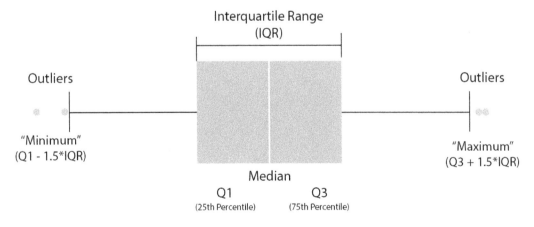

Figure 5.10 – Box plot elements

By analyzing the box plot shown in *Figure 5.9*, you could conclude that the ADA algorithm has presented some outliers during the cross-validation process, since one of the executions resulted in a very good model (around 92% accuracy). All the other executions of AdaBoost resulted in less than 85% accuracy, with a median value of around 80%.

Another conclusion you could make after analyzing *Figure 5.9* is that the CART algorithm presented the poorest performance during the cross-validation process (the lowest median and lower quartile).

Before you wrap up this section, note that you can also use a scatter plot to analyze data distributions when you have more than one variable. Next, you will look at another set of charts that is useful for showing compositions in your data.

Visualizing compositions in your data

Sometimes, you want to analyze the various elements that compose a feature – for example, the percentage of sales per region or percentage of queries per channel. In both examples, they are not considering any time dimension; instead, they are just looking at the entire data points. For these types of compositions, where you don't have the time dimension, you could show your data using **pie charts, stacked 100% bar charts, and tree maps.**

Figure 5.11 is a pie chart showing the number of queries per customer channel for a given company over a pre-defined period of time.

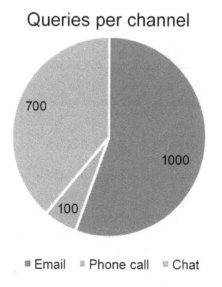

Figure 5.11 – Plotting compositions with a pie chart

If you want to show compositions while considering a time dimension, then your most common options are a **stacked area chart, a stacked 100% area chart, a stacked column chart, or a stacked 100% column chart.** For reference, take a look at *Figure 5.12*, which shows the sales per region from 2016 until 2020.

Figure 5.12 – Plotting compositions with a stacked 100% column chart

As you can see, stacked 100% column charts help us understand compositions across different periods.

Building key performance indicators

Before you wrap up these data visualization sections, you need to be introduced to **key performance indicators**, or **KPIs** for short.

A KPI is usually a single value that describes the results of a business indicator, such as the churn rate, **net promoter score (NPS), return on investment (ROI),** and so on. Although there are some standard indicators across different industries, you usually need to build custom metrics based on the company's needs.

To be honest, the most complex challenge associated with indicators is not in their visualization aspect itself, but in the way they have been built (the rules used) and the way they will be communicated and used across different levels of the company.

From a visualization perspective, just like any other single value, you can use all those charts that you have learned about to analyze your indicator, depending on your need. However, if you just want to show your KPI, with no time dimension, you can use a **widget**.

Alright, these are the most important topics about data visualization that you should know for the AWS Certified Machine Learning – Specialty exam. Now, let us have a look at QuickSight, an AWS service where you can implement all these visualization techniques you have just learned.

Introducing QuickSight

Amazon QuickSight is a cloud-based analytics service that allows you to build data visualizations and ad hoc analysis. QuickSight supports a variety of data sources, such as Redshift, Aurora, Athena, RDS, and your on-premises database solution.

Other sources of data include S3, where you can retrieve data from Excel, CSV, or log files, and **Software-as-a-Service (SaaS)** solutions, where you can retrieve data from Salesforce entities.

Amazon QuickSight has two versions:

- Standard edition
- Enterprise edition

The most important difference between these two versions is the possibility of integration with Microsoft **Active Directory (AD)** and encryption at rest. Both features are only provided in the Enterprise edition.

> **Important note**
>
> Keep in mind that AWS services are constantly evolving, so more differences between the Standard and Enterprise versions may crop up in the future. You should always consult the latest documentation of AWS services to check what is new.

In terms of access management, QuickSight offers a very simple interface you can use to control user access. In the Standard edition, you have pretty much two options for inviting a user to your QuickSight account:

- You can invite an IAM user.
- You can send an invitation to an email address.

If you invite IAM users, then they can automatically log in to your account and see or edit your visualization, depending on the type of permission you have provided during QuickSight user creation. If you have invited an email address, then the email owner has to access their mailbox to complete this operation.

Removing a user is also straightforward. The only extra information you have to provide while removing a user is whether you want to transfer the orphaned resources to another user into your account *or* delete all the user's resources.

If you are playing with the Enterprise edition, this process of authorizing users can be a little different, since you have AD working for you. In this case, you can grant access to AD groups, and all the users from those groups will be granted access to your account on QuickSight.

Also, remember that in both versions, all data transfer is encrypted; however, you will only find encryption at rest in the Enterprise edition.

When you are bringing data into QuickSight, you are technically creating what are known as **datasets**. Datasets, in turn, are imported in an optimized structure into QuickSight, known as the **Super-fast, Parallel, In-memory, Calculation Engine (SPICE)**. That is why QuickSight can perform data visualization on big data.

Finally, you should know that QuickSight does not only allow you to plot your data, but also perform some small data preparation tasks, such as renaming fields, computing new fields, changing data types, preparing queries to retrieve data from the source, and joining tables from the same source.

Summarizing the main steps for working with QuickSight:

1. User creation and authorization.
2. Connecting to a **data source.**
3. Bringing data into a **dataset**.
4. Your dataset will be imported into **SPICE**.
5. From a dataset, you can create an **analysis**.
6. Finally, inside your analysis, you can add **visuals**.
7. If you want to go further, you can create a snapshot of your analysis and place it in a **dashboard**. Alternatively, you can group your analysis into **stories**.

That brings you to the end of this chapter about data visualizations! Now, take some time to recap what you have learned.

Summary

You started this chapter by learning how to visualize relationships in the data. Scatter plots and bubble charts are the most important charts in this category to show relationships between two or three variables, respectively.

Then, you moved to another category of data visualization, which aimed to make comparisons in the data. The most common charts that you can use to show comparisons are bar charts, column charts, and line charts. Tables are also useful to show comparisons.

The next use case that you learned was visualizing data distributions. The most common types of charts that are used to show distributions are histograms and box plots.

Then, you moved to compositions. You can use this set of charts when you want to show the different elements that make up the data. While showing compositions, you must be aware of whether you want to present static data or data that changes over time. For static data, you should use a pie chart, a stacked 100% bar chart, or a tree map. For data that changes over time, you should use a stacked area chart, a stacked 100% area chart, a stacked column chart, or a stacked 100% column chart.

The last section of this chapter was reserved for QuickSight, which is an AWS service that you can use to visualize your data. You learned about the different versions and features of the service, and you were then introduced to SPICE.

Well done! In the next chapter, you will learn about machine learning algorithms. That is going to be a very important chapter for your certification journey, so make sure you are prepared! However, before you jump into that new chapter, take some time to practice a little more for the exam!

Exam Readiness Drill – Chapter Review Questions

Apart from a solid understanding of key concepts, being able to think quickly under time pressure is a skill that will help you ace your certification exam. That is why working on these skills early on in your learning journey is key.

Chapter review questions are designed to improve your test-taking skills progressively with each chapter you learn and review your understanding of key concepts in the chapter at the same time. You'll find these at the end of each chapter.

> **How To Access These Resources**
>
> To learn how to access these resources, head over to the chapter titled *Chapter 11*, *Accessing the Online Practice Resources*.

To open the Chapter Review Questions for this chapter, perform the following steps:

1. Click the link – `https://packt.link/MLSC01E2_CH05`.

    Alternatively, you can scan the following **QR code** (*Figure 5.13*):

Figure 5.13 – QR code that opens Chapter Review Questions for logged-in users

2. Once you log in, you'll see a page similar to the one shown in *Figure 5.14*:

Figure 5.14 – Chapter Review Questions for Chapter 5

3. Once ready, start the following practice drills, re-attempting the quiz multiple times.

Exam Readiness Drill

For the first three attempts, don't worry about the time limit.

ATTEMPT 1

The first time, aim for at least **40%**. Look at the answers you got wrong and read the relevant sections in the chapter again to fix your learning gaps.

ATTEMPT 2

The second time, aim for at least **60%**. Look at the answers you got wrong and read the relevant sections in the chapter again to fix any remaining learning gaps.

ATTEMPT 3

The third time, aim for at least **75%**. Once you score 75% or more, you start working on your timing.

Tip

You may take more than **three** attempts to reach 75%. That's okay. Just review the relevant sections in the chapter till you get there.

Working On Timing

Target: Your aim is to keep the score the same while trying to answer these questions as quickly as possible. Here's an example of how your next attempts should look like:

Attempt	Score	Time Taken
Attempt 5	77%	21 mins 30 seconds
Attempt 6	78%	18 mins 34 seconds
Attempt 7	76%	14 mins 44 seconds

Table 5.1 – Sample timing practice drills on the online platform

---

Note

The time limits shown in the above table are just examples. Set your own time limits with each attempt based on the time limit of the quiz on the website.

With each new attempt, your score should stay above **75%** while your "time taken" to complete should "decrease". Repeat as many attempts as you want till you feel confident dealing with the time pressure.

6
Applying Machine Learning Algorithms

In the previous chapter, you learned about understanding data and visualization. It is now time to move on to the modeling phase and study machine learning algorithms! In the earlier chapters, you learned that building machine learning models requires a lot of knowledge about AWS services, data engineering, data exploration, data architecture, and much more. This time, you will delve deeper into the algorithms that have been introduced and more.

Having a good sense of the different types of algorithms and machine learning approaches will put you in a very good position to make decisions during your projects. Of course, this type of knowledge is also crucial to the AWS Certified Machine Learning Specialty exam.

Bear in mind that there are thousands of algorithms out there. You can even propose your own algorithm for a particular problem. In this chapter, you will learn about the most relevant ones and, hopefully, the ones that you will probably face in the exam.

The main topics of this chapter are as follows:

- Storing the training data
- A word about ensemble models
- Supervised learning:
- Regression models
- Classification models
- Forecasting models
- Object2Vec
- Unsupervised learning:
- Clustering

- Anomaly detection

- Dimensionality reduction

- IP Insights

- Textual analysis (natural language processing)

- Image processing

- Reinforcement learning

Alright, grab a coffee and rock it!

Introducing this chapter

During this chapter, you will read about several algorithms, modeling concepts, and learning strategies. All these topics are beneficial for you to know for the exam and throughout your career as a data scientist.

This chapter has been structured in such a way that it not only covers the necessary topics of the exam but also gives you a good sense of the most important learning strategies out there. For example, the exam will check your knowledge regarding the basic concepts of K-Means. However, this chapter will cover it on a much deeper level, since this is an important topic for your career as a data scientist.

The chapter will follow this approach of looking deeper into the algorithms' logic for some types of models that every data scientist should master. Furthermore, keep this in mind: sometimes you may go deeper than what is expected of you in the exam, but that will be extremely important for you in your career.

Many times during this chapter, you will see the term **built-in algorithms**. This term will be used to refer to the list of algorithms implemented by AWS on their SageMaker SDK.

Here is a concrete example: you can use scikit-learn's **K-nearest neighbors** algorithm, or KNN for short (if you don't remember what scikit-learn is, refresh your memory by going back to *Chapter 1, Machine Learning Fundamentals*) to create a classification model and deploy it to SageMaker. However, AWS also offers its own implementation of the KNN algorithm on its SDK, which is optimized to run in the AWS environment. Here, KNN is an example of a built-in algorithm.

The possibilities on AWS are endless because you can either take advantage of built-in algorithms or bring in your own algorithm to create models on SageMaker. Finally, just to make this very clear, here is an example of how to import a built-in algorithm from the AWS SDK:

```
import sagemaker
knn = sagemaker.estimator.Estimator(get_image_uri(boto3.
Session().region_name, "knn"),
        get_execution_role(),
        train_instance_count=1,
        train_instance_type='ml.m5.2xlarge',
```

```
        output_path=output_path,
        sagemaker_session=sagemaker.Session())
knn.set_hyperparameters(**hyperparams)
```

You will learn how to create models on SageMaker in *Chapter 9, Amazon SageMaker Modeling*. For now, just understand that AWS has its own set of libraries where those built-in algorithms are implemented.

To train and evaluate a model, you need training and testing data. After instantiating your estimator, you should then feed it with those datasets. Not to spoil *Chapter 9, Amazon SageMaker Modeling*, but you should know about the concept of **data channels** in advance.

Data channels are configurations related to input data that you can pass to SageMaker when you are creating a training job. You should set these configurations just to inform SageMaker of how your input data is formatted.

In *Chapter 9, Amazon SageMaker Modeling*, you will learn how to create training jobs and how to set data channels. As of now, you should know that while configuring data channels, you can set a **content type** (ContentType) and an **input mode** (TrainingInputMode). You will now take a closer look at how and where the training data should be stored so that it can be integrated properly with AWS's built-in algorithms.

Storing the training data

First of all, you can use multiple AWS services to prepare data for machine learning, such as **Elastic MapReduce (EMR),** Redshift, Glue, and so on. After preprocessing the training data, you should store it in S3, in a format expected by the algorithm you are using. *Table 6.1* shows the list of acceptable data formats per algorithm.

Data format	Algorithm
Application/x-image	Object detection algorithm, semantic segmentation
Application/x-recordio	Object detection algorithm
Application/x-recordio-protobuf	Factorization machines, K-Means, KNN, latent Dirichlet allocation, linear learner, NTM, PCA, RCF, sequence-to-sequence
Application/jsonlines	BlazingText, DeepAR
Image/.jpeg	Object detection algorithm, semantic segmentation
Image/.png	Object detection algorithm, semantic segmentation
Text/.csv	IP Insights, K-Means, KNN, latent Dirichlet allocation, linear learner, NTM, PCA, RCF, XGBoost
Text/.libsvm	XGBoost

Table 6.1 – Data formats that are acceptable per AWS algorithm

As you can see, many algorithms accept `Text/.csv` format. You should follow these rules if you want to use that format:

- Your CSV file *cannot* have a header record.

- For supervised learning, the target variable must be in the first column.

- While configuring the training pipeline, set the input data channel as `content_type` equal to `text/csv`.

- For unsupervised learning, set `label_size` within `content_type`, as follows: `'content_type=text/csv;label_size=0'`.

Although `text/.csv` format is fine for many use cases, most of the time, AWS's built-in algorithms work better with `recordIO-protobuf`. This is an optimized data format that is used to train AWS's built-in algorithms, where SageMaker converts each observation in the dataset into a binary representation that is a set of 4-byte floats.

RecordIO-protobuf accepts two types of input modes: pipe mode and file mode. In pipe mode, the data will be streamed directly from S3, which helps optimize storage. In file mode, the data is copied from S3 to the training instance's store volume.

You are almost ready! Now you can take a quick look at some modeling definitions that will help you understand some more advanced algorithms.

A word about ensemble models

Before you start diving into the algorithms, there is an important modeling concept that you should be aware of – **ensemble**. The term ensemble is used to describe methods that use multiple algorithms to create a model.

A regular algorithm that *does not* implement ensemble methods will rely on a single model to train and predict the target variable. That is what happens when you create a decision tree or regression model. On the other hand, algorithms that *do* implement ensemble methods will rely on multiple models to predict the target variable. In that case, since each of these models might come up with a different prediction for the target variable, ensemble algorithms implement either a voting (for classification models) or averaging (for regression models) system to output the final results. *Table 6.2* illustrates a very simple voting system for an ensemble algorithm composed of three models.

Transaction	Model A	Model B	Model C	Prediction
1	Fraud	Fraud	Not Fraud	Fraud
2	Not Fraud	Not Fraud	Not Fraud	Not Fraud
3	Fraud	Fraud	Fraud	Fraud
4	Not Fraud	Not Fraud	Fraud	Not Fraud

Table 6.2 – An example of a voting system on ensemble methods

As described before, the same approach works for regression problems, where instead of voting, it could average the results of each model and use that as the outcome.

Voting and averaging are just two examples of ensemble approaches. Other powerful techniques include blending and stacking, where you can create multiple models and use the outcome of each model as a feature for a main model. Looking back at *Table 6.2*, columns *Model A*, *Model B*, and *Model C* could be used as features to predict the final outcome.

It turns out that many machine learning algorithms use ensemble methods while training, in an embedded way. These algorithms can be classified into two main categories:

- **Bootstrapping aggregation** or **bagging**: With this approach, several models are trained on top of different samples of data. Predictions are then made through the voting or averaging system. The most popular algorithm from this category is known as **Random Forest**.

- **Boosting**: With this approach, several models are trained on top of different samples of the data. One model then tries to correct the error of the next model by penalizing incorrect predictions. The most popular algorithms from this category are **stochastic gradient boosting** and **AdaBoost**.

Now that you know what ensemble models are, you can look at some machine learning algorithms that are likely to be present in your exam. Not all of them use ensemble approaches.

The next few sections are split based on AWS algorithm categories, as follows:

- Supervised learning
- Unsupervised learning
- Textual analysis
- Image processing

Finally, you will have an overview of reinforcement learning on AWS.

Supervised learning

AWS provides supervised learning algorithms for general purposes (regression and classification tasks) and more specific purposes (forecasting and vectorization). The list of built-in algorithms that can be found in these sub-categories is as follows:

- Linear learner algorithm
- Factorization machines algorithm
- XGBoost algorithm
- KNN algorithm
- Object2Vec algorithm
- DeepAR forecasting algorithm

You will start by learning about regression models and the linear learner algorithm.

Working with regression models

Looking at **linear regression** models is a nice way to understand what is going on inside **regression models** in general (linear and non-linear regression models). This is mandatory knowledge for every data scientist and can help you solve real challenges as well. You will now take a closer look at this in the following subsections.

Introducing regression algorithms

Linear regression models aim to predict a numeric value (y) according to one or more variables (x). Mathematically, such a relationship can be defined as $y = f(x)$, where y is known as the **dependent variable** and x is known as the **independent variable**.

With regression models, the component that you want to predict (y) is always a continuous number – for example, the price of houses or the number of transactions. You saw this in *Chapter 1, Machine Learning Fundamentals*, in *Figure 1.2*, when you were learning about the right type of supervised learning algorithm, given the target variable. Please feel free to go back and review it.

When you use *just one variable to predict y*, this problem is referred to as **simple linear regression**. On the other hand, when you use *more than one variable to predict y*, you have a **multiple linear regression** problem.

There is also another class of regression models, known as **non-linear regression**. However, let us put that aside for a moment and understand what simple linear regression means.

Regression models belong to the supervised side of machine learning (the other side is non-supervised) because algorithms try to predict values according to existing correlations between independent and dependent variables.

But what does f mean in $y=f(x)$? Here, f is the regression function responsible for predicting y based on x. In other words, this is the function that you want to find. When talking about simple linear regression, pay attention to the next three questions and answers:

- What is the shape of f in linear regression?

  Linear, of course!

- How can you represent a linear relationship?

  Using a *straight* line (you will understand why in a few minutes).

- So what is the function that defines a line?

  $ax + b$ (just check any *mathematics* book).

That is it! Linear regression models are given by $y = ax + b$. When you are trying to predict y given x, you just need to find out the values of a and b. You can adopt the same logic to figure out what is going on inside other kinds of regression.

Finding out the values of a and b is the only thing you are going to do. It is nice to know that a is also known as the **alpha coefficient**, or **slope**, and represents the line's inclination, while b is also known as the **beta coefficient**, or **y intercept**, and represents the place where the line crosses the y axis (into a two-dimensional plane consisting of x and y). You will learn about these two terms in a later subsection.

It is also nice to know that there is a bias (e) associated with every predictor that you do not have control over. That being said, the formal definition of simple linear regression is given by $y = ax + b + e$.

In the next subsection, you will learn how to find alpha and beta to solve a simple linear regression problem.

Least squares method

There are different ways to find the slope and y intercept of a line, but the most used method is known as the **least squares method**. The principle behind this method is simple: you have to find the *best line that reduces the sum of squared error*.

In *Figure 6.1*, you can see a Cartesian plane with multiple points and lines in it. *Line a* represents the best fit for this data – in other words, that would be the best linear regression function for those points. But how can you know that? It is simple: if you compute the error associated with each point, you will realize that *Line a* contains the least sum of squared errors.

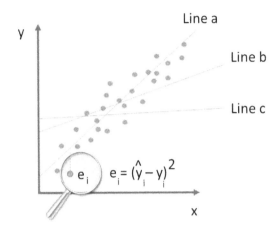

Figure 6.1 – Visualizing the principle of the least squares method

It is worth understanding linear regression from scratch not only for the certification exam but also for your career as a data scientist. To provide you with a complete example, a spreadsheet containing all the calculations that you are going to see has been developed! You are encouraged to jump on this support material and perform some simulations. In any case, you will see these calculations in action in the next subsection.

Creating a linear regression model from scratch

You are going to use a very simple dataset, with only two variables:

- x: Represents the person's number of years of work experience
- y: Represents the person's average salary

You want to understand the relationship between x and y and, if possible, predict the salary (y) based on years of experience (x). Real problems very often have far more independent variables and are not necessarily linear. However, this example will give you the baseline knowledge to master more complex algorithms.

To find out what the alpha and beta coefficients are (or slope and y intercept if you prefer), you need to find some statistics related to the dataset. In *Table 6.3*, you have the data and these auxiliary statistics.

X (INDEPENDENT)	Y (DEPENDENT)	X MEAN	Y MEAN	COVARIANCE (X,Y)	X VARIANCE	Y VARIANCE
1	1.000			21.015	20	21.808.900
2	1.500			14.595	12	17.388.900
3	3.700			4.925	6	3.880.900
4	5.000			1.005	2	448.900
5	4.000			835	0	2.788.900
6	6.500			415	0	688.900
7	7.000			1.995	2	1.768.900
8	9.000			8.325	6	11.088.900
9	9.000			11.655	12	11.088.900
10	10.000			19.485	20	18.748.900
COUNT	10	5,50	5.670,00	8.425,00	8,25	8.970.100,00

Table 6.3 – Dataset to predict average salary based on the amount of work experience

As you can see, there is an almost perfect linear relationship between x and y. As the amount of work experience increases, so does the salary. In addition to x and y, you need to compute the following statistics: the number of records, the mean of x, the mean of y, the covariance of x and y, the variance of x, and the variance of y. *Figure 6.2* depicts formulas that provide a mathematical representation of variance and covariance (respectively), where x bar, y bar, and n represent the mean of x, the mean of y, and the number of records, respectively:

$$S^2 = \frac{\Sigma\left(x_i - \overline{x}\right)}{n}$$

$$Cov\left(X,\ Y\right) = \frac{\sum_{i=1}^{n}\left(x_i - \overline{x}\right)\left(y_i - \overline{y}\right)}{n}$$

Figure 6.2 – Mathematical representation of variance and covariance respectively

If you want to check the calculation details of the formulas for each of those auxiliary statistics in *Table 6.2*, please refer to the support material provided along with this book. There, you will find these formulas already implemented for you.

These statistics are important because they will be used to compute the alpha and beta coefficients. *Figure 6.3* explains how you can compute both coefficients, along with the correlation coefficients R and R squared. These last two metrics will give you an idea about the quality of the model, where the closer they are to 1, the better the model is.

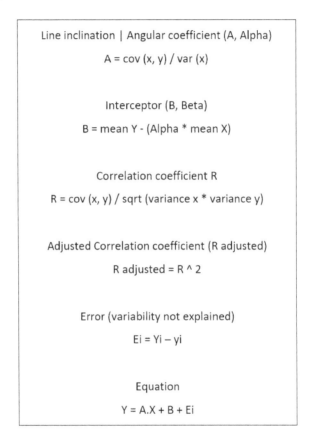

Figure 6.3 – Equations to calculate coefficients for simple linear regression

After applying these formulas, you will come up with the results shown in *Table 6.4*. It already contains all the information that you need to make predictions, on top of the new data. If you replace the coefficients in the original equation, $y = ax + b + e$, you will find the regression formula to be as follows: $y = 1021.212 * x + 53.3$.

Coefficient	Description	Value
Alpha	Line inclination	1,021,212,121
Beta	Interceptor	53
R	Correlation	0,979,364,354
R^2	Determination	0,959,154,538

Table 6.4 – Finding regression coefficients

From this point on, to make predictions, all you have to do is replace x with the number of years of experience. As a result, you will find y, which is the projected salary. You can see the model fit in *Figure 6.4* and some model predictions in *Table 6.5*.

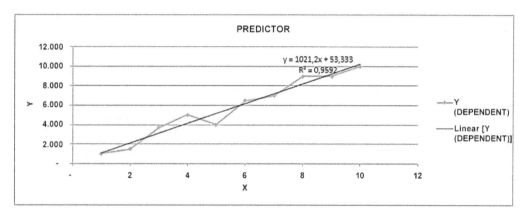

Figure 6.4 – Fitting data in the regression equation

INPUT	PREDICTION	ERROR
1	1.075	75
2	2.096	596
3	3.117	- 583
4	4.138	- 862
5	5.159	1.159
6	6.181	- 319
7	7.202	202
8	8.223	- 777
9	9.244	244

INPUT	PREDICTION	ERROR
10	10.265	265
11	11.287	
12	12.308	
13	13.329	
14	14.350	
15	15.372	
16	16.393	
17	17.414	
18	18.435	
19	19.456	
20	20.478	

Table 6.5 – Model predictions

While you are analyzing regression models, you should be able to know whether your model is of good quality or not. You read about many modeling issues (such as overfitting) in *Chapter 1, Machine Learning Fundamentals*, and you already know that you always have to check model performance.

A good approach to regression models is performing what is called residual analysis. This is where you plot the errors of the model in a scatter plot and check whether they are randomly distributed (as expected) or not. If the errors are *not* randomly distributed, this means that your model was unable to generalize the data. *Figure 6.5* shows a residual analysis based on the data from *Table 6.5*.

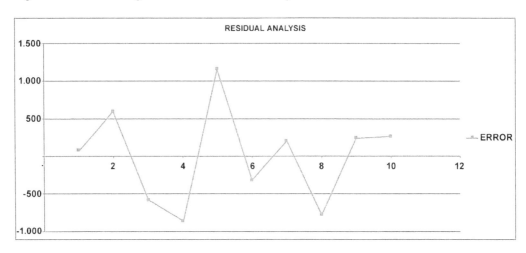

Figure 6.5 – Residual analysis

The takeaway here is that the errors are randomly distributed. Such evidence, along with a high R squared rating, can be used as arguments to support the use of this model.

> **Important note**
>
> In *Chapter 7, Evaluating and Optimizing Models*, you will learn about evaluation metrics. For instance, you will learn that each type of model may have its own set of evaluation metrics. Regression models are commonly evaluated with **Mean Squared Error (MSE)** and **Root Mean Squared Error (RMSE)**. In other words, apart from R, R squared, and residual analysis, ideally, you will execute your model on test sets to extract other performance metrics. You can even use a cross-validation system to check model performance, as you learned in *Chapter 1, Machine Learning Fundamentals*.

Very often, when the model residuals *do* present a pattern and are *not* randomly distributed, it is because the existing relationship in the data is not linear, but non-linear, so another modeling technique must be applied. In the next subsection, you will learn how you can interpret regression models.

Interpreting regression models

It is also good to know how to interpret a linear regression model. Sometimes, you use linear regression not necessarily to create a predictive model but to do a regression analysis. You can then use regression analysis to understand the relationship between the independent and dependent variables.

Looking back at the regression equation ($y = 1021.212 * x + 53.30$), you can see the two terms: alpha or slope (*1021.20*) and beta or *y* intercept (*53.3*). You can interpret this model as follows: *for each additional year of working experience, you will increase your salary by $1,021.20*. Also, note that when "years of experience" is equal to 0, the expected salary is going to be $53.30 (this is the point where the straight line crosses the *y* axis).

From a broad perspective, your regression analysis should answer the following question: for each extra unit that is added to the independent variable (slope), what is the average change in the dependent variable?

Checking adjusted R squared

At this point, you have a much better idea of regression models! There is just one other very important topic that you should be aware of, regardless of whether it will come up in the exam or not, which is the parsimony aspect of your model.

You have already heard about parsimony in *Chapter 1, Machine Learning Fundamentals*. This is the ability to prioritize simple models over complex ones. Looking into regression models, you might have to use more than one feature to predict your outcome. This is also known as a multiple regression model.

When that is the case, the R and R squared coefficients tend to reward more complex models with more features. In other words, if you keep adding new features to a multiple regression model, you will come up with higher R and R squared coefficients. That is why you *cannot* anchor your decisions *only* based on those two metrics.

Another additional metric that you could use (apart from R, R squared, MSE, and RMSE) is known as **adjusted R squared**. This metric is penalized when you add extra features to the model that do not bring any real value. In *Table 6.6*, you can see when a model is starting to lose parsimony.

Number of features	R squared	Adjusted R squared
1	81	79
2	83	82
3	88	87
4	90	86
5	92	85

Table 6.6 – Comparing R squared and adjusted R squared

Here, you can conclude that maintaining three variables in the model is better than maintaining four or five. Adding four or five variables to the model will increase the R squared (as expected), but decrease the adjusted R squared.

At this point, you should have a very good understanding of regression models. Now, let us check what AWS offers in terms of built-in algorithms for this class of models.

Regression modeling on AWS

AWS has a built-in algorithm known as **linear learner**, where you can implement linear regression models. The built-in linear learner uses **Stochastic Gradient Descent (SGD)** to train the model.

> **Important note**
> You will learn more about SGD when neural networks are discussed. For now, you can look at SGD as an alternative to the popular least squares error method that was just discussed.

The linear learner built-in algorithm provides a hyperparameter that can apply normalization to the data, prior to the training process. The name of this hyperparameter is `normalize_data`. This is very helpful since linear models are sensitive to the scale of the data and usually take advantage of data normalization.

> **Important note**
>
> Data normalization was discussed in *Chapter 4, Data Preparation and Transformation*. Please review that chapter if you need to.

Some other important hyperparameters of the linear learner algorithm are **L1** and **wd**, which play the roles of **L1 regularization** and **L2 regularization**, respectively.

L1 and L2 regularization help the linear learner (or any other regression algorithm implementation) to avoid overfitting. Conventionally, regression models that implement L1 regularization are called **lasso regression** models, while regression models with L2 regularization are called **ridge regression** models.

Although it might sound complex, it is not! The regression model equation is still the same: $y = ax + b + e$. The change is in the loss function, which is used to find the coefficients that best minimize the error. If you look back at *Figure 6.1*, you will see that the error function is defined as $e = (\hat{y} - y)\char`\^2$, where $\hat{y}$ is the regression function value and y is the real value.

L1 and L2 regularization add a penalty term to the loss function, as shown in the formulas in *Figure 6.6* (note that you are replacing $\hat{y}$ with $ax + b$):

$$L_1 = \left(ax + b - y\right)^2 + \lambda|a|$$

$$L_2 = \left(ax + b - y\right)^2 + \lambda a^2$$

Figure 6.6 – L1 and L2 regularization

The λ (lambda) parameter must be greater than 0 and manually tuned. A very high lambda value may result in an underfitting issue, while a very low lambda may not result in expressive changes in the end results (if your model is overfitted, it will stay overfitted).

In practical terms, the main difference between L1 and L2 regularization is that L1 will shrink the less important coefficients to 0, which will force the feature to be dropped (acting as a feature selector). In other words, if your model is overfitting because of the high number of features, L1 regularization should help you solve this problem.

> **Important note**
>
> During your exam, remember the basis of L1 and L2 regularization, especially the key difference between them, where L1 works well as a feature selector.

Finally, many built-in algorithms can serve multiple modeling purposes. The linear learner algorithm can be used for regression, binary classification, and multi-classification. Make sure you remember this during your exam (it is *not just* about regression models).

AWS has other built-in algorithms that work for regression and classification problems –that is, **factorization machines, KNN,** and the **XGBoost** algorithm. Since these algorithms can also be used for classification purposes, these will be covered in the section about classification algorithms.

> **Important note**
>
> You've just been given a very important tip to remember during the exam: linear learner, factorization machines, KNN, and XGBoost are suitable for both regression and classification problems. These algorithms are often known as algorithms for general purposes.

With that, you have reached the end of this section about regression models. Remember to check out the supporting material before you take the exam. You can also use the reference material when you are working on your daily activities! Now, let us move on to another classical example of a machine learning problem: classification models.

Working with classification models

You have been learning what classification models are throughout this book. However, now, you are going to look at some algorithms that are suitable for classification problems. Keep in mind that there are hundreds of classification algorithms out there, but since you are preparing for the AWS Certified Machine Learning Specialty exam, the ones that have been pre-built by AWS will be covered.

You will start with **factorization machines**. Factorization machines is considered an extension of the linear learner algorithm, optimized to find the relationship between features within high-dimensional sparse datasets.

> **Important note**
>
> A very traditional use case for factorization machines is *recommendation systems*, where you usually have a high level of sparsity in the data. During the exam, if you are faced with a general-purpose problem (either a regression or binary classification task) where the underlying datasets are sparse, then factorization machines is probably the best answer from an algorithm perspective.

When you use factorization machines in a regression model, the RMSE will be used to evaluate the model. On the other hand, in the binary classification mode, the algorithm will use log loss, accuracy, and F1 score to evaluate results. A deeper discussion about evaluation metrics will be provided in *Chapter 7, Evaluating and Optimizing Models*.

You should be aware that factorization machines only accepts input data in the **recordIO-protobuf** format. This is because of the data sparsity characteristic, in which recordIO-protobuf is supposed to do a better job on data processing compared to `text/.csv` format.

The next built-in algorithm suitable for classification problems is known as K-nearest neighbors, or KNN for short. As the name suggests, this algorithm will try to find the *K* closest points to the input data and return either of the following predictions:

- The most repeated class of the *K* closest points, if it is a classification task
- The average value of the label of the *K* closest points, if it is a regression task

KNN is an **index-based algorithm** because it computes distances between points, assigns indexes for these points, and then stores the sorted distances and their indexes. With that type of data structure, KNN can easily select the top *K* closest points to make the final prediction. Note that *K* is a hyperparameter of KNN and should be optimized during the modeling process.

The other AWS built-in algorithm available for general purposes, including classification, is known as **eXtreme Gradient Boosting**, or **XGBoost** for short. This is an ensemble, decision tree-based model.

XGBoost uses a set of **weaker** models (decision trees) to predict the target variable, which can be a regression task, binary class, or multi-class. This is a very popular algorithm and has been used in machine learning competitions by the top performers.

XGBoost uses a boosting learning strategy, in which one model tries to correct the error of the prior model. It carries the name "gradient" because it uses the gradient descent algorithm to minimize the loss when adding new trees.

> **Important note**
> The term *weaker* is used in this context to describe very simple decision trees.

Although XGBoost is much more robust than a single decision tree, it is important to go into the exam with a clear understanding of what decision trees are and their main configurations. By the way, they are the base model of many ensemble algorithms, such as AdaBoost, Random Forest, gradient boost, and XGBoost.

Decision trees are rule-based algorithms that organize decisions in the form of a tree, as shown in *Figure 6.7.*

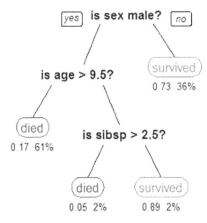

Figure 6.7 – Example of what a decision tree model looks like

They are formed by a root node (at the very top of the tree), intermediary or decision nodes (in the middle of the tree), and leaf nodes (bottom nodes with no splits). The depth of the tree is given by the difference between the root node and the very last leaf node. For example, in *Figure 6.7*, the depth of the tree is 3.

The depth of the tree is one of the most important hyperparameters of this type of model and it is often known as the **max depth**. In other words, the max depth controls the maximum depth that a decision tree can reach.

Another very important hyperparameter of decision tree models is the minimum number of samples/observations in the leaf nodes. It is also used to control the growth of the tree.

Decision trees have many other types of hyperparameters, but these two are especially important for controlling how the model overfits. Decision trees with a high depth or a very small number of observations in the leaf nodes are likely to face issues during extrapolation/prediction.

The reason for this is simple: decision trees use data from the leaf nodes to make predictions, based on the proportion (for classification tasks) or average value (for regression tasks) of each observation/target variable that belongs to that node. Thus, the node should have enough data to make good predictions outside the training set.

If you encounter the term **CART** during the exam, you should know that it stands for **Classification and Regression Trees**, since decision trees can be used for classification and regression tasks.

To select the best variables to split the data in the tree, the model will choose the ones that maximize the separation of the target variables across the nodes. This task can be performed by different methods, such as **Gini** and **information gain**.

Forecasting models

Time series refers to data points that are collected on a regular basis with a sequence dependency. Time series have a measure, a fact, and a time unit, as shown in *Figure 6.8*.

Figure 6.8 – Time series statement

Additionally, time series can be classified as **univariate** or **multivariate**. A univariate time series contains just one variable connected across a period of time, while a multivariate time series contains two or more variables connected across a period. *Figure 6.9* shows the univariate time series.

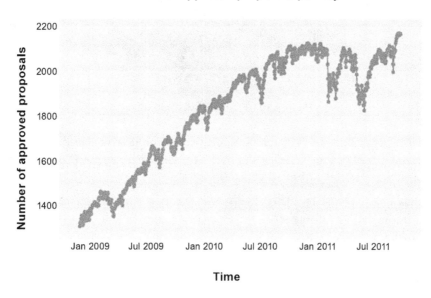

Figure 6.9 – Time series example

Time series can be decomposed as follows:

- **Observed** or **level**: The average values of the series
- **Trend**: Increasing, decreasing pattern (sometimes, there is no trend)
- **Seasonality**: Regular peaks at specific periods of time (sometimes, there is no seasonality)
- **Noise**: Something that cannot be explained

Sometimes, you can also find isolated peaks in the series that cannot be captured in a forecasting model. In such cases, you might want to consider those peaks as outliers. *Figure 6.10* is a decomposition of the time series shown in *Figure 6.9*.

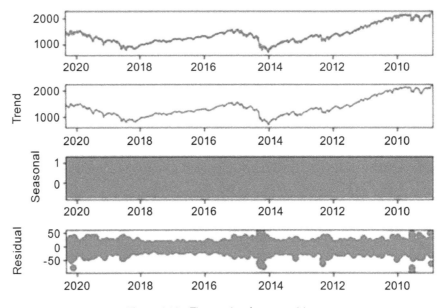

Figure 6.10 – Time series decomposition

It is also worth highlighting that you can use **additive** or **multiplicative** approaches to decompose time series. Additive models suggest that your time series *adds* each component to explain the target variable – that is, $y(t) = level + trend + seasonality + noise$.

Multiplicative models, on the other hand, suggest that your time series *multiplies* each component to explain the target variable – that is, $y(t) = level * trend * seasonality * noise$.

In the next section, you will take a closer look at time series components.

Checking the stationarity of time series

Decomposing time series and understanding how their components interact with additive and multiplicative models is a great achievement! However, the more you learn, the more you want to go deeper into the problem. Maybe you have realized that time series without trend and seasonality are easier to predict than the ones with all those components!

That is naturally right. If you do not have to understand trend and seasonality, and if you do not have control over the noise, all you have to do is explore the observed values and find their regression relationship.

A time series with constant mean and variance across a time period is known as **stationary**. In general, time series *with* trend and seasonality are *not* stationary. It is possible to apply data transformations to the series to transform it into a stationary time series so that the modeling task tends to be easier. This type of transformation is known as **differentiation**.

While you are exploring a time series, you can check stationarity by applying hypothesis tests, such as **Dickey-Fuller**, **KPSS**, and **Phillips-Perron**, just to mention a few. If you find it non-stationary, then you can apply differentiation to make it a stationary time series. Some algorithms already have that capability embedded.

Exploring, exploring, and exploring

At this point, it is important to remember that exploration tasks happen all the time in data science. Nothing is different here. While you are building time series models, you might want to take a look at the data and check whether it is suitable for this type of modeling.

Autocorrelation plots are one of the tools that you can use for time series analysis. Autocorrelation plots allow you to check the correlations between lags in the time series. *Figure 6.11* shows an example of this type of visualization.

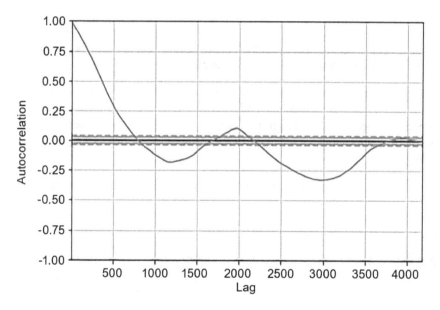

Figure 6.11 – Autocorrelation plot

Remember, if you are playing with univariate time series, your time series just contains one variable. Therefore, finding autocorrelation across the lags of your unique variable is crucial to understanding whether you can build a good model or not.

And yes, it turns out that, sometimes, it might happen that you do not have a time series in front of you. Furthermore, no matter your efforts, you will not be able to model this data as a time series. This type of data is often known as **white noise**.

Another type of series that you cannot predict is known as a **random walk**. Random walks are random by nature, but they have a dependency on the previous time step. For example, the next point of a random walk could be a random number between 0 and 1, and also the last point of the series.

> **Important note**
> Be careful if you come across those terms in the exam and remember to relate them to randomness in time series.

With that, you have covered the main theory behind time series modeling. You should also be aware that the most popular algorithms out there for working with time series are known as **Auto-Regressive Integrated Moving Average (ARIMA)** and **Exponential Smoothing (ETS)**. This book will not go into the details of these two models. Instead, you will see what AWS can offer in terms of time series modeling.

Understanding DeepAR

The **DeepAR** forecasting algorithm is a built-in SageMaker algorithm that is used to forecast a one-dimensional time series using a **Recurrent Neural Network (RNN)**.

Traditional time series algorithms, such as ARIMA and ETS, are designed to fit one model per time series. For example, if you want to forecast sales per region, you might have to create one model per region, since each region may have its own sales behaviors. DeepAR, on the other hand, allows you to operate more than one time series in a single model, which seems to be a huge advantage for more complex use cases.

The input data for DeepAR, as expected, is *one or more* time series. Each of these time series can be associated with the following:

- A vector of static (time-independent) categorical features, controlled by the `cat` field
- A vector of dynamic (time-dependent) time series, controlled by `dynamic_feat`

> **Important note**
> Note that the ability to train and make predictions on top of multiple time series is strictly related to the vector of static categorical features. While defining the time series that DeepAR will train on, you can set categorical variables to specify which group each time series belongs to.

Two of the main hyperparameters of DeepAR are `context_length`, which is used to control how far in the past the model can see during the training process, and `prediction_length`, which is used to control how far in the future the model will output predictions.

DeepAR can also handle missing values, which, in this case, refers to existing gaps in the time series. A very interesting functionality of DeepAR is its ability to create derived features from time series. These derived features, which are created from basic time frequencies, help the algorithm learn time-dependent patterns. *Table 6.7* shows all the derived features created by DeepAR, according to each type of time series that it is trained on.

Frequency of the time series	Derived feature
Minute	Minute of hour, hour of day, day of week, day of month, day of year
Hour	Hour of day, day of week, day of month, day of year
Day	Day of week, day of month, day of year
Week	Day of month, week of year
Month	Month of year

Table 6.7 – DeepAR derived features per frequency of time series

You have now completed this section about forecasting models. Next, you will take a look at the last algorithm regarding supervised learning – that is, the **Object2Vec** algorithm.

Object2Vec

Object2Vec is a built-in SageMaker algorithm that generalizes the well-known **Word2Vec** algorithm. Object2Vec is used to create **embedding spaces** for high dimensional objects. These embedding spaces are, per definition, compressed representations of the original object and can be used for multiple purposes, such as feature engineering or object comparison.

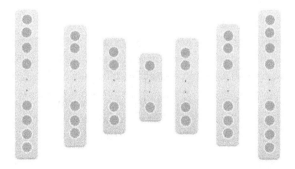

Figure 6.12 – A visual example of an embedding space

Figure 6.12 illustrates what is meant by an embedding space. The first and last layers of the neural network model just map the input data with itself (represented by the same vector size).

As you move on to the internal layers of the model, the data is compressed more and more until it hits the layer in the middle of this architecture, known as the embedding layer. On that particular layer, you have a smaller vector, which aims to be an accurate and compressed representation of the high-dimensional original vector from the first layer.

With this, you just completed the first section about machine learning algorithms in AWS. Coming up next, you will take a look at some unsupervised algorithms.

Unsupervised learning

AWS provides several unsupervised learning algorithms for the following tasks:

- Clustering: K-Means algorithm
- Dimension reduction: **Principal Component Analysis (PCA)**
- Pattern recognition: IP Insights
- Anomaly detection: The **Random Cut Forest (RCF)** algorithm

Let us start by talking about clustering and how the most popular clustering algorithm works: K-Means.

Clustering

Clustering algorithms are very popular in data science. Basically, they aim to identify similar groups in a given dataset, also known as *clusters*. Clustering algorithms belong to the field of non-supervised learning, which means that they do not need a label or response variable to be trained.

This is just fantastic since labeled data is very scarce! However, it comes with some limitations. The main one is that clustering algorithms provide clusters for you, but not the meaning of each cluster. Thus, someone, as a subject matter expert, has to analyze the properties of each cluster to define their meanings.

There are many types of clustering approaches, such as hierarchical clustering and partitional clustering. Inside each approach, you will find several algorithms. However, K-Means is probably the most popular clustering algorithm, and you are likely to come across it in your exam.

When you are playing with K-Means, somehow, you have to specify the number of clusters that you want to create. Then, you have to allocate the data points across each cluster, so that each data point will belong to a single cluster. This is exactly what you should expect as a result at the end of the clustering process!

You need to specify the number of clusters that you want to create and pass this number to the K-Means algorithm. Then, the algorithm will randomly initiate the central point of each cluster (this is known as **centroid initialization**).

Once you have the centroids of each cluster, all you need to do is assign a cluster to each data point. To do that, you have to use a proximity or distance metric! This book will use the term *distance metric*.

The **distance metric** is responsible for calculating the distance between data points and centroids. The data point will belong to the closer cluster centroid, according to the distance metric.

The most popular distance metric is called **Euclidean distance** and the math behind it is simple; imagine that the points of your dataset are composed of two dimensions, x and y. So, you could consider points *a* and *b* as follows:

- *a (x=1, y=1)*
- *b (x=2, y=5)*

The Euclidean distance between points *a* and *b* is given by the following formula, where x_1 and y_1 refer to the values of point *a*, and x_2 and y_2 refer to the values of point *b*: $\sqrt{((x1-x2)^2+(y1-y2)^2)}$. The same function can be generalized by the following equation: $\sqrt{\sum_{i=1}^{n}(y_i-x_i)^2}$. Once you have completed this process and assigned a cluster for each data point, you ▨▨▨ methods, such as **single link, average link,** and **complete link**.

Due to this centroid refreshment, you will have to keep checking the closest cluster for each data point and keep refreshing the centroids, iteratively, until the cluster centroids converge and no cluster reassignment is needed, or the maximum number of allowed iterations is reached.

Alright, the following is a summarization of the components and steps that compose the K-Means method:

- Centroid initialization, cluster assignment, centroid refreshment, and then redo the last two steps until it converges
- A distance metric to assign data points to each cluster (in this case, Euclidian distance)
- A linkage method to recalculate the cluster centroids (for the sake of our demonstration, you will learn about the average linkage)

With these definitions, you are now ready to walk through the following real example, step by step (some support material is also available for your reference).

Computing K-Means step by step

In this example, you will simulate K-Means in a very small dataset, with only two columns (*x* and *y*) and six data points (*A*, *B*, *C*, *D*, *E*, and *F*), as defined in *Table 6.8*.

Point	x	y
A	1	1
B	2	2
C	5	5
D	5	6
E	1	5
F	2	6
Cluster 1	**1**	**1**
Cluster 2	**2**	**2**
Cluster 3	**5**	**5**

Table 6.8 – Iteration input data for K-Means

Table 6.8 contains three clusters with the following centroids: *(1,1), (2,2), (5,5)*. The number of clusters (3) was defined *a priori* and the centroid for each cluster was randomly defined. *Figure 6.13* shows the stage of the algorithm that you are at right now.

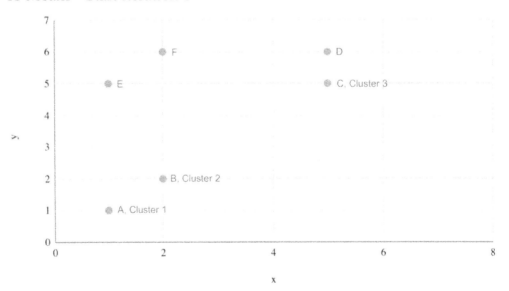

Figure 6.13 – Plotting the K-Means results before completing the first iteration

Here, you can't see points *A*, *B*, and *C* since they overlap with cluster centroids, but don't worry – they will appear soon. Next, you have to compute the distance of each data point to each cluster centroid, and then, you need to choose the cluster that is the closest to each point.

xc1	yc1	xc2	yc2	xc3	yc3	distance-c1	distance-c2	distance-c3	Cluster
1	1	2	2	5	5	0,0	1,4	5,7	Cluster 1
1	1	2	2	5	5	1,4	0,0	4,2	Cluster 2
1	1	2	2	5	5	5,7	4,2	0,0	Cluster 3
1	1	2	2	5	5	6,4	5,0	1,0	Cluster 3
1	1	2	2	5	5	4,0	3,2	4,0	Cluster 2
1	1	2	2	5	5	5,1	4,0	3,2	Cluster 3
Legend									
xc1 = x value of cluster 1									
yc1 = y value of cluster 1									

Table 6.9 – Processing iteration 1

Table 6.9 contains the following elements:

- Each row represents a data point.
- The first six columns represent the centroid axis (*x* and *y*) of each cluster.
- The next three columns represent the distance of each data point to each cluster centroid.
- The last column represents the clusters that are the closest to each data point.

Looking at data point *A* (first row), you can see that it was assigned to cluster 1 because the distance from data point *A* to cluster 1 is 0 (do you remember that they were overlapping?). The same calculation happens to all other data points to define a cluster for each data point.

Before you move on, you might want to see how those Euclidian distances between the clusters and the data points were computed. For demonstration purposes, the following simulation will consider the distance from data point *A* to cluster 3 (the first row in *Table 6.9*, column `distance-c3`, value *5,7*).

First of all, the following formula was used to calculate the Euclidian distance: $\sqrt{((x1 - x2)^2 + (y1 - y2)^2)}$

Here, you have the following:

- x_1 = x of data point A = 1
- y_1 = y of data point A = 1
- x_2 = x of cluster 3 = 5
- y_2 = y of cluster 3 = 5

Figure 6.14 applies the formula, step by step.

$$\sqrt{((1 - 5)^2 + (1 - 5)^2)}$$

$$\sqrt{((4)^2 + (4)^2)}$$

$$\sqrt{16 + 16}$$

$$\sqrt{32}$$

5,656 or ~5,7

Figure 6.14 – Computing the Euclidian distance step by step

That is just fantastic, isn't it? You have almost completed the first iteration of K-Means. In the very last step of iteration 1, you have to refresh the cluster centroids. Remember: initially, they were randomly defined, but now, you have just assigned some data points to each cluster, which means you should be able to identify where the central point of the cluster is.

In this example, the **linkage** method will be used to refresh the cluster centroids. This is a very simple step, and the results are presented in *Table 6.10*.

Point	x	y
A	1	1
B	2	2
C	5	5
D	5	6
E	1	5
F	2	6
Cluster 1	**1**	**1**
Cluster 2	**1,5**	**3,5**
Cluster 3	**4**	**5,7**

Table 6.10 – K-Means results after iteration 1

Table 6.10 shows the same data points (*A* to *F*) that you are dealing with (by the way, they will never change), and the centroids of clusters 1, 2, and 3. Those centroids are quite different from what they were initially, as shown in *Table 6.8*. This is because they were refreshed using average linkage! The method got the average value of all the *x* and *y* values of the data points of each cluster. In the next simulation, have a look at how *(1.5, 3.5)* were obtained as centroids of cluster 2.

If you look at *Table 6.9*, you will see that cluster 2 only has two data points assigned to it: *B* and *E*. These are the second and fifth rows in that figure. If you take the average values of the *x* axis of each point, then you will have *(2 + 1) / 2 = 1.5* and *(2 + 5) / 2 = 3.5*.

With that, you are done with iteration 1 of K-Means and you can view the results in *Figure 6.15*.

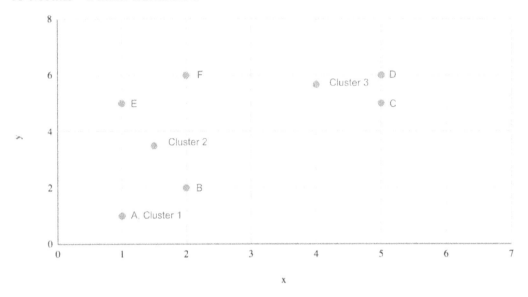

Figure 6.15 – Plotting the K-Means results after the first iteration

Now, you can see almost all the data points, except for data point A because it is still overlapping with the centroid of cluster 1. Moving on, you have to redo the following steps:

- Recalculate the distance between each data point and each cluster centroid and reassign clusters, if needed.

- Recalculate the cluster centroids.

You do those two tasks many times until the cluster centroids converge and they don't change anymore, *or* you reach the maximum number of allowed iterations, which can be set as a hyperparameter of K-Means. For demonstration purposes, after four iterations, your clusters will look like *Figure 6.16*.

K-Means - Finish iteration 4

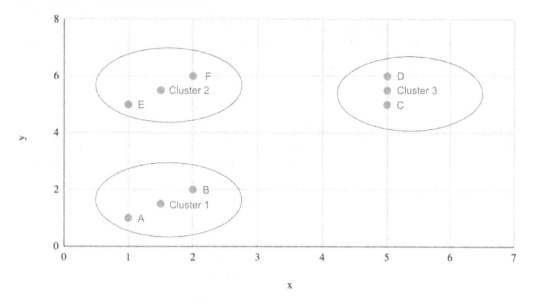

Figure 6.16 – Plotting the K-Means results after the fourth iteration

On the fourth iteration, all the cluster centroids look pretty consistent, and you can clearly see that all data points could be grouped according to their proximity.

> **Important note**
>
> In this example, you have only set two dimensions for each data point (dimensions x and y). In real use cases, you can see far more dimensions, and that is why clustering algorithms play a very important role in identifying groups in the data in a more automated fashion.

Hopefully, you have enjoyed how to compute K-Means from scratch! This knowledge will be beneficial for the exam and for your career as a data scientist. By the way, as advised many times, data scientists must be skeptical and curious, so you might be wondering why three clusters were defined in this example and not two or four. You may also be wondering how you measure the quality of the clusters.

You didn't think this explanation wouldn't be provided, did you?

Defining the number of clusters and measuring cluster quality

Although K-Means is a great algorithm for finding patterns in your data, it will not provide the meaning of each cluster, nor the number of clusters you have to create to maximize cluster quality.

In clustering, cluster quality means that you want to create groups with a high homogeneity among the elements of the same cluster, and a high heterogeneity among the elements of different clusters. In other words, the elements of the same clusters should be close/similar, whereas the elements of different clusters should be well separated.

One way to compute the cluster's homogeneity is by using a metric known as the **sum of square errors**, or **SSE** for short. This metric will compute the sum of squared differences between each data point and its cluster centroid. For example, when all the data points are located at the same point where the cluster centroid is, then the SSE will be 0. In other words, you want to minimize the SSE. The following equation formally defines the SSE: $SSE = \sum_{i=1}^{n}(x_i - x_p)^2$

Now that you know how to check the cluster quality, it is easier to understand how to define the number of appropriate clusters for a given dataset. All you have to do is find the optimal number of clusters to minimize the SSE. A very popular method that works around that logic is known as the **elbow method**.

The elbow method proposes executing the clustering algorithm many times. In each execution, you will test a different number of clusters, k. After each execution, you compute the SSE related to that k number of clusters. Finally, you can plot these results and select the number of k where the SSE stops to drastically decrease.

> **Important note**
> Adding more clusters will naturally decrease the SSE. In the elbow method, you want to find the point where that change becomes smoother, which means that the addition of new clusters will not bring too much value.

In the previous example, three clusters were created. *Figure 6.17* shows the elbow analysis that supports this decision.

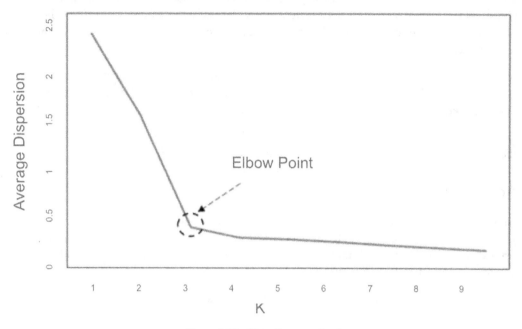

Figure 6.17 – The elbow method

You can conclude that adding more than three or four clusters will add unnecessary complexity to the clustering process.

Of course, you should always consider the business background while defining the number of clusters. For example, if you are creating a customer segmentation model and your company has prepared the commercial team and business processes to support four segments of customers, there is no harm in setting up four clusters instead of three.

Finally, you should know that AWS has implemented K-Means as part of its list of built-in algorithms. In other words, you don't have to use external libraries or bring your own algorithm to play with K-Means on AWS.

Conclusion

That was a really good accomplishment: you just mastered the basics of clustering algorithms and you should now be able to drive your own projects and research about this topic! For the exam, remember that clustering belongs to the unsupervised field of machine learning, so there is no need to have labeled data.

Also, make sure that you know how the most popular algorithm of this field works – that is, K-Means. Although clustering algorithms do not provide the meaning of each group, they are very powerful for finding patterns in the data, either to model a particular problem or just to explore the data.

Coming up next, you will keep studying unsupervised algorithms and see how AWS has built one of the most powerful algorithms out there for anomaly detection, known as **RCF**.

Anomaly detection

Finding anomalies in data is a very common task in modeling and data exploratory analysis. Sometimes, you might want to find anomalies in the data just to remove them before fitting a regression model, while other times, you might want to create a model that identifies anomalies as an end goal – for example, in fraud detection systems.

Again, you can use many different methods to find anomalies in the data. With some creativity, the possibilities are endless. However, there is a particular algorithm that works around this problem that you should definitely be aware of for your exam: RCF.

RCF is an unsupervised decision tree-based algorithm that creates multiple decision trees (forests) using random subsamples of the training data. Technically, it randomizes the data and then creates samples according to the number of trees. Finally, these samples are distributed across each tree.

These sets of trees are used to assign an anomaly score to the data points. To calculate the anomaly score for a particular data point, it is passed down each tree in the forest. As the data point moves through the tree, the path length from the root node to the leaf node is recorded for that specific tree. The anomaly score for that data point is then determined by considering the distribution of path lengths across all the trees in the forest.

If a data point follows a short path in most trees (i.e., it is close to the root node), it is considered a common point and will have a lower anomaly score.

On the other hand, if a data point follows a long path in many trees (i.e., it is far from the root node), it is considered an uncommon point and will have a higher anomaly score.

The most important hyperparameters of RCF are `num_trees` and `num_samples_per_tree`, which are the number of trees in the forest and the number of samples per tree, respectively.

Dimensionality reduction

Another unsupervised algorithm that was implemented by AWS in its list of built-in algorithms is known as principal component analysis, or PCA for short. PCA is a technique that's used to reduce the number of variables/dimensions in a dataset.

The main idea behind PCA is plotting the data points to another set of coordinates, known as **Principal Components (PCs)**, which aims to explain the most variance in the data. By definition, the first component will capture more variance than the second component, then the second component will capture more variance than the third one, and so on.

You can set up as many PCs as you need, as long as it does not surpass the number of variables in your dataset. *Figure 6.18* shows how these PCs are drawn:

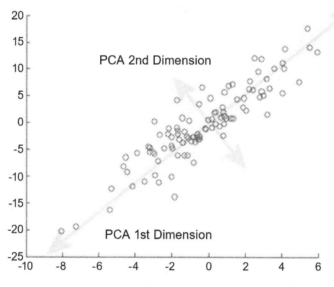

Figure 6.18 – Finding PCs in PCA

As mentioned previously, the first PC will be drawn in such a way that it will capture most of the variance in the data. That is why it passes near the majority of the data points in *Figure 6.18*.

Then, the second PC will be perpendicular to the first one, so that it will be the second component that explains the variance in the data. If you want to create more components (consequentially, capturing more variance), you just have to follow the same rule of adding perpendicular components. **Eigenvectors** and **eigenvalues** are the linear algebra concepts associated with PCA that compute the PCs.

So, what is the story with dimension reduction here? In case it is not clear yet, these PCs can be used to replace your original variables. For example, consider you have 10 variables in your dataset, and you want to reduce this dataset to three variables that best represent the others. A potential solution for that would be applying PCA and extracting the first three PCs!

Do these three components explain 100% of your dataset? Probably not, but ideally, they will explain most of the variance. Adding more PCs will explain more variance but at the cost of adding extra dimensions.

Using AWS's built-in algorithm for PCA

In AWS, PCA works in two different modes:

- **Regular**: For datasets with a moderate number of observations and features
- **Randomized**: For datasets with a large number of observations and features

The difference is that, in randomized mode, it is used as an approximation algorithm.

Of course, the main hyperparameter of PCA is the number of components that you want to extract, known as num_components.

IP Insights

IP Insights is an unsupervised algorithm that is used for pattern recognition. Essentially, it learns the usage pattern of IPv4 addresses.

The *modus operandi* of this algorithm is very intuitive: it is trained on top of pairs of events in the format of entity and IPv4 address so that it can understand the pattern of each entity that it was trained on.

> **Important note**
> For instance, you can understand "entity" as user IDs or account numbers.

Then, to make predictions, it receives a pair of events with the same data structure (entity, IPv4 address) and returns an anomaly score for that particular IP address, according to the input entity.

> **Important note**
> This anomaly score that is returned by IP Insights infers how anomalous the pattern of the event is.

You might come across many applications with IP Insights. For example, you can create an IP Insights model that was trained on top of your application login events (this is your entity). You should be able to expose this model through an API endpoint to make predictions in real time.

Then, during the authentication process of your application, you could call your endpoint and pass the IP address that is trying to log in. If you got a high score (meaning this pattern of logging in looks anomalous), you can request extra information before authorizing access (even if the password was right).

This is just one of the many applications of IP Insights you could think about. Next, you will learn about textual analysis.

Textual analysis

Modern applications use **Natural Language Processing (NLP)** for several purposes, such as text translation, document classifications, web search, **Named Entity Recognition (NER)**, and many others.

AWS offers a suite of algorithms for most NLP use cases. In the next few subsections, you will have a look at these built-in algorithms for textual analysis.

BlazingText algorithm

BlazingText does two different types of tasks: text classification, which is a supervised learning approach that extends the **fastText** text classifier, and Word2Vec, which is an unsupervised learning algorithm.

BlazingText's implementations of these two algorithms are optimized to run on large datasets. For example, you can train a model on top of billions of words in a few minutes.

This scalability aspect of BlazingText is possible due to the following:

- Its ability to use multi-core CPUs and a single GPU to accelerate text classification
- Its ability to use multi-core CPUs or GPUs, with custom CUDA kernels for GPU acceleration, when playing with the Word2Vec algorithm

The Word2Vec option supports **batch_skipgram** mode, which allows BlazingText to do distributed training across multiple CPUs.

> **Important note**
>
> The distributed training that's performed by BlazingText uses a mini-batching approach to convert **level-1 BLAS (Basic Linear Algebra Subprograms)** operations into **level-3 BLAS** operations. If you see these terms during your exam, you should know that they are related to BlazingText (Word2Vec mode).

Still in Word2Vec mode, BlazingText supports both the **skip-gram** and **Continuous Bag of Words (CBOW)** architectures.

Finally, note the following configurations of BlazingText, since they are likely to be present in your exam:

- In Word2Vec mode, only the train channel is available.

- BlazingText expects a single text file with space-separated tokens. Each line of the file must contain a single sentence. This means you usually have to preprocess your corpus of data before using BlazingText.

Sequence-to-sequence algorithm

This is a supervised algorithm that transforms an input sequence into an output sequence. This sequence can be a text sentence or even an audio recording.

The most common use cases for sequence-to-sequence are machine translation, text summarization, and speech-to-text. Anything that you think is a sequence-to-sequence problem can be approached by this algorithm.

Technically, AWS SageMaker's Seq2Seq uses two types of neural networks to create models: an **RNN** and a **Convolutional Neural Network (CNN)** with an attention mechanism.

Latent Dirichlet allocation, or **LDA** for short, is used for topic modeling. Topic modeling is a textual analysis technique where you can extract a set of topics from a corpus of text data. LDA learns these topics based on the probability distribution of the words in the corpus of text.

Since this is an unsupervised algorithm, there is no need to set a target variable. Also, the number of topics must be specified up-front, and you will have to analyze each topic to find its domain meaning.

Neural Topic Model algorithm

Just like the LDA algorithm, the **Neural Topic Model (NTM)** also aims to extract topics from a corpus of data. However, the difference between LDA and NTM is their learning logic. While LDA learns from probability distributions of the words in the documents, NTM is built on top of neural networks.

The NTM network architecture has a bottleneck layer, which creates an embedding representation of the documents. This bottleneck layer contains all the necessary information to predict document composition, and its coefficients can be considered topics.

With that, you have completed this section on textual analysis. In the next section, you will learn about image processing algorithms.

Image processing

Image processing is a very popular topic in machine learning. The idea is pretty self-explanatory: creating models that can analyze images and make inferences on top of them. By inference, you can understand this as detecting objects in an image, classifying images, and so on.

AWS offers a set of built-in algorithms you can use to train image processing models. In the next few sections, you will have a look at those algorithms.

Image classification algorithm

As the name suggests, the image classification algorithm is used to classify images using supervised learning. In other words, it needs a label within each image. It supports multi-label classification.

The way it operates is simple: during training, it receives an image and its associated labels. During inference, it receives an image and returns all the predicted labels. The image classification algorithm uses a CNN (**ResNet**) for training. It can either train the model from scratch or take advantage of transfer learning to pre-load the first few layers of the neural network.

According to AWS's documentation, the `.jpg` and `.png` file formats are supported, but the recommended format is **MXNet's RecordIO**.

Semantic segmentation algorithm

The semantic segmentation algorithm provides a pixel-level capability for creating computer vision applications. It tags each pixel of the image with a class, which is an important feature for complex applications such as self-driving and medical image diagnostics.

In terms of its implementation, the semantic segmentation algorithm uses the **MXNet Gluon framework** and the **Gluon CV toolkit**. You can choose any of the following algorithms to train a model:

- **Fully Convolutional Network (FCN)**
- **Pyramid Scene Parsing (PSP)**
- DeepLabV3

All these options work as an **encoder-decoder** neural network architecture. The output of the network is known as a **segmentation mask**.

Object detection algorithm

Just like the image classification algorithm, the main goal of the object detection algorithm is also self-explanatory: it detects and classifies objects in images. It uses a supervised approach to train a deep neural network.

During the inference process, this algorithm returns the identified objects and a score of confidence regarding the prediction. The object detection algorithm uses **Single Shot MultiBox Detector (SSD)** and supports two types of network architecture: **Visual Geometry Group (VGG)** and **Residual Network (ResNet)**.

Summary

That was such a journey! Take a moment to recap what you have just learned. This chapter had four main topics: supervised learning, unsupervised learning, textual analysis, and image processing. Everything that you have learned fits into those subfields of machine learning.

The list of supervised learning algorithms that you have studied includes the following:

- Linear learner
- Factorization machines
- XGBoost
- KNN
- Object2Vec
- DeepAR forecasting

Remember that you can use linear learner, factorization machines, XGBoost, and KNN for multiple purposes, including solving regression and classification problems. Linear learner is probably the simplest algorithm out of these four; factorization machines extends linear earner and is good for sparse datasets, XGBoost uses an ensemble method based on decision trees, and KNN is an index-based algorithm.

The other two algorithms, Object2Vec and DeepAR, are used for specific purposes. Object2Vec is used to create vector representations of the data, while DeepAR is used to create forecast models.

The list of unsupervised learning algorithms that you have studied includes the following:

- K-Means
- PCA
- IP Insights
- RCF

K-Means is a very popular algorithm that is used for clustering. PCA is used for dimensionality reduction, IP Insights is used for pattern recognition, and RCF is used for anomaly detection.

You then looked at regression models and K-Means in more detail. You did this because, as a data scientist, you should at least master these two very popular algorithms so that you can go deeper into other algorithms by yourself.

Then, you moved on to the second half of this chapter, where you learned about textual analysis and the following algorithms:

- BlazingText
- Sequence-to-sequence
- LDA
- NTM

Finally, you learned about image processing and looked at the following:

- Image classification algorithm
- Semantic segmentation algorithm
- Object detection algorithm

Since the topics covered in this chapter are very important with regard to the AWS Certified Machine Learning Specialty exam, you are highly encouraged to jump into the AWS website and search for machine learning algorithms. There, you will find the most recent information about the algorithms that you have just learned about. Please make sure you do it before taking the exam.

That brings you to the end of this quick refresher and the end of this chapter. In the next chapter, you will learn about the existing mechanisms provided by AWS that you can use to optimize and evaluate these algorithms.

Exam Readiness Drill – Chapter Review Questions

Apart from a solid understanding of key concepts, being able to think quickly under time pressure is a skill that will help you ace your certification exam. That is why working on these skills early on in your learning journey is key.

Chapter review questions are designed to improve your test-taking skills progressively with each chapter you learn and review your understanding of key concepts in the chapter at the same time. You'll find these at the end of each chapter.

> **How To Access These Resources**
>
> To learn how to access these resources, head over to the chapter titled *Chapter 11, Accessing the Online Practice Resources*.

To open the Chapter Review Questions for this chapter, perform the following steps:

1. Click the link – https://packt.link/MLSC01E2_CH06.

    Alternatively, you can scan the following **QR code** (*Figure 6.19*):

Figure 6.19 – QR code that opens Chapter Review Questions for logged-in users

2. Once you log in, you'll see a page similar to the one shown in *Figure 6.20*:

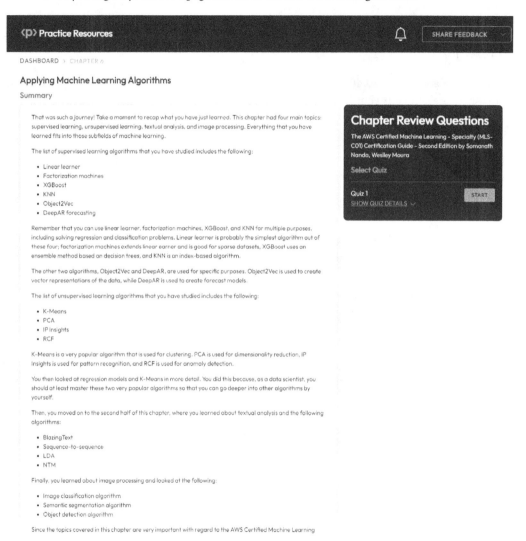

Figure 6.20 – Chapter Review Questions for Chapter 6

3. Once ready, start the following practice drills, re-attempting the quiz multiple times.

Exam Readiness Drill

For the first three attempts, don't worry about the time limit.

ATTEMPT 1

The first time, aim for at least **40%**. Look at the answers you got wrong and read the relevant sections in the chapter again to fix your learning gaps.

ATTEMPT 2

The second time, aim for at least **60%**. Look at the answers you got wrong and read the relevant sections in the chapter again to fix any remaining learning gaps.

ATTEMPT 3

The third time, aim for at least **75%**. Once you score 75% or more, you start working on your timing.

> Tip
> You may take more than **three** attempts to reach 75%. That's okay. Just review the relevant sections in the chapter till you get there.

Working On Timing

Target: Your aim is to keep the score the same while trying to answer these questions as quickly as possible. Here's an example of how your next attempts should look like:

Attempt	Score	Time Taken
Attempt 5	77%	21 mins 30 seconds
Attempt 6	78%	18 mins 34 seconds
Attempt 7	76%	14 mins 44 seconds

Table 6.11 – Sample timing practice drills on the online platform

> Note
> The time limits shown in the above table are just examples. Set your own time limits with each attempt based on the time limit of the quiz on the website.

With each new attempt, your score should stay above **75%** while your "time taken" to complete should "decrease". Repeat as many attempts as you want till you feel confident dealing with the time pressure.

7

Evaluating and Optimizing Models

It is now time to learn how to evaluate and optimize machine learning models. During the process of modeling, or even after model completion, you might want to understand how your model is performing. Each type of model has its own set of metrics that can be used to evaluate performance, and that is what you are going to study in this chapter.

Apart from model evaluation, as a data scientist, you might also need to improve your model's performance by tuning the hyperparameters of your algorithm. You will take a look at some nuances of this modeling task.

In this chapter, the following topics will be covered:

- Introducing model evaluation
- Evaluating classification models
- Evaluating regression models
- Model optimization

Alright, time to rock it!

Introducing model evaluation

There are several different scenarios in which you might want to evaluate model performance. Some of them are as follows:

- You are creating a model and testing different approaches and/or algorithms. Therefore, you need to compare these models to select the best one.

- You have just completed your model and you need to document your work, which includes specifying the model's performance metrics that you got from the modeling phase.

- Your model is running in a production environment, and you need to track its performance. If you encounter model drift, then you might want to retrain the model.

> **Important note**
>
> The term model drift is used to refer to the problem of model deterioration. When you are building a machine learning model, you must use data to train the algorithm. This set of data is known as training data, and it reflects the business rules at a particular point in time. If these business rules change over time, your model will probably fail to adapt to those changes. This is because it was trained on top of another dataset, which was reflecting another business scenario. To solve this problem, you must retrain the model so that it can consider the rules of the new business scenario.

Model evaluations are commonly inserted in the context of testing. You have learned about holdout validation and cross-validation before. However, both testing approaches share the same requirement: they need a metric in order to evaluate performance.

These metrics are specific to the problem domain. For example, there are specific metrics for regression models, classification models, clustering, natural language processing, and more. Therefore, during the design of your testing approach, you have to consider what type of model you are building in order to define the evaluation metrics.

In the following sections, you will take a look at the most important metrics and concepts that you should know to evaluate your models.

Evaluating classification models

Classification models are one of the most traditional classes of problems that you might face, either during the exam or during your journey as a data scientist. A very important artifact that you might want to generate during the classification model evaluation is known as a confusion matrix.

A confusion matrix compares your model predictions against the real values of each class under evaluation. *Figure 7.1* shows what a confusion matrix looks like in a binary classification problem:

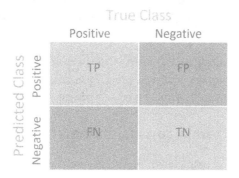

Figure 7.1 – A confusion matrix

There are the following components in a confusion matrix:

- TP: This is the number of true positive cases. Here, you have to count the number of cases that have been predicted as true and are, indeed, true. For example, in a fraud detection system, this would be the number of fraudulent transactions that were correctly predicted as fraud.

- TN: This is the number of true negative cases. Here, you have to count the number of cases that have been predicted as false and are, indeed, false. For example, in a fraud detection system, this would be the number of non-fraudulent transactions that were correctly predicted as not fraud.

- FN: This is the number of false negative cases. Here, you have to count the number of cases that have been predicted as false but are, instead, true. For example, in a fraud detection system, this would be the number of fraudulent transactions that were wrongly predicted as not fraud.

- FP: This is the number of false positive cases. Here, you have to count the number of cases that have been predicted as true but are, instead, false. For example, in a fraud detection system, this would be the number of non-fraudulent transactions that were wrongly predicted as fraud.

In a perfect scenario, your confusion matrix will have only true positive and true negative cases, which means that your model has an accuracy of 100%. In practical terms, if that type of scenario occurs, you should be skeptical instead of happy, since it is expected that your model will contain some level of errors. If your model does not contain errors, you are likely to be suffering from overfitting issues, so be careful.

Once false negatives and false positives are expected, the best you can do is prioritize one of them. For example, you can reduce the number of false negatives by increasing the number of false positives and vice versa. This is known as the precision versus recall trade-off. Let's take a look at these metrics next.

Extracting metrics from a confusion matrix

The simplest metric that can be extracted from a confusion matrix is known as **accuracy**. Accuracy is given by the following equation, as shown in *Figure 7.2*:

$$Accuracy = \frac{True\,Negatives + True\,Positive}{True\,Positive + False\,Positive + True\,Negative + False\,Negative}$$

Figure 7.2 – Formula for accuracy

For the sake of demonstration, *Figure 7.3* shows a confusion matrix with data.

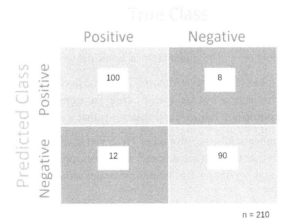

Figure 7.3 – A confusion matrix filled with some examples

According to *Figure 7.3*, the accuracy would be (100 + 90) / 210, which is equal to 0.90. There is a common issue that occurs when utilizing an accuracy metric, which is related to the balance of each class. Problems with highly imbalanced classes, such as 99% positive cases and 1% negative cases, will impact the accuracy score and make it useless.

For example, if your training data has 99% positive cases (the majority class), your model is likely to correctly classify most of the positive cases but work badly in the classification of negative cases (the minority class). The accuracy will be very high (due to the correctness of the classification of the positive cases), regardless of the bad results in the minority class classification.

The point is that on highly imbalanced problems, you usually have more interest in correctly classifying the minority class, not the majority class. That is the case in most fraud detection systems, for example, where the minority class corresponds to fraudulent cases. For imbalanced problems, you should look for other types of metrics, which you will learn about next.

Another important metric that you can extract from a confusion matrix is known as recall, which is given by the following equation, as shown in *Figure 7.4*:

$$\text{Recall} = \frac{True\ Positive}{True\ Positive + False\ Negative}$$

Figure 7.4 – Formula for recall

In other words, recall is the number of true positives over the total number of positive cases. Recall is also known as sensitivity.

With the values in *Figure 7.3*, recall is given by 100 / 112, which is equal to 0.89. Precision, on the other hand, is given by the following formula, as shown in *Figure 7.5*:

$$\text{Precision} = \frac{True\ Positive}{True\ Positive + False\ Positive}$$

Figure 7.5 – Formula for precision

In other words, precision is the number of true positives over the total number of predicted positive cases. Precision is also known as positive predictive power.

With the values in *Figure 7.3*, precision is given by 100 / 108, which is equal to 0.93. In general, you can increase precision at the cost of decreasing recall and vice versa. There is another model evaluation artifact in which you can play around with this precision versus recall trade-off. It is known as a precision-recall curve.

Precision-recall curves summarize the precision versus recall trade-off by using different probability thresholds. For example, the default threshold is 0.5, where any prediction above 0.5 will be considered true; otherwise, it is false. You can change the default threshold according to your need so that you can prioritize recall or precision. *Figure 7.6* shows an example of a precision-recall curve:

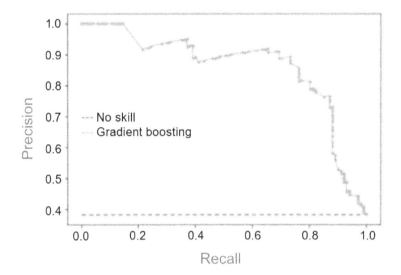

Figure 7.6 – A precision-recall curve

As you can see in *Figure 7.6*, increasing the precision will reduce the amount of recall and vice versa. *Figure 7.6* shows the precision/recall for each threshold for a **gradient boosting model** (as shown by the orange line) compared to a **no-skill model** (as shown by the blue dashed line). A perfect model will approximate the curve to the point (1,1), forming a squared corner on the top right-hand side of the chart.

Another visual analysis you can use on top of confusion matrixes is known as a **Receiver Operating Characteristic** (**ROC**) curve. ROC curves summarize the trade-off between the **true positive rate** and the **false positive rate** according to different thresholds, as in the precision-recall curve.

You already know about the true positive rate, or sensitivity, which is the same as what you have just learned about with the precision-recall curve. The other dimension of an ROC curve is the **false positive rate**, which is the number of false positives over the number of false positives plus true negatives.

In literature, you might find the false positive rate referred to as **inverted specificity**, represented by *1 – specificity*. Specificity is given as the number of true negatives over the number of true negatives plus false positives. Furthermore, false-positive rates or inverted specificity are the same. *Figure 7.7* shows what an ROC curve looks like:

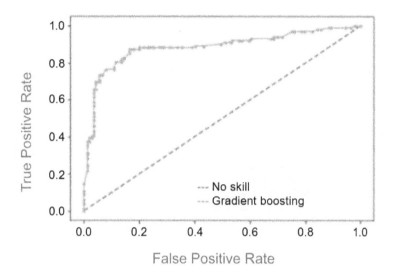

Figure 7.7 – ROC curve

A perfect model will approximate the curve to the point (0,1), forming a squared corner on the top left-hand side of the chart. The orange line represents the trade-off between the true positive rate and the false positive rate of a gradient-boosting classifier. The dashed blue line represents a no-skill model, which cannot predict the classes properly.

To summarize, you can use ROC curves for fairly balanced datasets and precision-recall curves for moderate to imbalanced datasets.

Summarizing precision and recall

Sometimes, you might want to use a metric that summarizes precision and recall, instead of prioritizing one over the other. Two very popular metrics can be used to summarize precision and recall: **F1 score** and **Area Under Curve (AUC)**.

The F1 score, also known as the **F-measure**, computes the harmonic mean of precision and recall. AUC summarizes the approximation of the area under the precision-recall curve.

That brings us to the end of this section on classification metrics. Let's now take a look at the evaluation metrics for regression models.

Evaluating regression models

Regression models are quite different from classification models since the outcome of the model is a continuous number. Therefore, the metrics around regression models aim to monitor the difference between real and predicted values.

The simplest way to check the difference between a predicted value (*yhat*) and its actual value (*y*) is by performing a simple subtraction operation, where the error will be equal to the absolute value of *yhat – y*. This metric is known as the **Mean Absolute Error (MAE)**.

Since you usually have to evaluate the error of each prediction, *i*, you have to take the mean value of the errors. *Figure 7.8* depicts formula that shows how this error can be formally defined:

$$MAE = \frac{1}{N} \sum_{i=1}^{N} |y_i - \hat{y}_i|$$

Figure 7.8 – Formula for error of each prediction

Sometimes, you might want to penalize bigger errors over smaller errors. To achieve this, you can use another metric, known as the **Mean Squared Error (MSE)**. The MSE will square each error and return the mean value.

By squaring errors, the MSE will penalize bigger ones. *Figure 7.9* depicts formula that shows how the MSE can be formally defined:

$$\text{MSE} = \underbrace{\frac{1}{n} \sum_{i=1}^{n}}_{\text{test set}} (\underbrace{y_i}_{\text{predicted vaue}} - \underbrace{\hat{y}_i}_{\text{actual value}})^2$$

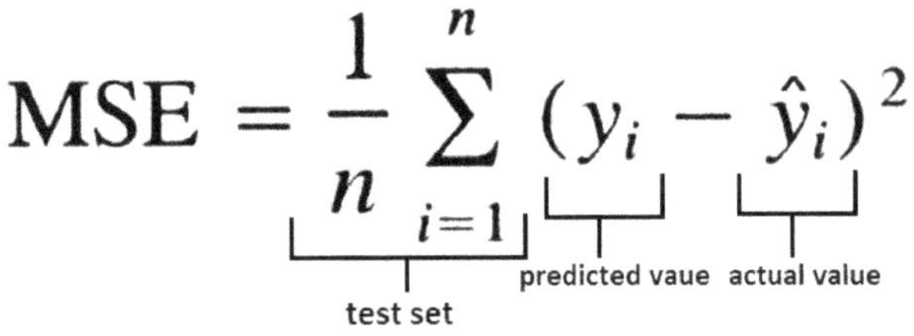

Figure 7.9 – Formula for MSE

There is a potential interpretation problem with the MSE. Since it has to compute the squared error, it might be difficult to interpret the final results from a business perspective. The **Root Mean Squared Error** (**RMSE**) works around this interpretation issue, by taking the square root of the MSE. *Figure 7.10* depicts the RMSE equation:

$$RMSE = \sqrt{\sum_{i=1}^{n} \frac{(\hat{y}_i - y_i)^2}{n}}$$

Figure 7.10 – Formula for RMSE

The RMSE is one of the most used metrics for regression models, since it can penalize larger errors and remains easy to interpret.

Exploring other regression metrics

There are many more metrics that are suitable for regression problems, in addition to the ones that you have just learned. You will not learn about most of them here, but you will be introduced to a few more metrics that might be important for you to know.

One of these metrics is known as the **Mean Absolute Percentage Error** (**MAPE**). As the name suggests, the MAPE will compute the absolute percentage error of each prediction and then take the average value. *Figure 7.11* depicts formula that shows how this metric is computed:

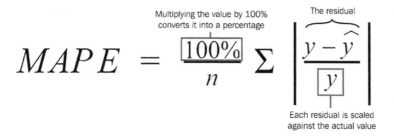

Figure 7.11 – Formula for MAPE

The MAPE is broadly used in forecasting models since it is very simple to interpret, and it provides a very good sense of how far (or close) the predictions are from the actual values (in terms of a percentage).

You have now completed this section on regression metrics. Next, you will learn about model optimization.

Model optimization

As you know, understanding evaluation metrics is very important in order to measure your model's performance and document your work. In the same way, when you want to optimize your current models, evaluating metrics also plays a very important role in defining the baseline performance that you want to challenge.

The process of model optimization consists of finding the best configuration (also known as hyperparameters) of the machine learning algorithm for a particular data distribution. You do not want to find hyperparameters that overfit the training data, in the same way that you do not want to find hyperparameters that underfit the training data.

You learned about overfitting and underfitting in *Chapter 1, Machine Learning Fundamentals*. In the same chapter, you also learned how to avoid these two types of modeling issues.

In this section, you will learn about some techniques that you can use to find the best configuration for a particular algorithm and dataset. You can combine these techniques of model optimization with other methods, such as cross-validation, to find the best set of hyperparameters for your model and avoid fitting issues.

> **Important note**
>
> Always remember that you do not want to optimize your algorithm to the underlying training data but to the data distribution behind the training data, so that your model will work on the training data as well as the production data (the data that has never been exposed to your model during the training process). A machine learning model that works only on the training data is useless. That is why combining model-tuning techniques (such as the ones you will learn about next) with sampling techniques (such as cross-validation) makes all the difference when it comes to creating a good model.

Grid search

Grid search is probably the most popular method for model optimization. It consists of testing different combinations of the algorithm and selecting the best one. Here, there are two important points that you need to pay attention to:

- How to define the best configuration of the model
- How many configurations should be tested

The best model is defined based on an evaluation metric. In other words, you have to first define which metric you are going to use to evaluate the model's performance. Secondly, you have to define how you are going to evaluate the model. Usually, cross-validation is used to evaluate the model on multiple datasets that have never been used for training.

In terms of the number of combinations/configurations, this is the most challenging part when playing with grid search. Each hyperparameter of an algorithm may have multiple or, sometimes, infinite possibilities of values. If you consider that an algorithm will usually have multiple hyperparameters, this becomes a function with quadratic cost, where the number of unique combinations to test is given as *the number of values of hyperparameter a * the number of values of hyperparameter b * the number of values of hyperparameter i. Table 7.1* shows how you could potentially set a grid search configuration for a decision tree model:

Criterion	Max depth	Min samples leaf
Gini, Entropy	2, 5 =, 10	10, 20, 30

Table 7.1 – Grid search configuration

In *Table 7.1*, there are three hyperparameters: **Criterion**, **Max depth**, and **Min samples leaf**. Each of these hyperparameters has a list of values for testing. That means by the end of the grid search process, you will have tested 18 models (2 * 3 * 3), where only the best one will be selected.

As you might have noticed, all the different combinations of those three hyperparameters will be tested. For example, consider the following:

- Criterion = Gini, Max depth = 2, Min samples leaf = 10

- Criterion = Gini, Max depth = 5, Min samples leaf = 10

- Criterion = Gini, Max depth = 10, Min samples leaf = 10

Some other questions that you might have could be as follows:

- Considering that a particular algorithm might have several hyperparameters, which ones should I tune?

- Considering that a particular hyperparameter might accept infinite values, which values should I test?

These are good questions, and grid search will not give you a straight answer for them. Instead, this is closer to an empirical process, where you have to test as much as you need to achieve your target performance.

Important note

Of course, grid search cannot guarantee that you will come up with your target performance. That depends on the algorithm and the training data.

A common practice, though, is to define the values for testing by using a **linear space** or **log space**, where you can manually set the limits of the hyperparameter you want to test and the number of values for testing. Then, the intermediate values will be drawn by a linear or log function.

As you might imagine, grid search can take a long time to run. A number of alternative methods have been proposed to work around this time issue. **Random search** is one of them, where the list of values for testing is randomly selected from the search space.

Another method that has gained rapid adoption across the industry is known as **Bayesian optimization**. Algorithm optimizations, such as **gradient descent**, try to find what is called the **global minima**, by calculating derivatives of the cost function. The global minima are the points where you find the algorithm configuration with the least associated cost.

Bayesian optimization is useful when calculating derivatives is not an option. So you can use the **Bayes theorem**, a probabilistic approach, to find the global minima using the smallest number of steps.

In practical terms, Bayesian optimization will start testing the entire search space to find the most promising set of optimal hyperparameters. Then, it will perform more tests specifically in the place where the global minima are likely to be.

Summary

In this chapter, you learned about the main metrics for model evaluation. You started with the metrics for classification problems and then you moved on to the metrics for regression problems.

In terms of classification metrics, you have been introduced to the well-known confusion matrix, which is probably the most important artifact for performing a model evaluation on classification models.

You learned about true positives, true negatives, false positives, and false negatives. Then, you learned how to combine these components to extract other metrics, such as accuracy, precision, recall, the F1 score, and AUC.

You then went even deeper and learned about ROC curves, as well as precision-recall curves. You learned that you can use ROC curves to evaluate fairly balanced datasets and precision-recall curves for moderate to imbalanced datasets.

By the way, when you are dealing with imbalanced datasets, remember that using accuracy might not be a good idea.

In terms of regression metrics, you learned that the most popular ones, and the ones most likely to be present in the *AWS Machine Learning Specialty* exam, are the MAE, MSE, RMSE, and MAPE. Make sure you know the basics of each of them before taking the exam.

Finally, you learned about methods for hyperparameter optimization, such as grid search and Bayesian optimization. In the next chapter, you will have a look at AWS application services for AI/ML. But first, take a moment to practice these questions about model evaluation and model optimization.

Exam Readiness Drill – Chapter Review Questions

Apart from a solid understanding of key concepts, being able to think quickly under time pressure is a skill that will help you ace your certification exam. That is why working on these skills early on in your learning journey is key.

Chapter review questions are designed to improve your test-taking skills progressively with each chapter you learn and review your understanding of key concepts in the chapter at the same time. You'll find these at the end of each chapter.

> **How To Access These Resources**
>
> To learn how to access these resources, head over to the chapter titled *Chapter 11, Accessing the Online Practice Resources*.

To open the Chapter Review Questions for this chapter, perform the following steps:

1. Click the link – https://packt.link/MLSC01E2_CH07.

   Alternatively, you can scan the following **QR code** (*Figure 7.12*):

Figure 7.12 – QR code that opens Chapter Review Questions for logged-in users

2. Once you log in, you'll see a page similar to the one shown in *Figure 7.13*:

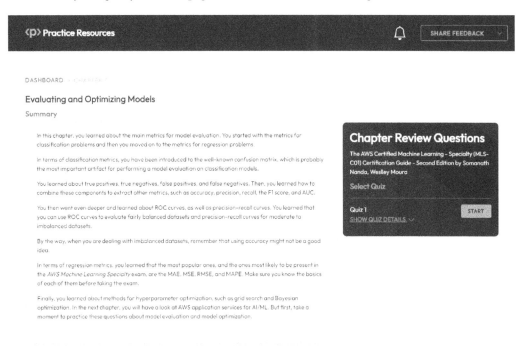

Figure 7.13 – Chapter Review Questions for Chapter 7

3. Once ready, start the following practice drills, re-attempting the quiz multiple times.

Exam Readiness Drill

For the first three attempts, don't worry about the time limit.

ATTEMPT 1

The first time, aim for at least **40%**. Look at the answers you got wrong and read the relevant sections in the chapter again to fix your learning gaps.

ATTEMPT 2

The second time, aim for at least **60%**. Look at the answers you got wrong and read the relevant sections in the chapter again to fix any remaining learning gaps.

ATTEMPT 3

The third time, aim for at least **75%**. Once you score 75% or more, you start working on your timing.

> **Tip**
>
> You may take more than **three** attempts to reach 75%. That's okay. Just review the relevant sections in the chapter till you get there.

Working On Timing

Target: Your aim is to keep the score the same while trying to answer these questions as quickly as possible. Here's an example of how your next attempts should look like:

Attempt	Score	Time Taken
Attempt 5	77%	21 mins 30 seconds
Attempt 6	78%	18 mins 34 seconds
Attempt 7	76%	14 mins 44 seconds

Table 7.2 – Sample timing practice drills on the online platform

> **Note**
>
> The time limits shown in the above table are just examples. Set your own time limits with each attempt based on the time limit of the quiz on the website.

With each new attempt, your score should stay above **75%** while your "time taken" to complete should "decrease". Repeat as many attempts as you want till you feel confident dealing with the time pressure.

8

AWS Application Services for AI/ML

In this chapter, you will learn about the AWS AI services for building chatbots, advanced text analysis, document analysis, transcription, and so on. This chapter has been designed in such a way that you can solve different use cases by integrating AWS AI services and get an idea of how they work. AWS is growing every day, and they are adding new AI services regularly.

In this chapter, you will approach different use cases programmatically or from the console. This will help you understand different APIs and how to use them. You will use S3 for storage and AWS Lambda to execute any code. The examples in this chapter are in Python, but you can use other supported languages such as Java, Node.js, .NET, PowerShell, Ruby, and so on.

You will cover the following topics:

- Analyzing images and videos with Amazon Rekognition
- Text to speech with Amazon Polly
- Speech to text with Amazon Transcribe
- Implementing natural language processing with Amazon Comprehend
- Translating documents with Amazon Translate
- Extracting text from documents with Amazon Textract
- Creating chatbots on Amazon Lex
- Time series forecasting with Amazon Forecast

Technical requirements

All you need for this chapter is an AWS account.

You can download the code examples for this chapter from GitHub at `https://github.com/PacktPublishing/AWS-Certified-Machine-Learning-Specialty-MLS-C01-Certification-Guide-Second-Edition/tree/main/Chapter08`.

Analyzing images and videos with Amazon Rekognition

If you need to add powerful visual analysis to your applications, then **Amazon Rekognition** is the service to choose. **Rekognition Image** lets you easily build powerful applications to search, verify, and organize millions of images. It lets you extract motion-based context from stored or live stream videos, and helps you analyze them. Rekognition Video also allows you to index metadata such as objects, activities, scenes, celebrities, and faces, making video searches easy. Rekognition Image uses deep neural network models to detect and label numerous objects and scenes in your images. It helps you capture text in an image, a bit like **Optical Character Recognition (OCR)**. A perfect example is a T-shirt with quotes on it. If you were to take a picture of one and ask Amazon Rekognition to extract the text from it, it would be able to tell you what the text says. You can also perform celebrity recognition using Amazon Rekognition. Somebody who is not a celebrity won't use the celebrity recognition API for their face; instead, they will use the face comparison API.

The official documentation, available at `https://aws.amazon.com/rekognition/faqs/`, states the following:

"With Rekognition Image, you only pay for the images you analyze and the face metadata you store. You will not be charged for the compute resources if, at any point of time, your training fails."

Some common uses of Amazon Rekognition include the following:

- Image and video analysis
- Searchable image library
- Face-based user verification
- Sentiment analysis
- Text in image
- Facial recognition
- Image moderation
- Search index for video archives
- Easy filtering of explicit and suggestive content in videos

- Examples of explicit nudity – sexual activity, graphical nudity, adult toys, and so on

- Examples of suggestive content – partial nudity, swimwear or underwear, and so on

Exploring the benefits of Amazon Rekognition

Here are some of the benefits of using Amazon Rekognition:

- AWS manages the infrastructure it runs on. In short, just use the API for your image analysis. You need to only focus on building and managing your deep learning pipelines.

  With or without knowledge of image processing, you can perform image and video analysis just by using the APIs provided in Amazon Rekognition, which can be used for any application or service on several platforms.

- The Labels API's response will identify real-world entities within an image through the DetectLabels API. These labels include city, town, table, home, garden, animal, pets, food, drink, electronics, flowers, and more. The entities are classified based on their **confidence score**, which indicates the probability that a given prediction is correct — the higher the score, the better. Similarly, you can use the DetectText API to extract the text in an image. Amazon Rekognition may detect multiple lines based on the gap between words. Periods do not represent the end of a line.

- Amazon Rekognition can be integrated with AWS Kinesis Video Stream, AWS S3, and AWS Lambda for seamless and affordable image and video analysis. With the AWS IAM service, Amazon Rekognition API calls can easily be secured and controlled.

- Low cost: you only pay for the images and videos that are analyzed.

- Through AWS CloudTrail, all the API calls for Amazon Rekognition can be captured as events. It captures all calls made from the console, the CLI, or code calls for APIs, which further enables the user to create Amazon SNS notifications based on CloudTrail events.

- You can create a VPC endpoint policy for specific API calls to establish a private connection between your VPC and Amazon Rekognition. This helps you leverage enhanced security. As per the AWS Shared Responsibility Model, AWS takes care of the security of the infrastructure and software, and you have to take care of the security of your content in the cloud.

Getting hands-on with Amazon Rekognition

In this section, you will learn how to integrate AWS Lambda with Amazon Rekognition to detect the labels in our image (uploaded at `https://github.com/PacktPublishing/AWS-Certified-Machine-Learning-Specialty-MLS-C01-Certification-Guide-Second-Edition/tree/main/Chapter08/Amazon%20Rekognition%20Demo/images`) and print the detected objects in the CloudWatch console. You will use the `detect_labels` API from Amazon Rekognition in the code.

You will begin by creating an IAM role for Lambda:

1. Navigate to the IAM console page.

2. Select **Roles** from the left-hand menu.

3. Select **Create role**.

4. Select **Lambda** from the **Choose a use case** section.

5. Add the following managed policies:

    *   `AmazonS3ReadOnlyAccess`

    *   `AmazonRekognitionFullAccess`

    *   `CloudWatchLogsFullAccess`

6. Name the role `rekognition-lambda-role`:

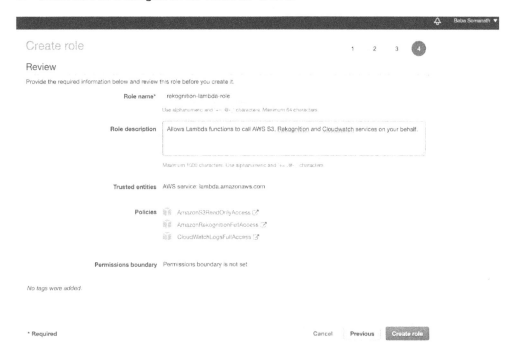

Figure 8.1 – The Create role dialog

Next, you will create a Lambda function.

7. Navigate to the AWS Lambda console page.

8. Select **Create function**.

9. Create a function:

    - Select **Author from scratch**.

    - Give the function a name, such as `lambda-rekognition`.

    - Choose `Python 3.6` from the **Runtime** dropdown.

    - Select **Use an existing role**. Add the name of the role you created previously; that is, `rekognition-lambda-role`:

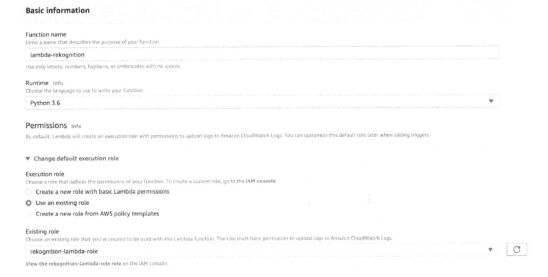

Figure 8.2 – Creating the Lambda function

10. Enter the following code in `lambda_function.py`:

```python
from __future__ import print_function
import boto3
def lambda_handler(event, context):
    print("=========lambda_handler started=======")
    # read the bucket name (key) from the event
    name_of_the_bucket=event['Records'][0]['s3']
['bucket']
['name']
    # read the object from the event
    name_of_the_photo=event['Records'][0]['s3']['object']
['key']
    detect_labels(name_of_the_photo,name_of_the_bucket)
    print("Labels detected Successfully")
```

```
def detect_labels(photo, bucket):
    client=boto3.client('rekognition')
   response=client.detect_
labels(Image={'S3Object':{'Bucket':bucket,'Name':photo}})
    print('Detected labels for ' + photo)
    print('==============================')
    for label in response['Labels']:
        print ("Label: " + label['Name'])
        print ("Confidence: " +
str(label['Confidence']))
        print ("Instances:")
        for instance in label['Instances']:
            print ("  Bounding box")
            print ("Top:
"+str(instance['BoundingBox']['Top']))
            print ("Left: \
"+str(instance['BoundingBox']['Left']))
            print ("Width: \
"+str(instance['BoundingBox']['Width']))
            print ("Height: \
"+str(instance['BoundingBox']['Height']))
            print ("Confidence:
"+str(instance['Confidence']))
            print()
        print ("Parents:")
        for parent in label['Parents']:
            print ("   " + parent['Name'])
        print ("----------")
        print('==============================')
    return response
```

Now, you will create a trigger for the Lambda Function.

11. Navigate to the AWS S3 console page. Create a bucket, for example, `rekognition-test-baba`, as shown in *Figure 8.3*:

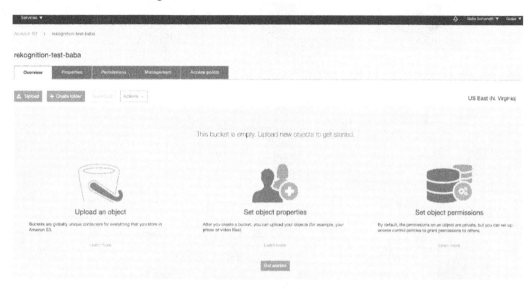

Figure 8.3 – AWS S3 console page

12. Click on **Create folder** and name it `images`. Click **Save**.

13. Click the **Properties** tab of our bucket.

14. Scroll to **Events** for that bucket.

15. Inside the **Events** window, select **Add notification** and set the following properties:

- **Name**: `rekognition_event`
- **Events**: `All object create events`
- **Prefix**: `images/`
- **Send to**: `Lambda Function`

- **Lambda**: `lambda-rekognition`:

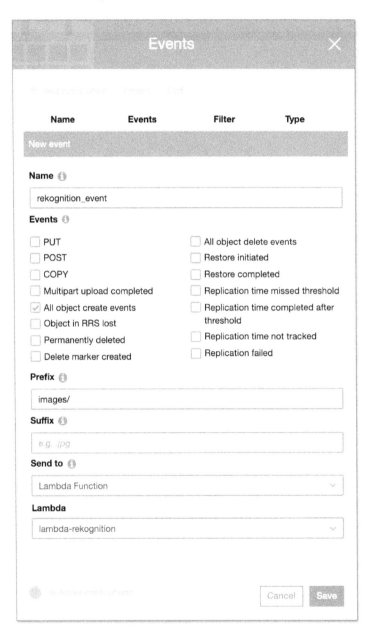

Figure 8.4 – S3 bucket Events window

Next, you will upload the image from the shared GitHub repository to the S3 bucket `images` folder.

16. As soon as you upload, you can check the **Monitoring** tab in the Lambda console to monitor the events, as shown in *Figure 8.5*:

Figure 8.5 – CloudWatch monitoring the event in the Lambda console

17. Navigate to `CloudWatch > CloudWatch Logs > Log groups > /aws/lambda/ lambda-rekognition`. Select the latest stream from all the streams listed on the AWS console and scroll down in the logs to see your output.

In this section, you learned how to implement the Amazon Rekognition AI service to detect objects in an image and get a confidence score for each. You will see more use cases for Amazon Rekognition in the upcoming sections, where you will detect text in images. In the next section, you will learn about Amazon's text-to-speech service and implement it.

Text to speech with Amazon Polly

Amazon Polly is all about converting text into speech, and it does so by using pretrained deep learning models. It is a fully managed service, so you do not have to do anything. You provide the plain text as input for synthesizing or in **Speech Synthesis Markup Language** (**SSML**) format so that an audio stream is returned. It also gives you different languages and voices to choose from, with both male and female options. The output audio from Amazon Polly can be saved in MP3 format for further use in the application (web or mobile) or can be a JSON output for written speech.

For example, if you were to input the text "Baba went to the library" into Amazon Polly, the output speech mark object would look as follows:

```
{"time":370,"type":"word","start":5,"end":9,"value":"went"}
```

The word `"went"` begins 370 milliseconds after the audio stream begins, and starts at byte 5 and ends at byte 9 of the given input text.

It also returns output in `ogg_vorbis` and `pcm` format. When `pcm` is used, the content that is returned as an output is `audio/pcm` in a signed 16-bit, 1-channel (mono), little-endian format.

Some common uses of Amazon Polly include the following:

- Can be used as an accessibility tool for reading web content.

- Can be integrated with Amazon Rekognition to help visually impaired people read signs. You can click a picture of the sign with text and feed it to Amazon Rekognition to extract text. The output text can be used as input for Polly, and it will return a voice as output.

- Can be used in a public address system, where the admin team can just pass on the text to be announced and Amazon Polly does the magic.

- By combining Amazon Polly with **Amazon Connect** (telephony backend service), you can build an `audio/video receiver` (**AVR**) system.

- Smart devices such as smart TVs, smart watches, and **Internet of Things** (**IoT**) devices can use this for audio output.

- Narration generation.

- When combined with Amazon Lex, full-blown voice user interfaces for applications can be developed.

Now, let's explore the benefits of Amazon Polly.

Exploring the benefits of Amazon Polly

Some of the benefits of using Amazon Polly include the following:

- This service is fully managed and does not require any admin cost to maintain or manage resources.

- It provides an instant speech correction and enhancement facility.

- You can develop your own access layer using the HTTP API from Amazon Polly. Development is easy due to the huge amount of language support that's available, such as Python, Ruby, Go, C++, Java, and Node.js.

- For certain neural voices, speech can be synthesized using the Newscaster style, to make them sound like a TV or radio broadcaster.

- Amazon Polly also allows you to modify the pronunciation of particular words or the use of new words.

Next, you'll get hands-on with Amazon Polly.

Getting hands-on with Amazon Polly

In this section, you will build a pipeline where you can integrate AWS Lambda with Amazon Polly. The pipeline reads a text file and generates an MP3 file, saving it to another folder in the same bucket. You will monitor the task's progress in CloudWatch logs.

You will begin by creating an IAM role for Lambda. Let's get started:

1. Navigate to the IAM console page.
2. Select **Roles** from the left-hand menu.
3. Select **Create role**.
4. Select **Lambda** as the trusted entity.

5. Add the following managed policies:

   - `AmazonS3FullAccess`

   - `AmazonPollyFullAccess`

   - `CloudWatchFullAccess`

6. Save the role as `polly-lambda-role`.

   Next, you will create a Lambda function:

7. Navigate to `Lambda > Functions > Create Function`.

   - Name the function `polly-lambda`

   - Set the runtime to `python 3.6`.

   - Use an existing role; that is, `polly-lambda-role`.

8. Paste the code at `https://github.com/PacktPublishing/AWS-Certified-Machine-Learning-Specialty-MLS-C01-Certification-Guide-Second-Edition/tree/main/Chapter08/Amazon%20Rekognition%20Demo/lambda_code` into your Lambda function and check its progress in the CloudWatch console. You will be using the `start_speech_synthesis_task` API from Amazon Polly for this code; it is an asynchronous synthesis task.

9. Scroll down and in the **Basic Settings** section, change **Timeout** to `59 sec`, as shown in *Figure 8.6*, and click **Save**:

Important note

The default is 3 seconds. Since this is an asynchronous operation, any retried attempts will create more files.

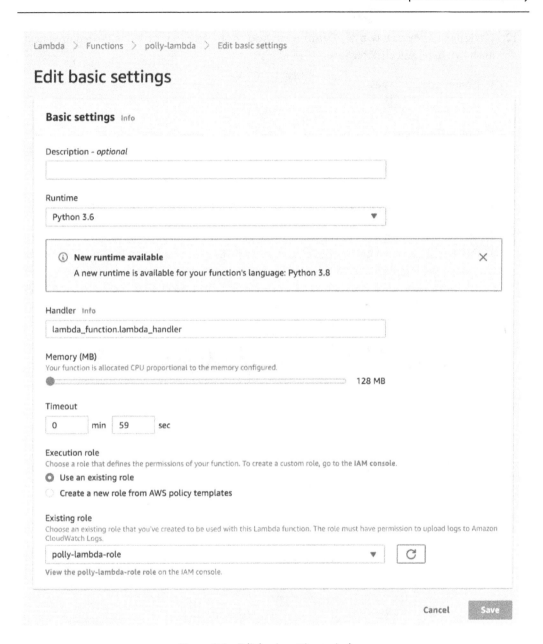

Figure 8.6 – Edit basic settings window

Now, you will create a bucket to trigger an event.

10. Navigate to the AWS S3 console and create a bucket called `polly-test-baba`.

11. Create a folder called `input-text` (in this example, you will only upload `.txt` files).

12. Navigate to `Properties > Events > Add notification`. Fill in the required fields, as shown here, and click on **Save**:

- **Name**: `polly_event`

- **Events**: `All object create events`

- **Prefix**: `input-text/`

- **Suffix**: `.txt`

- **Send to**: `Lambda Function`

- **Lambda**: `polly-lambda`

13. Next, you will upload a file to trigger an event and check its progress in CloudWatchUpload, in this case, a file called `test_file.txt` in `input-text`, as shown in *Figure 8.7*. You can download the sample file from this book's GitHub repository at `https://github.com/PacktPublishing/AWS-Certified-Machine-Learning-Specialty-MLS-C01-Certification-Guide-Second-Edition/tree/main/Chapter08/Amazon%20Polly%20Demo/text_file`:

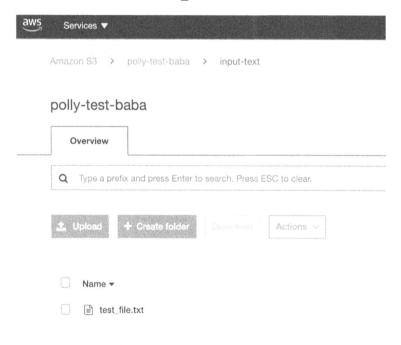

Figure 8.7 – The S3 bucket after uploading a text file for further processing

14. This will trigger the Lambda function. You can monitor your logs by going to `CloudWatch>`
    `CloudWatch Logs> Log groups> /aws/lambda/polly-lambda`.

15. Click on the latest stream; the log will look as follows:

```
File Content:  Hello Everyone, Welcome to Dublin. How
are you doing today?
{'ResponseMetadata': {'RequestId': '74ca4afd-5844-
47d8-9664-3660a26965e4', 'HTTPStatusCode': 200,
'HTTPHeaders': {'x-amzn-requestid': '74ca4afd-5844-
47d8-9664-3660a26965e4', 'content-type':
'application/json', 'content-length': '471', 'date':
'Thu, 24 Sep 2020 18:50:57 GMT'}, 'RetryAttempts': 0},
'SynthesisTask': {'Engine': 'standard', 'TaskId':
'57548c6b-d21a-4885-962f-450952569dc7', 'TaskStatus':
'scheduled', 'OutputUri': 'https://s3.us-east-
1.amazonaws.com/polly-test-baba/output-
audio/.57548c6b-d21a-4885-962f-450952569dc7.mp3',
'CreationTime': datetime.datetime(2020, 9, 24, 18, 50,
57, 769000, tzinfo=tzlocal()), 'RequestCharacters':
59, 'OutputFormat': 'mp3', 'TextType': 'text',
'VoiceId': 'Aditi', 'LanguageCode': 'en-GB'}}
```

The logs sample is shown in *Figure 8.8*:

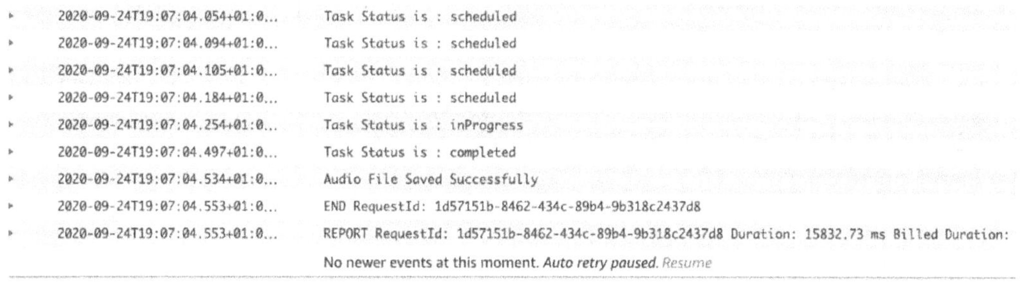

```
▶    2020-09-24T19:07:04.054+01:0...    Task Status is : scheduled
▶    2020-09-24T19:07:04.094+01:0...    Task Status is : scheduled
▶    2020-09-24T19:07:04.105+01:0...    Task Status is : scheduled
▶    2020-09-24T19:07:04.184+01:0...    Task Status is : scheduled
▶    2020-09-24T19:07:04.254+01:0...    Task Status is : inProgress
▶    2020-09-24T19:07:04.497+01:0...    Task Status is : completed
▶    2020-09-24T19:07:04.534+01:0...    Audio File Saved Successfully
▶    2020-09-24T19:07:04.553+01:0...    END RequestId: 1d57151b-8462-434c-89b4-9b318c2437d8
▶    2020-09-24T19:07:04.553+01:0...    REPORT RequestId: 1d57151b-8462-434c-89b4-9b318c2437d8 Duration: 15832.73 ms Billed Duration:
                                        No newer events at this moment. Auto retry paused. Resume
```

Figure 8.8 – The logs in the CloudWatch console

16. It will create output in MP3 format, as shown in *Figure 8.9*. Download and listen to it:

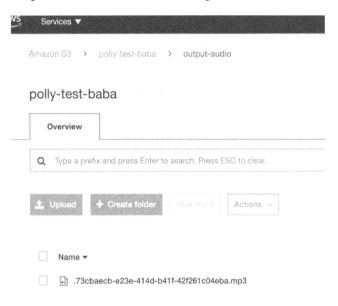

Figure 8.9 – The output file that was created in the S3 bucket

> **Important note**
>
> The most scalable and cost-effective way for your mobile apps or web apps is to generate an AWS pre-signed URL for S3 buckets and provide it to your users. These S3 Put events asynchronously invoke downstream AI workflows to generate results and send a response to the end users. Many users can be served at the same time through this approach, and it may increase performance and throughput.

In this section, you learned how to implement text to speech. In the next section, you will learn about Amazon Transcribe, a speech-to-text AI service.

Speech to text with Amazon Transcribe

In the previous section, you learned about text to speech. In this section, you will learn about speech to text and the service that provides it: **Amazon Transcribe**. It is an automatic speech recognition service that uses pre-trained deep learning models, which means that you do not have to train on petabytes of data to produce a model; Amazon does this for us. You just have to use the APIs that are available to transcribe audio files or video files; it supports a number of different languages and custom vocabulary too. Accuracy is the key, and through custom vocabulary, you can enhance it based on the desired domain or industry:

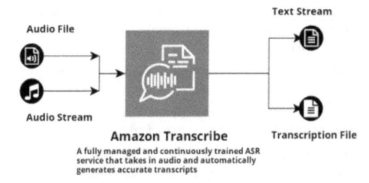

Figure 8.10 – Block diagram of Amazon Transcribe's input and output

Some common uses of Amazon Transcribe include the following:

- Real-time audio streaming and transcription
- Transcripting pre-recorded audio files
- Enable text searching from a media file by combining AWS Elasticsearch and Amazon Transcribe
- Performing sentiment analysis on recorded audio files for voice helpdesk (contact center analytics)
- Channel identification separation

Next, you will explore the benefits of Amazon Transcribe.

Exploring the benefits of Amazon Transcribe

Let's look at some of the benefits of using Amazon Transcribe:

- **Content redaction**: Customer privacy can be ensured by instructing Amazon Transcribe to identify and redact **personally identifiable information (PII)** from the language transcripts. You can filter unwanted words from your transcript by supplying a list of unwanted words with `VocabularyFilterName` and `VocabularyFilterMethod`, which are provided by the `StratTranscriptionJob` operation. For example, in financial organizations, this can be used to redact a caller's details.

- **Language identification**: It can automatically identify the most used language in an audio file and generate transcriptions. If you have several audio files, then this service will help you classify them by language.

- **Streaming transcription**: You can send recorded audio files or live audio streams to Amazon Transcribe and output a stream of text in real time.

- **Custom vocabulary or customized transcription**: You can use your custom vocabulary list as per your custom needs to generate accurate transcriptions.

- **Timestamp generation**: If you want to build or add subtitles to your videos, then Amazon Transcribe can return the timestamp for each word or phrase from the audio.

- **Cost effectiveness**: Being a managed service, there is no infrastructure cost.

Now, let's get hands-on with Amazon Transcribe.

Getting hands-on with Amazon Transcribe

In this section, you will build a pipeline where you can integrate AWS Lambda with Amazon Transcribe to read an audio file stored in a folder in an S3 bucket, and then store the output JSON file in another S3 bucket. You will monitor the task's progress in CloudWatch Logs too. You will use the `start_transcription_job` asynchronous function to start our job and you will constantly monitor the job through `get_transcription_job` until its status becomes COMPLETED. Let's get started:

1. First, create an IAM role called `transcribe-demo-role` for the Lambda function to execute. Ensure that it can read and write from/to S3, use Amazon Transcribe, and print the output in CloudWatch logs. Add the following policies to the IAM role:

   - `AmazonS3FullAccess`

   - `CloudWatchFullAccess`

   - `AmazonTranscribeFullAccess`

2. Now, you will create a Lambda function called `transcribe-lambda` with our existing IAM role, `transcribe-demo-role`, and save it.

    Please make sure you change the default timeout to a higher value in the **Basic settings** section of your Lambda function. I have set it to 10 min and 20 sec to avoid timeout errors. You will be using an asynchronous API call called `start_transcription_job` to start the task and monitor it by using the `get_transcription_job` API.

3. Paste the code available at `https://github.com/PacktPublishing/AWS-Certified-Machine-Learning-Specialty-MLS-C01-Certification-Guide-Second-Edition/blob/main/Chapter08/Amazon%20Transcribe%20Demo/lambda_function/lambda_function.py` and click on **Deploy**.

    This should give us the following output:

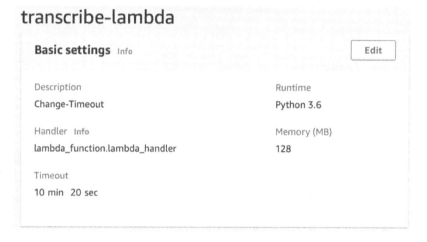

Figure 8.11 – The Basic settings section of our created lambda function

4. Next, you will be creating an S3 bucket called `transcribe-demo-101` and a folder called `input`. Create an event by going to the **Properties** tab of the **Create event notification** section. Enter the following details:

*   **Name**: `audio-event`
*   **Events**: `All object create events`
*   **Prefix**: `input/`
*   **Destination**: `Lambda Function`
*   **Lambda**: `transcribe-lambda`

5.   Upload the audio file in .mp4 format to the input folder. This will trigger the Lambda function. As per the code, the output will be stored in the S3 bucket in JSON format, which you can then use to read the contents of the file.

6.   Navigate to CloudWatch > CloudWatch Logs > Log groups > aws/lambda/transcribe-lambda. Choose the latest stream from the list. It will look as follows:

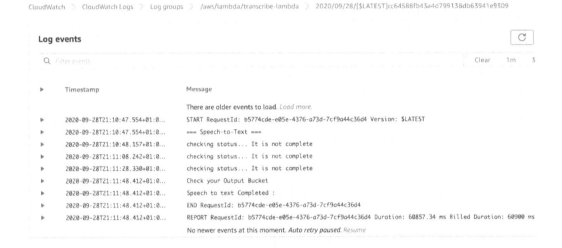

Figure 8.12 – The logs in a Log Stream for the specified log groups in the CloudWatch console

7.   The output is saved to the S3 bucket in JSON format, as per the job name mentioned in your code (you can use the S3 getObject API to download and read it):

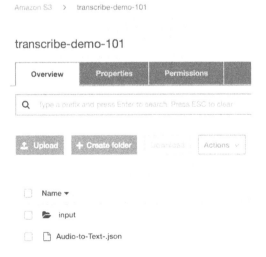

Figure 8.13 – The output JSON file in an S3 bucket

> **Important note**
> It is a best practice not to overprovision your function's timeout settings. Always understand your code performance and set a function timeout accordingly. Overprovisioning a function timeout results in Lambda functions running longer, causing unexpected costs. If you are using asynchronous API calls in your Lambda function, then it is good to write them into SNS topics on success and trigger another Lambda function from that. If it needs human intervention, then it is suggested that you use AWS Step Functions.

In this section, you learned and applied Amazon Transcribe to convert speech into text. In the next section, you will learn about one of the most powerful AWS AI services you can use to get the maximum amount of insight from our text data.

Implementing natural language processing with Amazon Comprehend

This service helps you extract insights from unstructured text. Unstructured text information is growing exponentially. A few data source examples are as follows:

- **Customer engagement**: Call center, issue triage, customer surveys, and product reviews
- **Business processes**: Customer/vendor emails, product support messages, and operation support feedback
- **Records and research**: Whitepapers and medical records
- **News and social media**: Social media analytics, brand trends, and correlated events

Now, the question is, what can you do with this data? How can you analyze it and extract any value out of it? The answer is Amazon Comprehend, which is used to get insights from unstructured data.

Some common uses of Amazon Comprehend include the following:

- Information management system
- More accurate search system on organized topics
- Sentiment analysis of users
- Support ticket classification
- Language detection from a document and then translating it into English using Amazon Translate
- Creating a system to label unstructured clinical data to assist in research and analysis purposes
- Extracting topics from saved audio files of company meetings or TV news

Next, you'll explore the benefits of Amazon Comprehend.

Exploring the benefits of Amazon Comprehend

Some of the advantages of using Comprehend can be seen in the following image:

Figure 8.14 – A block diagram showing Amazon Comprehend's capabilities

Let's look at these in more detail:

- It detects the language of the text and extracts key phrases. Amazon Comprehend can be used for sentiment analysis and topic modeling too.

- Amazon Comprehend Medical can be used to extract medical information.

- You pay for what you use since this is a fully managed service; you do not have to pay for the infrastructure. You do not need to train, develop, and deploy your own model.

- The topic modeling service works by extracting up to 100 topics. A topic is a keyword bucket so that you can see what is in the actual corpus of documents.

- It is accurate, continuously trained, and easy to use.

Next, you'll get hands-on with Amazon Comprehend.

Getting hands-on with Amazon Comprehend

In this section, you will build a pipeline where you can integrate AWS Lambda with Amazon Rekognition and Amazon Comprehend. You will then read an image file stored in an S3 bucket and detect the language of the text that has been extracted from the image. You will also use CloudWatch to print out the output. The following is a diagram of our use case:

Figure 8.15 – Architecture diagram of the required use case

Let's begin by creating an IAM role:

1. Navigate to the IAM console page.

2. Select **Roles** from the left-hand menu.

3. Select **Create role.**

4. Select **Lambda** as the trusted entity.

5. Add the following managed `policies`:

   - `AmazonS3ReadOnlyAccess`

   - `AmazonRekognitionFullAccess`

   - `ComprehendFullAccess`

   - `CloudWatchFullAccess`

6. Save the role as `language-detection-from-image-role`.

7. Now, let's create the Lambda function. Navigate to `Lambda > Functions > Create Function`.

8. Name the function `language-detection-from-image`.

9. Set the runtime to `Python 3.6`.

10. Use our existing role; that is, `language-detection-from-image-role`.

11. Download the code from `https://github.com/PacktPublishing/AWS-Certified-Machine-Learning-Specialty-MLS-C01-Certification-Guide-Second-Edition/tree/main/Chapter08/Amazon%20Transcribe%20Demo/lambda_function`, paste it into the function, and click **Deploy**.

    This code will read the text from the image that you uploaded and detect the language of the text. You have used the `detect_text` API from Amazon Rekognition to detect text from an image and the `batch_detect_dominant_language` API from Amazon Comprehend to detect the language of the text.

12. Now, go to your AWS S3 console and create a bucket called *language-detection-image*.

13. Create a folder called `input-image` (in this example, you will only upload `.jpg` files).

14. Navigate to `Properties > Events> Add notification`.

15. Fill in the required fields in the **Events** section with the following information; then, click on **Save**:

    - **Name**: `image-upload-event`
    - **Events**: `All object create events`
    - **Prefix**: `input-image/`
    - **Suffix**: `.jpg`
    - **Send to**: `Lambda Function`
    - **Lambda**: `language-detection-from-image`

16. Navigate to `Amazon S3>language-detection-image>input-image`. Upload the `sign-image.jpg` image in the folder. (This file is available in this book's GitHub repository at `https://github.com/PacktPublishing/AWS-Certified-Machine-Learning-Specialty-MLS-C01-Certification-Guide-Second-Edition/tree/main/Chapter08/Amazon%20Comprehend%20Demo/input_image`).

17. This file upload will trigger the Lambda function. You can monitor the logs from `CloudWatch> CloudWatch Logs> Log groups> /aws/lambda/language-detection-from-image`.

18. Click on the streams and select the latest one. The detected language is printed in the logs, as shown in *Figure 8.16*:

Figure 8.16 – The logs in CloudWatch for verifying the output

---

Important note

It is suggested that you use batch operations such as `BatchDetectSentiment` or `BatchDetectDominantLanguage` in your production environment. This is because single API operations can cause API-level throttling. More details are available here: `https://docs.aws.amazon.com/comprehend/latest/dg/functionality.html`.

In this section, you learned how to use Amazon Comprehend to detect the language of texts. The text is extracted into our Lambda function using Amazon Rekognition. In the next section, you will learn about translating the same text into English via Amazon Translate.

Translating documents with Amazon Translate

Most of the time, people prefer to communicate in their own language, even on digital platforms. Amazon Translate is a text translation service. You can provide documents or strings of text in various languages and get it back in a different language. It uses pre-trained deep learning techniques, so you should not be worried about the models, nor how they are managed. You can make API requests and get the results back.

Some common uses of Amazon Translate include the following:

- If there is an organization-wide requirement to prepare documents in different languages, then Translate is the solution for converting one language into many.

- Online chat applications can be translated in real time to provide a better customer experience.

- To localize website content faster and more affordably into more languages.

- Sentiment analysis can be applied to different languages once they have been translated.

- To provide non-English language support for a news publishing website.

Next, you will explore the benefits of Amazon Translate.

Exploring the benefits of Amazon Translate

Some of the benefits of using Amazon Translate include the following:

- It uses neural machine translation, which mimics the way the human brain works.

- You do not need to maintain resources or infrastructures for the Translation action.

- Produces high-quality results and maintains their consistency.

- You can customize brand names and model names. Other unique terms too can get translated using the custom terminology feature.

- Can be easily integrated with applications through APIs.

- Amazon Translate scales itself when you need it to do more.

Next, you will get hands-on with Amazon Translate.

Getting hands-on with Amazon Translate

In this section, you will build a product by integrating AWS Lambda with Amazon Rekognition, Amazon Comprehend, and Amazon Translate to read an image file stored in an S3 bucket. Then, you will detect the language of the text that has been extracted from the image so that you can translate it into English. You will also use CloudWatch to print the translated output. The following is a diagram of our use case:

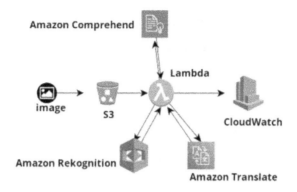

Figure 8.17 – Architecture diagram of the required use case

Let's start by creating an IAM role:

1. Navigate to the IAM console page.

2. Select **Roles** from the left-hand menu.

3. Select **Create role**.

4. Select **Lambda** as the trusted entity.

5. Add the following managed policies:

   - `AmazonS3ReadOnlyAccess`

   - `AmazonRekognitionFullAccess`

   - `ComprehendFullAccess`

   - `CloudWatchFullAccess`

   - `TranslateFullAccess`

6. Save the role as `language-translation-from-image`.

7. The next immediate step is to create a Lambda function. Navigate to `Lambda > Functions > Create Function`.

8. Name the function `language-detection-from-image`.

9. Set the runtime to `Python 3.6`.

10. Use an existing role; that is, `language-detection-from-image-role`.

11. Paste the code available at `https://github.com/PacktPublishing/AWS-Certified-Machine-Learning-Specialty-MLS-C01-Certification-Guide-Second-Edition/blob/main/Chapter08/Amazon%20Translate%20Demo/lambda_function/lambda_function.py` and click **Deploy**. You will use the `translate_text` API to translate the input text.

12. The next step is to create a bucket called `language-translation-from-image`.

    Create a folder named `image`. Then, navigate to `Properties > Events> Add notification`.

13. Fill in the required fields, as shown here, and click on Save (please make sure you select `.jpg` as the suffix; otherwise, it will trigger the Lambda function for any object creation process):

    • **Name**: *translate-language-image*

    • **Events**: `All object create events`

    • **Prefix**: `image/`

    • **Suffix**: `.jpg`

    • **Send to**: `Lambda Function`

    • **Lambda**: `language-translation-from-image`

14. Navigate to `Amazon S3 > language-detection-image > input-image`. Upload the `sign-image.jpg` image into the folder. This file is available in this book's GitHub repository: `https://github.com/PacktPublishing/AWS-Certified-Machine-Learning-Specialty-MLS-C01-Certification-Guide-Second-Edition/tree/main/Chapter08/Amazon%20Translate%20Demo/input_image`.

15. Uploading this image will trigger the Lambda function. You can monitor the logs by going to `CloudWatch > CloudWatch Logs > Log groups > /aws/lambda/language-translation-from-image`.

16. Click on the streams and select the latest one. It will look as follows:

Figure 8.18 – The logs in CloudWatch for verifying the output

The translation is as follows:

```
Translation of the text from the Image :
{'PREVENCION DEL COVID-19': 'PREVENTION OF COVID-19',
'LAVATE LAS MANOS EVITA EL CONTACTO NO TE TOQUES oJOs,
EVITA': 'WASHE HANDS AVOID CONTACT DO NOT TOUCH EYES',
'60 SEGUNDOS CON CONTAGIADOS NARIZ O BOCA
AGLOMERACIONES': '60 SECONDS WITH CONTAGIOUS NOSE OR
MOUTH AGGLOMERATIONS', 'NO COMPARTAS NO VIAJES A MENOS
SI TE PONES ENFERMO': "DON'T SHARE NOT TRAVEL UNLESS
YOU GET SICK", 'CUBIERTOS NI COMIDA QUE SEA NECESARIO
BUSCA AYUDA MEDICA': 'CUTLERY OR FOOD NEEDED SEEK
MEDICAL HELP'}
```

> **Important note**
>
> For production use cases, it is recommended to use AWS Lambda with AWS Step Functions if you have dependent services or a chain of services.
>
> Using the same S3 bucket to store input and output objects is not recommended. Output object creation in the same bucket may trigger recursive Lambda invocation. If you are using the same bucket, then you recommend that you use a prefix and suffix to trigger events. Similarly, you recommend using a prefix to store output objects.

In this section, you learned how to combine multiple services and chain their output to achieve a particular use case outcome. You learned how to integrate Amazon Rekognition to detect text in an image. The language can then be detected by using Amazon Comprehend. Then, you used the same input and translated it into English with the help of Amazon Translate. The translated output was then printed on CloudWatch logs for verification. In the next section, you will learn about Amazon Textract, which can be used to extract text from a document.

Extracting text from documents with Amazon Textract

Manually extracting information from documents is slow, expensive, and prone to errors. Traditional optical character recognition software needs a lot of customization, and it will still give erroneous output. To avoid such manual processes and errors, you should use **Amazon Textract**. Generally, you convert the documents into images to detect bounding boxes around the texts in images. You then apply character recognition to read the text from it. Textract does all this for you, and also extracts text, tables, forms, and other data for you with minimal effort. If you get low-confidence results from Amazon Textract, then Amazon A2I is the best solution.

Textract reduces the manual effort of extracting text from millions of scanned document pages. Once the information has been captured, actions can be taken on the text, such as storing it in different data stores, analyzing sentiments, or searching for keywords. The following diagram shows how Amazon Textract works:

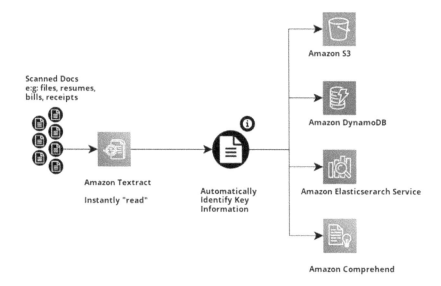

Figure 8.19 – Block diagram representation of Amazon Textract and how it stores its output

Some common uses of Amazon Textract include the following:

- Documenting processing workflows to extract tables or forms
- Creating search indexes from documents using Amazon Elasticsearch
- Redacting personally identifiable information in a workflow; Textract identifies data types and form labels automatically

Next, you will explore the benefits of Amazon Textract.

Exploring the benefits of Amazon Textract

There are several reasons to use Textract:

- Zero infrastructure cost
- Fully managed service (reduced development and management overhead)
- Helps you extract both structured and unstructured data
- Handwritten reviews can be analyzed

- Amazon Textract performs better than OCR apps, which use a flat bag of words

- Next, you will get hands-on with Amazon Textract.

Getting hands-on with Amazon Textract

In this section, you will use the Amazon Textract API to read an image file from our S3 bucket and print the FORM details on Cloudwatch. The same can be stored in S3 in your desired format for further use or can be stored in DynamoDB as a key-value pair. Let's get started:

1. First, create an IAM role called `textract-use-case-role` with the following policies. This will allow the Lambda function to execute so that it can read from S3, use Amazon Textract, and print the output in CloudWatch logs:

    - `CloudWatchFullAccess`

    - `AmazonTextractFullAccess`

    - `AmazonS3ReadOnlyAccess`

2. Let's create an S3 bucket called `textract-document-analysis` and upload the `receipt.png` image file. This will be used to contain the FORM details that will be extracted. The image file is available at `https://github.com/PacktPublishing/AWS-Certified-Machine-Learning-Specialty-MLS-C01-Certification-Guide-Second-Edition/tree/main/Chapter08/Amazon%20Textract%20Demo/input_doc`:

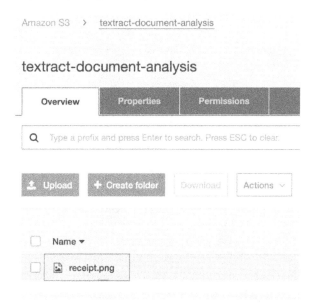

Figure 8.20 – An S3 bucket with an image (.png) file uploaded to the input folder

3. The next step is to create a Lambda function called `read-scanned-doc`, as shown in *Figure 8.21*, with an existing execution role called `textract-use-case-role`:

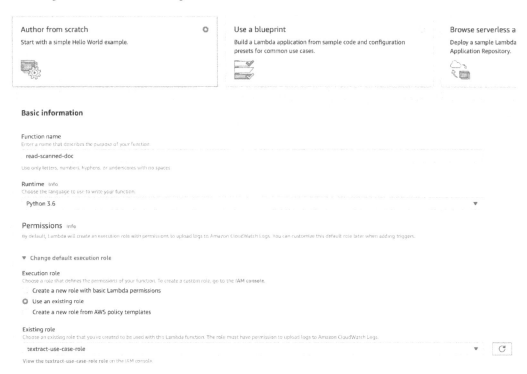

Figure 8.21 – The AWS Lambda Create function dialog

4. Once the function has been created, paste the following code and deploy it. Scroll down to **Basic Settings** to change the default timeout to a higher value (40 seconds) to prevent timeout errors. You have used the `analyze_document` API from Amazon Textract to get the `Table` and `Form` details via the `FeatureTypes` parameter of the API:

```
import boto3
import time
from trp import Document
textract_client=boto3.client('textract')
def lambda_handler(event, context):
    print("- - - Amazon Textract Demo - - -")
    # read the bucket name from the event
    name_of_the_bucket=event['Records'][0]['s3']
['bucket']['name']
```

```
    # read the object from the event
    name_of_the_doc=event['Records'][0]['s3']['object']
['key']
    print(name_of_the_bucket)
    print(name_of_the_doc)
    response =
textract_client.analyze_document(Document={'S3Object':
{'Bucket': name_of_the_bucket,'Name':
name_of_the_doc}},FeatureTypes=["TABLES","FORMS"])
    print(str(response))
    doc=Document(response)
    for page in doc.pages:
        # Print tables
        for table in page.tables:
            for r, row in enumerate(table.rows):
                for c, cell in enumerate(row.cells):
                    print("Table[{}][{}] =
{}".format(r, c, cell.text))
    for page in doc.pages:
        # Print fields
        print("Fields:")
        for field in page.form.fields:
            print("Key: {}, Value:
{}".format(field.key, field.value))
```

Unlike the previous examples, you will create a test configuration to run our code.

5. Click on the dropdown left of the **Test** button.

6. Select **Configure test events** and choose **Create new test event**.

7. Select **Amazon S3 Put** from the **Event template** dropdown.

8. In the JSON body, change the highlighted values as per our bucket name and key, as shown here:

```
"x-amz-id-2": "EXAMPLE123/5678abcdefghijklambdaisawesome/
},
"s3": {
  "s3SchemaVersion": "1.0",
  "configurationId": "testConfigRule",
  "bucket": {
    "name": "textract-document-analysis",
    "ownerIdentity": {
      "principalId": "EXAMPLE"
    },
    "arn": "arn:aws:s3:::textract-document-analysis"
  },
  "object": {
    "key": "receipt.png",
    "size": 1024,
    "eTag": "0123456789abcdef0123456789abcdef",
    "sequencer": "0A1B2C3D4E5F678901"
  }
}
```

Figure 8.22 – The Event template for testing the Lambda function

9. In the **Event name** field, name the test configuration `TextractDemo`.

10. Click **Save**.

11. Select your test configuration (`TextractDemo`) and click on **Test**:

Figure 8.23 – Selecting the test configuration before running your test

12. This will trigger the Lambda function. You can monitor the logs from `CloudWatch >
CloudWatch Logs > Log groups > /aws/lambda/ read-scanned-doc`.

13. Click on the streams and select the latest one. It will look as follows; the key-value pairs can
be seen in *Figure 8.24*:

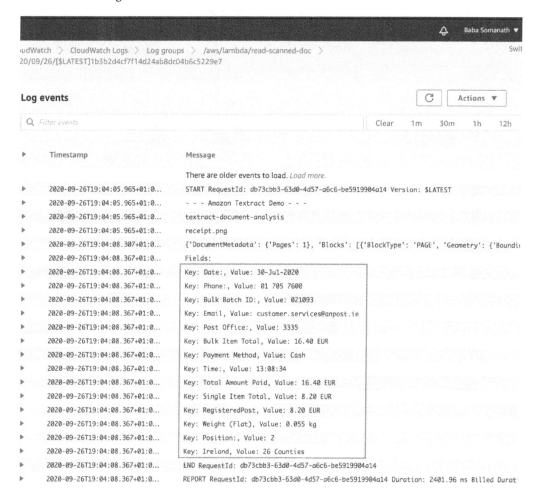

Figure 8.24 – The logs in CloudWatch for verifying the output

> **Important note**
>
> The most scalable and cost-effective way to generate S3 PJUT events for asynchronously invoking downstream AI workflows via Lambda is to generate an AWS pre-signed URL, and then provide it to your mobile or web application users. Many users can be served at the same time via this approach, and it may increase performance and throughput.
>
> Considering the same region for your AWS AI services and S3 bucket may improve performance and reduce network latency. AWS VPC endpoints can leverage enhanced security without using the public internet. You can store the AWS AI results in an AWS S3 bucket and encrypt the rest to attain better security.

In this section, you learned how to extract text from a scanned document and print the form data out of it. Unlike the other sections, you used the testing feature of a Lambda function by creating a test configuration that includes an event template. In the next section, you will learn about creating a chatbot for organizations and learn how to use it.

Creating chatbots on Amazon Lex

Most of the features that are available in Alexa are powered by **Amazon Lex**. You can easily build a chatbot using Amazon Lex. It uses natural language understanding and automatic speech recognition behind the scenes. An Amazon Lex bot can be created either from the console or via APIs. Its basic requirements are shown in the upcoming diagram.

Some common uses of Amazon Lex include the following:

- Apps that both listen and take input as text
- Chatbots
- Conversational AI products to provide a better customer and sales experience
- Custom business bots for assistance through AWS Lambda functions

- Voice assistants for your call center, which can speak to a user, schedule a meeting, or request the details of your account

- By integrating with Amazon Cognito, a few aspects such as user management, authentication, and sync across all your devices can be controlled

Next, you will explore the benefits of Amazon Lex.

Exploring the benefits of Amazon Lex

Some reasons for using Lex include the following:

- Chatbots can be directly built and tested from the AWS Management Console. These chatbots can be easily integrated into Facebook Messenger, Slack, and Twilio SMS via its rich formatting capabilities.

- Conversation logs can be stored in Amazon CloudWatch for further analysis. You can use them to monitor your bot and derive insights to improve your user experience.

- Amazon Lex can be integrated into other AWS services such as Amazon Cognito, AWS Lambda, Amazon DynamoDB, Amazon CloudWatch, and AWS Mobile Hub to leverage application security, monitoring, user authentication, business logic, storage, and mobile app development in AWS platforms.

- Amazon Lex chatbots can be integrated into your custom web applications too. You just need to build a chatbot widget and integrate it into your UI.

Next, you'll get hands-on with Amazon Lex.

Getting hands-on with Amazon Lex

Let's get started:

1. Log in to `https://console.aws.amazon.com/lex/`.
2. Click on **Get Started** and select **Custom bot**.

3. Fill in the following details and click on **Create**:

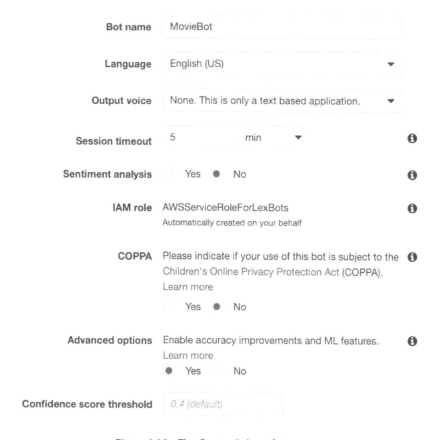

Figure 8.25 – The Create dialog of Amazon Lex

4. Click on **Create Intent**. A dialog will appear. Select **Create Intent**.
5. Name the new intent MovieIntent and click on **Add**.

6.   Go to the **Slots** section and use the following details:

  - Name: `movie_type`

  - Slot type: `AMAZON.Genre`

  - Prompt: `Which movie do you like?`

7.   Click on the + in **Settings**.

Some sample utterances can be seen in *Figure 8.26*. In this example, `movie_type` is my variable:

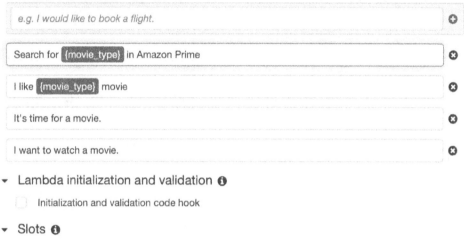

Figure 8.26 – The Sample utterances section

8. Scroll down to the **Response** section to add a message:

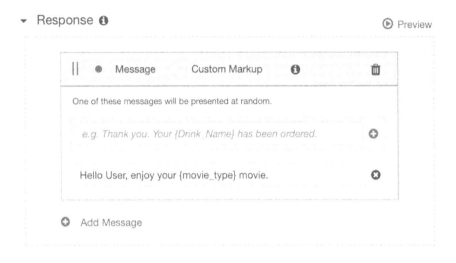

Figure 8.27 – The Response section of Amazon Lex

9. Scroll down to **Save Intent** and click on **Build**. Upon successfully building the prompt, the following success message will appear:

Figure 8.28 – The Response section of Amazon Lex

10. Now, you can test your bot, as shown in *Figure 8.29*:

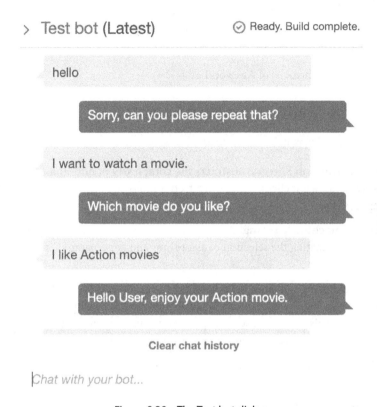

Figure 8.29 – The Test bot dialog

In the next section, you will learn about Amazon Forecast and learn how to use it for different use cases.

Amazon Forecast

Amazon Forecast is a powerful service that enables you to build highly accurate time-series forecasting models without the need for deep expertise in machine learning. Whether you are predicting sales, demand for inventory, or any time-dependent metric, Amazon Forecast simplifies the process, making it accessible to a broader audience.

Amazon Forecast is designed to tackle a variety of forecasting challenges, including:

- **Demand forecasting**: Predict future demand for products or services based on historical data, helping optimize inventory and supply chain management.

- **Financial planning**: Forecast financial metrics, such as revenue and expenses, aiding in budgeting and financial decision-making.

- **Resource planning**: Efficiently plan resources like workforce scheduling based on predicted demand patterns.

- **Traffic and user engagement**: Predict website or application traffic, enhancing resource allocation and user experience.

Next, you will explore the benefits of Amazon Lex.

Exploring the benefits of Amazon Forecast

Some reasons for using Amazon Forecast are as follows:

- **Ease of use**: Amazon Forecast abstracts the complexity of building accurate forecasting models. With just a few clicks, you can create, train, and deploy models without deep machine learning expertise.

- **Automated machine learning**: Amazon Forecast employs advanced machine learning techniques, automating the selection of algorithms and hyperparameter tuning to deliver the best possible model.

- **Forecast backtesting**: Enhance the reliability of your forecasts through backtesting. Amazon Forecast enables you to assess the accuracy of your models by comparing predictions against historical data. This iterative process helps fine-tune your models, adjusting hyperparameters and algorithms to achieve optimal forecasting performance.

- **Scalability**: Amazon Forecast seamlessly scales with your data, ensuring accurate predictions even with vast datasets.

- **Integration with AWS**: Leverage the power of integration with other AWS services like Amazon S3, AWS Lambda, and Amazon CloudWatch to create end-to-end forecasting solutions. Easily integrate Amazon Forecast into your existing applications and workflows, ensuring a seamless forecasting experience.

- **Accuracy and precision**: Amazon Forecast utilizes cutting-edge forecasting algorithms to deliver accurate and precise predictions, minimizing errors in your forecasts.

- **Cost-effective**: Pay only for what you use. The pay-as-you-go pricing model ensures cost-effectiveness, especially for businesses with varying forecasting needs.

- **Customization**: Tailor forecasting models to your specific business needs, accommodating various forecasting scenarios.

Next, you'll get hands-on with Amazon Lex.

Sales Forecasting Model with Amazon Forecast

Let's dive into a hands-on example of using Amazon Forecast to build a sales forecasting model. In this example, you'll predict future sales based on historical data.

Set up your dataset: Prepare a dataset containing historical sales data, ensuring it includes relevant timestamps and corresponding sales figures.

Create a dataset group: Use the Amazon Forecast console or API to create a dataset group, grouping related datasets for forecasting.

Import your data: Upload your historical sales dataset to Amazon Forecast, allowing the service to learn patterns from the provided data.

Train your model: Initiate model training using the Forecast console or API. Amazon Forecast will automatically select suitable algorithms and optimize hyperparameters.

Generate forecasts: Once the model is trained, generate forecasts for future sales based on the patterns identified in your historical data.

By leveraging advanced features and implementing optimization strategies, you can elevate your Amazon Forecast experience. The flexibility and adaptability of the service allow you to tailor forecasting solutions to the specific needs of your business. For example, you can improve the precision of your forecasts by integrating external variables. Amazon Forecast allows you to include additional information, such as promotions, holidays, or economic indicators, that might impact the time series you are forecasting. By considering these external factors, your models can adapt to changing circumstances and provide more nuanced predictions.

Summary

In this chapter, you learned about a few of the AWS AI services that can be used to solve various problems. You used the Amazon Rekognition service, which detects objects and faces (including celebrity faces), and can also extract text from images. For text to speech, you used Amazon Polly, while for speech to text, you used Amazon Transcribe. Toward the end of this chapter, you built a chatbot in Amazon Lex and learned the usage and benefits of Amazon Forecast.

For language detection and translation in an image, you used Amazon Rekognition, Amazon Comprehend, and Amazon Translate. You learned how to combine all of them into one Lambda function to solve our problem.

For the certification exam, you do not need to remember all the APIs you used in this chapter. There may be questions on a few of the best practices that you learned or on the names of services that solve a specific problem. It is always good to practice using these AWS AI services as it will enhance your architecting skills.

In the next chapter, you will learn about data preparation and transformation, which is the most important aspect of machine learning.

Exam Readiness Drill – Chapter Review Questions

Apart from a solid understanding of key concepts, being able to think quickly under time pressure is a skill that will help you ace your certification exam. That is why working on these skills early on in your learning journey is key.

Chapter review questions are designed to improve your test-taking skills progressively with each chapter you learn and review your understanding of key concepts in the chapter at the same time. You'll find these at the end of each chapter.

> **How To Access These Resources**
>
> To learn how to access these resources, head over to the chapter titled *Chapter 11, Accessing the Online Practice Resources*.

To open the Chapter Review Questions for this chapter, perform the following steps:

1. Click the link – `https://packt.link/MLSC01E2_CH08`.

    Alternatively, you can scan the following **QR code** (*Figure 8.30*):

Figure 8.30 – QR code that opens Chapter Review Questions for logged-in users

2. Once you log in, you'll see a page similar to the one shown in *Figure 8.31*:

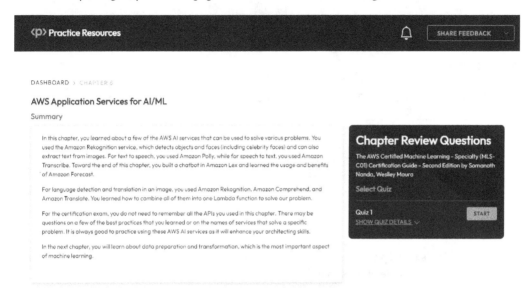

Figure 8.31 – Chapter Review Questions for Chapter 8

3. Once ready, start the following practice drills, re-attempting the quiz multiple times.

Exam Readiness Drill

For the first three attempts, don't worry about the time limit.

ATTEMPT 1

The first time, aim for at least **40%**. Look at the answers you got wrong and read the relevant sections in the chapter again to fix your learning gaps.

ATTEMPT 2

The second time, aim for at least **60%**. Look at the answers you got wrong and read the relevant sections in the chapter again to fix any remaining learning gaps.

ATTEMPT 3

The third time, aim for at least **75%**. Once you score 75% or more, you start working on your timing.

Tip

You may take more than **three** attempts to reach 75%. That's okay. Just review the relevant sections in the chapter till you get there.

Working On Timing

Target: Your aim is to keep the score the same while trying to answer these questions as quickly as possible. Here's an example of how your next attempts should look like:

Attempt	Score	Time Taken
Attempt 5	77%	21 mins 30 seconds
Attempt 6	78%	18 mins 34 seconds
Attempt 7	76%	14 mins 44 seconds

Table 8.1 – Sample timing practice drills on the online platform

---

Note

The time limits shown in the above table are just examples. Set your own time limits with each attempt based on the time limit of the quiz on the website.

With each new attempt, your score should stay above **75%** while your "time taken" to complete should "decrease". Repeat as many attempts as you want till you feel confident dealing with the time pressure.

9

Amazon SageMaker Modeling

In the previous chapter, you learned several methods of model optimization and evaluation techniques. You also learned various ways of storing data, processing data, and applying different statistical approaches to data. So, how can you now build a pipeline for this? Well, you can read data, process data, and build **machine learning (ML)** models on the processed data. But what if my first ML model does not perform well? Can I fine-tune my model? The answer is *yes*; you can do nearly everything using Amazon SageMaker. In this chapter, you will walk you through the following topics using Amazon SageMaker:

- Understanding different instances of Amazon SageMaker
- Cleaning and preparing data in Jupyter Notebook in Amazon SageMaker
- Model training in Amazon SageMaker
- Using SageMaker's built-in ML algorithms
- Writing custom training and inference code in SageMaker

Technical requirements

You can download the data used in this chapter's examples from GitHub at `https://github.com/PacktPublishing/AWS-Certified-Machine-Learning-Specialty-MLS-C01-Certification-Guide-Second-Edition/tree/main/Chapter09`.

Creating notebooks in Amazon SageMaker

If you are working with ML, then you need to perform actions such as storing data, processing data, preparing data for model training, model training, and deploying the model for inference. They are complex, and each of these stages requires a machine to perform the task. With Amazon SageMaker, life becomes much easier when carrying out these tasks.

What is Amazon SageMaker?

SageMaker provides training instances to train a model using the data and provides endpoint instances to infer by using the model. It also provides notebook instances running on the Jupyter Notebook to clean and understand the data. If you are happy with your cleaning process, then you should store the cleaned data in S3 as part of the staging for training. You can launch training instances to consume this training data and produce an ML model. The ML model can be stored in S3, and endpoint instances can consume the model to produce results for end users.

If you draw this in a block diagram, then it will look similar to *Figure 9.1*:

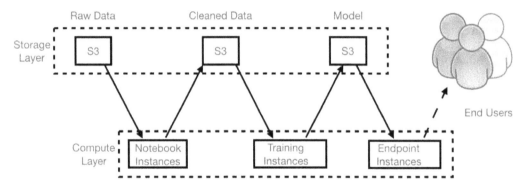

Figure 9.1 – A pictorial representation of the different layers of the Amazon SageMaker instances

Now, you will take a look at the Amazon SageMaker console and get a better feel for it. Once you log in to your AWS account and go to Amazon SageMaker, you will see something similar to *Figure 9.2*:

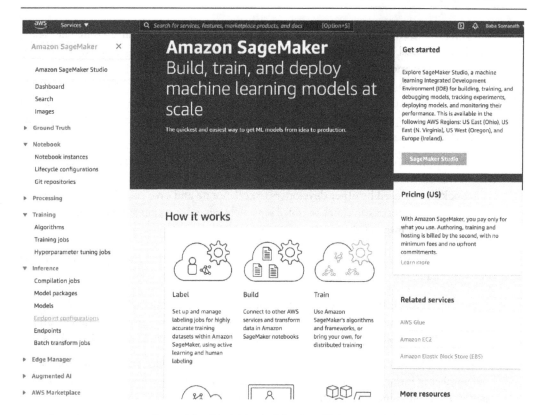

Figure 9.2 – A quick look at the SageMaker console

There are three different sections in the menu on the left, labeled **Notebook**, **Training**, and **Inference**, that have been expanded in *Figure 9.2* so that you can dive in and understand them better.

Notebook has three different options that you can use:

- **Notebook instances**: This helps you create, open, start, and stop notebook instances. These instances are responsible for running Jupyter Notebooks. They allow you to choose the instance type based on the workload of the use case. The best practice is to use a notebook instance to orchestrate the data pipeline for processing a large dataset. For example, making a call from a notebook instance to AWS Glue for ETL services or Amazon EMR to run Spark applications. If you are asked to create a secure notebook instance outside AWS, then you need to take care of endpoint security, network security, launching the machine, managing storage on it, and managing Jupyter Notebook applications running on the instance. The user does not need to manage any of these with SageMaker.

- **Lifecycle configurations**: This is useful when there is a use case that requires a different library, which is not available in the notebook instances. To install the library, the user will do either `pip install` or `conda install`. However, as soon as the notebook instance is terminated, the customization will be lost. To avoid such a scenario, you can customize your notebook instance through a script provided through **Lifecycle configurations**. You can choose any of the environments present in `/home/ec2-user/anaconda3/envs/` and customize the specific environment as required.

- **Git repositories**: AWS CodeCommit, GitHub, or any other Git server can be associated with the notebook instance for the persistence of your notebooks. If access is given, then the same notebook can be used by other developers to collaborate and save code in a source-control fashion. Git repositories can either be added separately using this option or they can be associated with a notebook instance during the creation.

As you can see in *Figure 9.2*, **Training** offers **Algorithms**, **Training jobs**, and **Hyperparameter tuning jobs**. Let's understand their usage:

- **Algorithms**: This is the first step toward deciding on an algorithm that you are going to run on our cleaned data. You can either choose a custom algorithm or create a custom algorithm based on the use case. Otherwise, you can run SageMaker algorithms on the cleaned data.

- **Training jobs**: You can create training jobs from a notebook instance via API calls. You can set the number of instances, input the data source details, perform checkpoint configuration, and output data configuration. Amazon SageMaker manages the training instances and stores the model artifacts as output in the specified location. Both incremental training (that is, to train the model from time to time for better results) and managed spot training (that is, to reduce costs) can also be achieved.

- **Hyperparameter tuning jobs**: Usually, hyperparameters are set for an algorithm prior to the training process. During the training process, you let the algorithm figure out the best values for these parameters. With hyperparameter tuning, you obtain the best model that has the best value of hyperparameters. This can be done through a console or via API calls. The same can be orchestrated from a notebook instance too.

Inference has many offerings and is evolving every day:

- **Compilation jobs**: If your model is trained using an ML framework such as Keras, MXNet, ONNX, PyTorch, TFLite, TensorFlow, or XGBoost, and your model artifacts are available on a S3 bucket, then you can choose either **Target device** or **Target platform**. The Target device option is used to specify where you will deploy your model, such as an AWS SageMaker ML instance or an AWS IoT Greengrass device. The Target platform option is used to decide the operating system, architecture, and accelerator on which you want your model to run. You can also store the compiled module in your S3 bucket for future use. This essentially helps you in cross-platform model deployment.

- **Model packages**: These are used to create deployable SageMaker models. You can create your own algorithm, package it using the model package APIs, and publish it to AWS Marketplace.

- **Models**: Models are created using model artifacts. They are similar to mathematical equations with variables; that is, you input the values for the variables and get an output. These models are stored in S3 and will be used for inference by the endpoints.

- **Endpoint configurations**: Amazon SageMaker allows you to deploy multiple weighted models to a single endpoint. This means you can route a specific number of requests to one endpoint. *What does this mean?* Well, let's say you have one model in use. You want to replace it with a new model. However, you cannot simply remove the first model that is already in use. In this scenario, you can use the `VariantWeight` API to make the endpoints serve 80% of the requests with the old model and 20% of the requests with the new model. This is the most common production scenario where the data changes rapidly and the model needs to be trained and tuned periodically. Another possible use case is to test the model results with live data, then a certain percentage of the requests can be routed to the new model, and the results can be monitored to ascertain the accuracy of the model on real-time unseen data.

- **Endpoints**: These are used to create a URL to which the model is exposed and can be requested to give the model results as a response.

- **Batch transform jobs**: If the use case demands that you infer results on several million records, then instead of individual inference jobs, you can run batch transform jobs on the unseen data. Note that there can be some confusion when you receive thousands of results from your model after parsing thousands of pieces of unseen data as a batch. To overcome this confusion, the `InputFilter`, `JoinSource`, and `OutputFilter` APIs can be used to associate input records with output results.

You have got an overview of Amazon SageMaker. Now, put your knowledge to work in the next section.

> **Important note**
> The Amazon SageMaker console keeps changing. There's a possibility that when you are reading this book, the console might look different.

Training Data Location and Formats

As you embark on the journey of setting up your AWS SageMaker training job, understanding the diverse data storage and reading options is crucial. To ensure a seamless training experience, delve into the supported options and their benefits.

First you will look at the **supported data storage options**:

- **Amazon Simple Storage Service (Amazon S3):**

  - **Overview**: Amazon SageMaker provides robust support for storing training datasets in Amazon S3, offering reliability and scalability.

  - **Usage Example**: You can configure your dataset using an Amazon S3 prefix, manifest file, or augmented manifest file.

- **Amazon Elastic File System (Amazon EFS):**

  - **Overview**: SageMaker extends its support to Amazon EFS, facilitating file system access to the dataset.

  - **Usage Example**: Data stored in Amazon EFS must be pre-existing before initiating the training job.

- **Amazon FSx for Lustre:**

  - **Overview**: Achieving high throughput and low-latency file retrieval, SageMaker mounts the FSx for Lustre file system to the training instance.

  - **Usage Example**: FSx for Lustre can scale seamlessly, providing a performant option for your training data.

Here are the **input modes for data access:**

- **File Mode:**

  - **Overview**: Default input mode where SageMaker downloads the entire dataset to the Docker container before training starts.

  - **Usage Example**: Compatible with SageMaker local mode and supports sharding for distributed training.

- **Fast File Mode:**

  - **Overview**: Combining file system access with the efficiency of pipe mode, fast file mode identifies data files at the start but delays the download until necessary.

  - **Usage Example**: Streamlines training startup time, particularly beneficial when dealing with a large dataset.

- **Pipe Mode:**

  - **Overview**: Streams data directly from an Amazon S3 data source, providing faster start times and better throughput.

  - **Usage Example**: Historically used, but largely replaced by the simpler-to-use fast file mode.

And lastly, look at the **specialized storage classes**:

- **Amazon S3 Express One Zone:**

  - **Overview**: A high-performance, single Availability Zone storage class, optimizing compute performance and costs.

  - **Usage Example**: Supports file mode, fast file mode, and pipe mode for SageMaker model training.

- **Amazon EFS and Amazon FSx for Lustre:**

  - **Overview**: SageMaker supports both Amazon EFS and Amazon FSx for Lustre, offering flexibility in choosing the right storage solution for your training data.

  - **Usage Example**: Mounting the file systems to the training instance ensures seamless access during training.

Understanding the nuances of data storage and reading options for AWS SageMaker training jobs empowers you to tailor your setup to specific requirements. In the upcoming sections, you'll explore more facets of AWS SageMaker to deepen your understanding and proficiency in machine learning workflows. Let's put our knowledge to work in the next section.

Getting hands-on with Amazon SageMaker notebook instances

The very first step, in this section, is to create a Jupyter Notebook, and this requires a notebook instance. You can start by creating a notebook instance, as follows:

1. Sign in to your AWS account.

2. Navigate to `Services > Amazon SageMaker`.

3. In the left navigation pane, click on **Notebook instances** and then click on the **Create notebook instance** button.

4. Provide a **Notebook instance name** value such as `notebookinstance` and leave the **Notebook instance type** at its default `ml.t2.medium` setting. In the **Permissions and encryption** section, select `Create a new role` in **IAM role**. You will be asked to specify the bucket name. For the purpose of this example, it's chosen as any bucket.

5. Following the successful creation of a role, you should see something similar to *Figure 9.3*:

Figure 9.3 – Amazon SageMaker role creation

6. Leave everything else on their default settings and click on the **Create notebook instance** button.

7. Once the instance is in the InService state, select the instance. Click on the **Actions** drop-down menu and choose **Open Jupyter**. This opens your Jupyter Notebook.

8. Now, you are all set to run our Jupyter Notebook on the newly created instance. You will perform **Exploratory Data Analysis (EDA)** and plot different types of graphs to visualize the data. Once you are familiar with the Jupyter Notebook, you will build some models to predict house prices in Boston. You will apply the algorithms that you have learned in previous chapters and compare them to find the best model that offers the best prediction according to our data. Let's dive in.

9. In the Jupyter Notebook, click on **New** and select **Terminal**. Run the following commands in Command Prompt to download the code to the instance:

```
sh-4.2$ cd ~/SageMaker/
sh-4.2$ git clone https://github.com/PacktPublishing/
AWS-Certified-Machine-Learning-Specialty-MLS-C01-Certification-
Guide-Second-Edition.git
```

10. Once the Git repository is cloned to the SageMaker notebook instance, type `exit` into Command Prompt to quit. Now, your code is ready to execute.

11. Navigate to `Chapter-9` in the Jupyter Notebook's Files section, as shown in *Figure 9.4*:

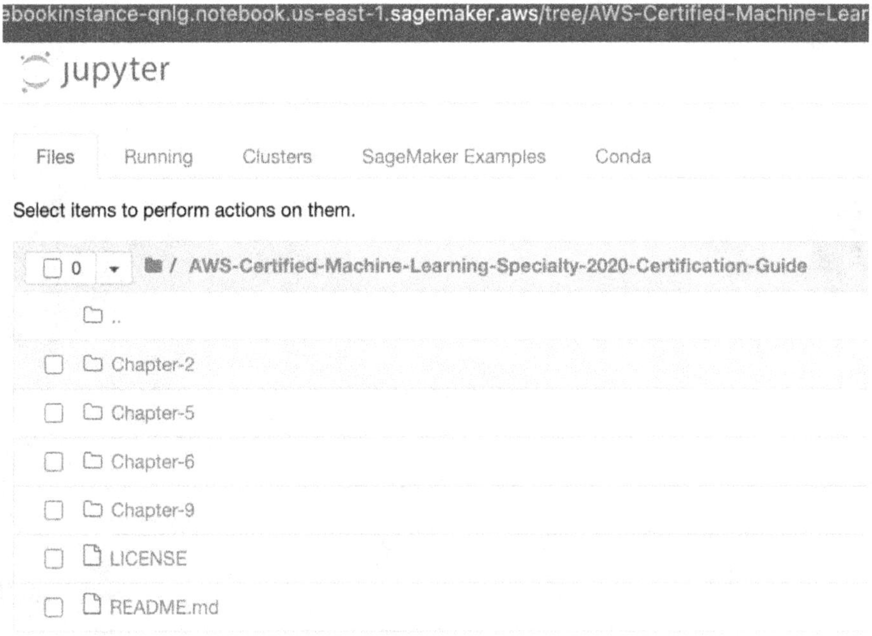

Figure 9.4 – Jupyter Notebook

12. Click on the first notebook in `1.Boston-House-Price-SageMaker-Notebook-Instance-Example.ipynb`. It will prompt you to choose the kernel for the notebook. Please select `conda_python3`, as shown in *Figure 9.5*:

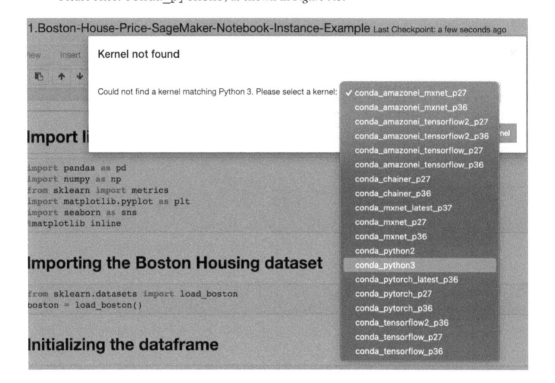

Figure 9.5 – Jupyter Notebook kernel selection

13. From the notebook, navigate to `Kernel > Restart & Clear Output`. Click on the play icon to run the cells one after another. Please ensure you have run each individual cell and inspect the output from each execution/run.

14. You can experiment by adding cells and deleting cells to familiarize yourself with the Jupyter Notebook operations. In one of the paragraphs, there is a bash command that allows you to install the `xgboost` libraries from the notebook.

15. The final cell explains how you have compared the different scores of various modeling techniques to draw a conclusion mathematically. *Figure 9.6* clearly shows that the best model for predicting house prices in Boston is XGBoost:

```
models = pd.DataFrame({
    'Model': ['Linear Regression', 'Random Forest', 'XGBoost', 'Support Vector Machines'],
    'R-squared Score': [acc_linreg*100, acc_rf*100, acc_xgb*100, acc_svm*100],
    'Adjusted R-squared Score': [adj_R2_linreg*100, adj_R2_rf*100, adj_R2_xgb*100, adj_R2_svm*100],
    'MAE': [mae_linreg, mae_rf, mae_xgb, mae_svm],
    'MSE': [mse_linreg, mse_rf, mse_xgb, mse_svm],
    'RMSE': [rmse_linreg, rmse_rf, rmse_xgb, rmse_svm]})
models.sort_values(by='R-squared Score', ascending=False)
```

	Model	R-squared Score	Adjusted R-squared Score	MAE	MSE	RMSE
2	XGBoost	85.799520	84.461793	2.530958	14.828152	3.850734
1	Random Forest	82.181317	80.502745	2.500316	18.606282	4.313500
0	Linear Regression	71.218184	68.506853	3.859006	30.053993	5.482152
3	Support Vector Machines	59.001585	55.139415	3.756145	42.810575	6.542979

Figure 9.6 – Comparing the models

16. Once you've completed the execution of this notebook, please feel free to shut down the kernel and stop your notebook instance from the SageMaker console. This is a best practice to reduce costs.

In the next hands-on section, you will familiarize ourselves with Amazon SageMaker's training and inference instances. You will also use the Amazon SageMaker API to make this process easier. You will use the same notebook instance as you did in the previous example.

Getting hands-on with Amazon SageMaker's training and inference instances

In this section, you will learn about training a model and hosting the model to generate its predicted results. Let's dive in by using the notebook instance from the previous example:

1. Sign in to your AWS account at `https://console.aws.amazon.com/sagemaker/home?region=us-east-1#/notebook-instances`.

2. Click on **Start** next to the instance that you created in the previous example, `notebookinstance`. Once the status moves to `InService`, open it in a new tab, as shown in *Figure 9.7*:

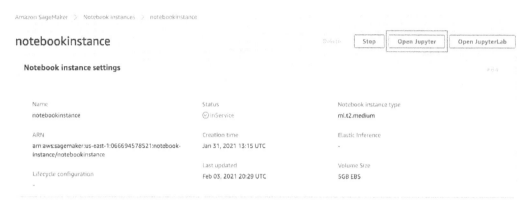

Figure 9.7 – The InService instance

3. Navigate to the tab named **SageMaker Examples** from the Jupyter Notebook home page.

4. Select the `k_nearest_neighbors_covtype.ipynb` notebook. Click on **Use** and create a copy.

5. When you run the following code block, as shown in *Figure 9.8*, you can also check a training job in `Training > Training jobs` of the SageMaker home page:

```
hyperparams = {"feature_dim": 54, "k": 10, "sample_size": 200000, "predictor_type": "classifier"}
output_path = f"s3://{bucket}/{prefix}/default_example/output"
knn_estimator = trained_estimator_from_hyperparams(
    s3_train_data, hyperparams, output_path, s3_test_data=s3_test_data
)

The method get_image_uri has been renamed in sagemaker>=2.
See: https://sagemaker.readthedocs.io/en/stable/v2.html for details.
Defaulting to the only supported framework/algorithm version: 1. Ignoring framework/algorithm version: 1.

2021-02-03 22:00:05 Starting - Starting the training job...
2021-02-03 22:00:30 Starting - Launching requested ML instancesProfilerReport-1612389605: InProgress
.........
2021-02-03 22:01:51 Starting - Preparing the instances for training...
2021-02-03 22:02:32 Downloading - Downloading input data...
2021-02-03 22:02:52 Training - Downloading the training image...
2021-02-03 22:03:33 Training - Training image download completed. Training in progress..Docker entrypoint called with
argument(s): train
Running default environment configuration script
[02/03/2021 22:03:35 INFO 140457495148352] Reading default configuration from /opt/amazon/lib/python2.7/site-package
s/algorithm/resources/default-conf.json: {u'index_metric': u'L2', u'_tuning_objective_metric': u'', u'_num_gpus': u'a
uto', u'_log_level': u'info', u'feature_dim': u'auto', u'faiss_index_ivf_nlists': u'auto', u'epochs': u'1', u'index_t
ype': u'faiss.Flat', u'_faiss_index_nprobe': u'5', u'_kvstore': u'dist_async', u'_num_kv_servers': u'1', u'mini_batch
_size': u'5000'}
[02/03/2021 22:03:35 INFO 140457495148352] Merging with provided configuration from /opt/ml/input/config/hyperparamet
```

Figure 9.8 – The SageMaker fit API call

6. The training job looks similar to *Figure 9.9*. It launches an ECS container in the backend and uses the IAM execution role created in the previous example to run the training job for this request:

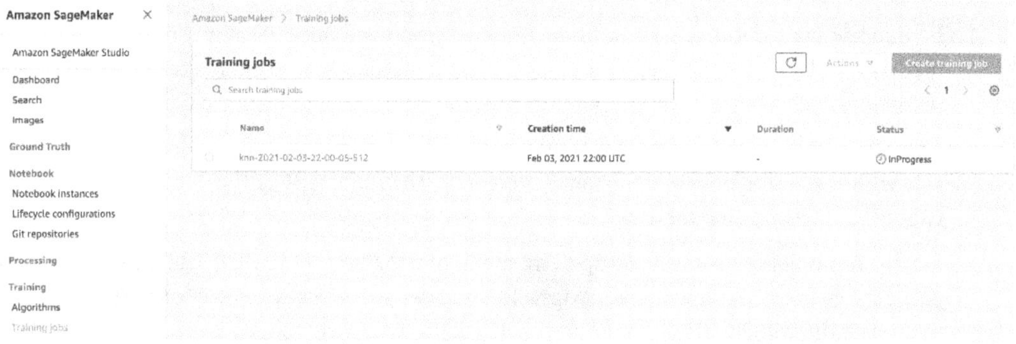

Figure 9.9 – Training jobs

7. If you go inside and check the logs in CloudWatch, it gives you more details about the containers and the steps they performed. As an ML engineer, it's worth going in and checking the CloudWatch metrics for your algorithm.

8. Now, if you run the following paragraph, as shown in *Figure 9.10*, in the notebook, then it will create an endpoint configuration and an endpoint where the model from the earlier training job is deployed.

9. I have changed the instance type to reduce costs. It is the instance or the machine that will host your model. Please choose your instance wisely. You will learn about choosing instance types in the next section. I have also changed endpoint_name so that it can be recognized easily:

```
import time

instance_type = "ml.t2.medium"
model_name = "knn_%s" % instance_type
endpoint_name = "knn-baba-test-%s" % (str(time.time()).replace(".", "-"))
print("setting up the endpoint..")
predictor = predictor_from_estimator(
    knn_estimator, model_name, instance_type, endpoint_name=endpoint_name
)
```

```
setting up the endpoint..
-
```

Figure 9.10 – Creating the predictor object with endpoint details

10. Navigate to `Inference > Endpoints`. This will show you the endpoint that was created as a result of the previous paragraph's execution. This endpoint has a configuration and can be navigated and traced through `Inference > Endpoint Configurations`.

11. If you view the **Inference** section in the notebook, you will notice that it uses the test data to predict results. It uses the predictor object from the SageMaker API to make predictions. The predictor object contains the endpoint details, model name, and instance type.

12. The API call to the endpoint occurs in the **Inference** section and is authenticated via the IAM role with which the notebook instance is created. The same API calls can be traced through CloudWatch invocation metrics.

13. Finally, running the `delete_endpoint` method in the notebook will delete the endpoint. To delete the endpoint configurations, navigate to `Inference > Endpoint Configurations` and select the configuration on the screen. Click on `Actions > Delete > Delete`.

14. Now, please feel free to shut down the kernel and stop your notebook instance from the SageMaker console. This is a best practice to reduce costs.

In this section, you learned how to use the notebook instance, training instances, inference endpoints, and endpoint configurations to clean our data, train models, and generate predicted results from them. In the next section, you will learn about model tuning.

Model tuning

In *Chapter 7, Evaluating and Optimizing Models*, you learned many important concepts about model tuning. Let's now explore this topic from a practical perspective.

In order to tune a model on SageMaker, you have to call `create_hyper_parameter_tuning_job` and pass the following main parameters:

- `HyperParameterTuningJobName`: This is the name of the tuning job. It is useful to track the training jobs that have been started on behalf of your tuning job.

- `HyperParameterTuningJobConfig`: Here, you can configure your tuning options. For example, which parameters you want to tune, the range of values for them, the type of optimization (such as random search or Bayesian search), the maximum number of training jobs you want to spin up, and more.

- `TrainingJobDefinition`: Here, you can configure your training job. For example, the data channels, the output location, the resource configurations, the evaluation metrics, and the stop conditions.

In SageMaker, the main metric that you want to use to evaluate the models to select the best one is known as an **objective metric**.

In the following example, you are configuring HyperParameterTuningJobConfig for a decision tree-based algorithm. You want to check the best configuration for a max_depth hyperparameter, which is responsible for controlling the depth of the tree.

In IntegerParameterRanges, you have to specify the following:

- The hyperparameter name

- The minimum value that you want to test

- The maximum value that you want to test

> **Important note**
>
> Each type of hyperparameter must fit in one of the parameter range sections, such as categorical, continuous, or integer parameters.

In ResourceLimits, you are specifying the number of training jobs along with the number of parallel jobs that you want to run. Remember that the goal of the tuning process is to execute many training jobs with different hyperparameter settings. This is so that the best one will be selected for the final model. That's why you have to specify these training job execution rules.

You then set up our search strategy in Strategy and, finally, set up the objective function in HyperParameterTuningJobObjective:

```
tuning_job_config = {
    "ParameterRanges": {
        "CategoricalParameterRanges": [],
        "ContinuousParameterRanges": [],
        "IntegerParameterRanges": [
            {
                "MaxValue": "10",
                "MinValue": "1",
                "Name": "max_depth"
            }
        ]
    },
    "ResourceLimits": {
        "MaxNumberOfTrainingJobs": 10,
        "MaxParallelTrainingJobs": 2
    },
    "Strategy": "Bayesian",
```

```
    "HyperParameterTuningJobObjective": {
      "MetricName": "validation:auc",
      "Type": "Maximize"
    }
  }
```

The second important configuration you need to set is `TrainingJobDefinition`. Here, you have to specify all the details regarding the training jobs that will be executed. One of the most important settings is the `TrainingImage` setting, which refers to the container that will be started to execute the training processes. This container, as expected, must have your training algorithm implemented.

Here, you present an example of a built-in algorithm, eXtreme Gradient Boosting, so that you can set the training image as follows:

```
training_image = sagemaker.image_uris.retrieve('xgboost',
region, '1.0-1')
```

Then, you can go ahead and set your training definitions:

```
training_job_definition = {
    "AlgorithmSpecification": {
      "TrainingImage": training_image,
      "TrainingInputMode": "File"
    },
```

Next, you have to specify the data input configuration, which is also known as the data channels. In the following section of code, you are setting up two data channels – train and validation:

```
    "InputDataConfig": [
      {
        "ChannelName": "train",
        "CompressionType": "None",
        "ContentType": "csv",
        "DataSource": {
          "S3DataSource": {
            "S3DataDistributionType": "FullyReplicated",
            "S3DataType": "S3Prefix",
            "S3Uri": s3_input_train
          }
        }
      },
      {
        "ChannelName": "validation",
        "CompressionType": "None",
        "ContentType": "csv",
```

```
            "DataSource": {
              "S3DataSource": {
                "S3DataDistributionType": "FullyReplicated",
                "S3DataType": "S3Prefix",
                "S3Uri": s3_input_validation
              }
            }
          }
      ],
```

You also need to specify where the results will be stored:

```
      "OutputDataConfig": {
        "S3OutputPath": "s3://{}/{}/output".format(bucket,prefix)
      },
```

Finally, you set the resource configurations, roles, static parameters, and stopping conditions. In the following section of code, you want to use two instances of type ml.c4.2xlarge with 10 GB of storage:

```
      "ResourceConfig": {
        "InstanceCount": 2,
        "InstanceType": "ml.c4.2xlarge",
        "VolumeSizeInGB": 10
      },
      "RoleArn": <<your_role_name>>,
      "StaticHyperParameters": {
        "eval_metric": "auc",
        "num_round": "100",
        "objective": "binary:logistic",
        "rate_drop": "0.3",
        "tweedie_variance_power": "1.4"
      },
      "StoppingCondition": {
        "MaxRuntimeInSeconds": 43200
      }
  }
```

> **Important note**
>
> Please note that you are using other variables in this configuration file, bucket and prefix, which should be replaced by your bucket name and prefix key (if needed), respectively. You are also referring to s3_input_train and s3_input_validation, which are two variables that point to the train and validation datasets in S3.

Once you have set your configurations, you can spin up the tuning process:

```
smclient.create_hyper_parameter_tuning_job(
    HyperParameterTuningJobName = "my-tuning-example",
    HyperParameterTuningJobConfig = tuning_job_config,
    TrainingJobDefinition = training_job_definition
)
```

Next, let's find out how to track the execution of this process.

Tracking your training jobs and selecting the best model

Once you have started the tuning process, there are two additional steps that you might want to check: tracking the process of tuning and selecting the winner model (that is, the one with the best set of hyperparameters).

In order to find your training jobs, you should go to the SageMaker console and navigate to Hyperparameter training jobs. You will then find a list of executed tuning jobs, including yours:

Figure 9.11 – Finding your tuning job

If you access your tuning job, by clicking under its name, you will find a summary page, which includes the most relevant information regarding the tuning process. On the **Training jobs** tab, you will see all the training jobs that have been executed:

Figure 9.12 – Summary of the training jobs in the tuning process

Finally, if you click on the **Best training job** tab, you will find the best set of hyperparameters for your model, including a handy button for creating a new model based on those best hyperparameters that have just been found:

Figure 9.13 – Finding the best set of hyperparameters

As you can see, SageMaker is very intuitive, and once you know the main concepts behind model optimization, playing with SageMaker should be easier. Now, you understand how to use SageMaker for our specific needs. In the next section, you will explore how to select the instance type for various use cases and the security of our notebooks.

Choosing instance types in Amazon SageMaker

SageMaker uses a pay-for-usage model. There is no minimum fee for it.

When you think about instances on SageMaker, it all starts with an EC2 instance. This instance is responsible for all your processing. It's a managed EC2 instance. These instances won't show up in the EC2 console and cannot be SSHed either. The names of this instance type start with ml.

SageMaker offers instances of the following families:

- The **t** family: This is the burstable CPU family. With this family, you get a balanced ratio of CPU and memory. This means that if you have a long-running training job, then you lose performance over time as you spend the CPU credits. If you have very small jobs, then they are cost-effective. For example, if you want a notebook instance to launch training jobs, then this family is the most appropriate and cost-effective.

- The **m** family: In the previous family, you saw that CPU credits are consumed faster due to their burstable nature. If you have a long-running ML job that requires constant throughput, then this is the right family. It comes with a similar CPU and memory ratio as the **t** family.

- The **r** family: This is a memory-optimized family. *When do you need this?* Well, imagine a use case where you have to load the data in memory and do some data engineering on the data. In this scenario, you will require more memory and your job will be memory-optimized.

- The **c** family: c-family instances are compute-optimized. This is a requirement for jobs that need higher compute power and less memory to store the data. If you refer to the following table, c5.2x large has 8 vCPU and 16 GiB memory, which makes it compute-optimized with less memory. For example, if a use case needs to be tested on fewer records and it is compute savvy, then this instance family is the to-go option to get some sample records from a huge **DataFrame** and test your algorithm.

- The **p** family: This is a GPU family that supports accelerated computing jobs such as training and inference. Notably, **p**-family instances are ideal for handling large, distributed training jobs that result in less time required for training and are thus much more cost-effective. The p3/p3dn GPU compute instance can go up to 1 petaFLOP per second compute with up to 256 GB of GPU memory and 100 Gbps (gigabits) of networking with 8x NVIDIA v100 GPUs. They are highly optimized for training and are not fully utilized for inference.

- The **g** family: For cost-effective, small-scale training jobs, **g**-family GPU instances are ideal. G4 has the lowest cost per inference for GPU instances. It uses T4 NVIDIA GPUs. The G4 GPU compute instance goes up to 520 TeraFLOPs of compute time with 8x NVIDIA T4 GPUs. This instance family is the best for simple networks.

In the following table, you have a visual comparison between the CPU and memory ratio of 2x large instance types from each family:

t3.2x large	m5.2x large	r5.2x large	c5.2x large	p3.2x large	g4dn.2x large
8 vCPU, 32 GiB	8 vCPU, 32 GiB	8 vCPU, 64 GiB	8 vCPU, 16 GiB	8 vCPU, 61 GiB	8 vCPU, 32 GiB

Table 9.1 – A table showing the CPU and memory ratio of different instance types

> **Important note**
>
> To remember this easily, you can think of t for Tiny, m for Medium, c for Compute, and p and g for GPU. The CPU-related family instance types are t, m, r, and c. The GPU-related family instance types are p and g.

Choosing the right instance type for a training job

There is no rule of thumb to determine the instance type that you require. It changes based on the size of the data, the complexity of the network, the ML algorithm in question, and several other factors such as time and cost. Asking the right questions will allow you to save money and make your project cost-effective.

If the deciding factor is *instance size*, then classifying the problem as one for CPUs or GPUs is the right step. Once that is done, then it is good to consider whether it could be multi-GPU or multi-CPU, answering the question about distributed training. This also solves your *instance count* factor. If it's compute intensive, then it would be wise to check the memory requirements too.

The next deciding factor is the *instance family*. The right question here is, *is the chosen instance optimized for time and cost?* In the previous step, you figured out whether the problem can be solved best by either a CPU or GPU, and this narrows down the selection process. Now, let's learn about inference jobs.

Choosing the right instance type for an inference job

The majority of the cost and complexity of ML in production is inference. Usually, inference runs on a single input in real time. Inference jobs are usually less compute/memory-intensive. They have to be highly available as they run all the time and serve end-user requests or are integrated into a wider application.

You can choose any of the instance types that you learned about so far based on the given workload. Other than that, AWS has **Inf1** and **Elastic Inference** type instances for inference. Elastic inference allows you to attach a fraction of a GPU instance to any CPU instance.

Let's look at an example where an application is integrated with inference jobs. In this case, the CPU and memory requirements for the application are different from the inference jobs' CPU and memory requirements. For use cases such as this, you need to choose the right instance type and size. In such scenarios, it is good to have a separation between your application fleets and inference fleets. This might require some management. If such management is a problem for your requirement, then choose Elastic Inference, where the application and inference jobs can be colocated. This means that you can host multiple models on the same fleet, and you can load all of these different models on different accelerators in memory, and concurrent requests can be served.

It's always recommended that you run some examples in a lower environment before deciding on your instance types and family in the production environment. For Production environments, you need to manage your scalability configurations for your Amazon SageMaker hosted models. You will understand this in the next section.

Taking care of Scalability Configurations

To kickstart auto scaling for your model, you can take advantage of the SageMaker console, **AWS Command Line Interface (AWS CLI)**, or an **AWS SDK** through the **Application Auto Scaling API**. For those inclined towards the CLI or API, the process involves registering the model as a scalable target, defining the scaling policy, and then applying it. If you opt for the SageMaker console, simply navigate to **Endpoints** under **Inference** in the navigation pane, locate your model's endpoint name, and choose it along with the variant name to activate auto scaling.

Let's now dive into the intricacies of scaling policies.

Scaling Policy Overview

Auto scaling is driven by scaling policies, which determine how instances are added or removed in response to varying workloads. Two options are at your disposal: target tracking and step scaling policies.

Target Tracking Scaling Policies: Our recommendation is to leverage target tracking scaling policies. Here, you select a CloudWatch metric and set a target value. Auto scaling takes care of creating and managing CloudWatch alarms, adjusting the number of instances to maintain the metric close to the specified target value. For instance, a scaling policy targeting the InvocationsPerInstance metric with a target value of 70 ensures the metric hovers around that value.

Step Scaling Policies: Step scaling is for advanced configurations, allowing you to specify instance deployment under specific conditions. However, for simplicity and full automation, target tracking scaling is preferred. Note that step scaling is managed exclusively through the AWS CLI or Application Auto Scaling API.

Creating a target tracking scaling policy involves specifying the metric, such as the average number of invocations per instance, and the target value, for example, 70 invocations per instance per minute. You have the flexibility to create target tracking scaling policies based on predefined or custom metrics. Cooldown periods, which prevent rapid capacity fluctuations, can also be configured optionally.

Scale Based on a Schedule

Scheduled actions enable scaling activities at specific times, either as a one-time event or on a recurring schedule. These actions can work in tandem with your scaling policy, allowing dynamic decisions based on changing workloads. Scheduled scaling is managed exclusively through the AWS CLI or Application Auto Scaling API.

Minimum and Maximum Scaling Limits

Before crafting a scaling policy, it's essential to set minimum and maximum scaling limits. The minimum value, set to at least 1, represents the minimum number of instances, while the maximum value signifies the upper cap. SageMaker auto scaling adheres to these limits and automatically scales in to the minimum specified instances when traffic becomes zero.

You have three options to specify these limits:

- Use the console to update the Minimum instance count and Maximum instance count settings.

- Use the AWS CLI, including the --min-capacity and --max-capacity options with the register-scalable-target command.

- Call the RegisterScalableTarget API, specifying the MinCapacity and MaxCapacity parameters.

Cooldown Period

The cooldown period is pivotal for preventing over-scaling during scale-in or scale-out activities. It slows down subsequent scaling actions until the period expires, safeguarding against rapid capacity fluctuations. You can configure the cooldown period within your scaling policy.

If not specified, the default cooldown period is 300 seconds for both scale-in and scale-out. Adjust this value based on your model's traffic characteristics; consider increasing for frequent spikes or multiple scaling policies, and decrease if instances need to be added swiftly.

As you embark on optimizing your model's scalability, keep these configurations in mind to ensure a seamless and cost-effective experience. In the next section, you will dive into and understand the different ways of securing our Amazon SageMaker notebooks.

Securing SageMaker notebooks

If you are reading this section of the chapter, then you have already learned how to use notebook instances, which type of training instances should be chosen, and how to configure and use endpoints. Now, let's learn about securing those instances. The following aspects will help to secure the instances:

- **Encryption**: When you talk about securing something via encryption, you are talking about safeguarding data. But what does this mean? It means protecting data at rest using encryption, protecting data in transit with encryption, and using KMS for better role separation and internet traffic privacy through TLS 1.2 encryption. SageMaker instances can be launched with encrypted volumes by using an AWS-managed KMS key. This helps you to secure the Jupyter Notebook server by default.

- **Root access**: When a user opens a shell terminal from the Jupyter Web UI, they will be logged in as ec2-user, which is the default username in Amazon Linux. Now the user can run sudo to the root user. With root access, users can access and edit files. In many use cases, an administrator might not want data scientists to manage, control, or modify the system of the notebook server. This requires restrictions to be placed on the root access. This can be done by setting the `RootAccess` field to `Disabled` when you call `CreateNotebookInstance` or `UpdateNotebookInstance`. The data scientist will have access to their user space and can install Python packages. However, they cannot sudo into the root user and make changes to the operating system.

- **IAM role**: During the launch of a notebook instance, it is necessary to create an IAM role for execution or to use an existing role for execution. This is used to launch the service-managed EC2 instance with an instance profile associated with the role. This role will restrict the API calls based on the policies attached to this role.

- **VPC connection**: When you launch a SageMaker notebook instance, by default, it gets created within the SageMaker service account, which has a service-managed VPC, and it will, by default, have access to the internet via an internet gateway, and that gateway is managed by the service. If you are only dealing with AWS-related services, then it is recommended that you launch a SageMaker notebook instance in your VPC within a private subnet and with a well-customized security group. The AWS services can be invoked or used from this notebook instance via VPC endpoints attached to that VPC. The best practice is to control them via endpoint policies for better API controls. This enforces the restriction on data egress outside your VPC and secured environment. In order to capture all network traffic, you can turn on the VPC flow logs, which can be monitored and tracked via CloudWatch.

- **Internet access**: You can launch a Jupyter Notebook server without direct internet access. It can be launched in a private subnet with a NAT or to access the internet through a virtual private gateway. To train and deploy inference containers, you can set the `EnableNetworkIsolation` parameter to `True` when you call `CreateTrainingJob`, `CreateHyperParameterTuningJob`, or `CreateModel`. Network isolation can be used along with the VPC, which ensures that containers cannot make any outbound network calls.

- **Connecting a private network to your VPC**: You can launch your SageMaker notebook instance inside the private subnet of your VPC. This can access data from your private network by communicating with the private network, which can be done by connecting your private network to your VPC by using Amazon VPN or AWS Direct Connect.

In this section, you learned several ways in which you can secure our SageMaker notebooks. In the next section, you will learn about SageMaker Debugger.

SageMaker Debugger

In this section, you will learn about Amazon SageMaker Debugger, unraveling the intricacies of monitoring, profiling, and debugging ML model training:

- **Monitoring and profiling**: SageMaker Debugger captures model metrics and keeps a real-time eye on system resources during training, eliminating the need for additional code. It not only provides a window into the training process but empowers instant issue correction, expediting training and elevating model quality.

- **Automatic detection and analysis**: A true time-saver, Debugger automatically spots and notifies you of common training errors, such as oversized or undersized gradient values. Say goodbye to days of troubleshooting; Debugger reduces it to mere hours.

- **Profiling capabilities**: Venture into the realm of profiling with Debugger, which meticulously monitors system resource utilization metrics and allows you to profile training jobs. This involves collecting detailed metrics from your ML framework, identifying anomalies in resource usage, and swiftly pinpointing bottlenecks.

- **Built-in analysis and actions**: Debugger introduces built-in analysis rules that tirelessly examine the training data emitted, encompassing input, output, and transformations (tensors). But that's not all—users have the freedom to craft custom rules, analyze specific conditions, and even dictate actions triggered by rule events, such as stopping training or sending notifications.

- **Integration with SageMaker Studio**: It is possible to visualize Debugger results seamlessly within SageMaker Studio, treating yourself to charts depicting CPU utilization, GPU activity, network usage, and more. There is also a heat map, offering a visual timeline of system resource utilization.

- **Profiler output**: Peek into profiling results, an exhaustive dossier on system resource usage covering GPU, CPU, network, memory, and I/O. It's your one-stop shop for understanding the inner workings of your training job.

- **Debugger insights and optimization**: Beyond detection, Debugger evolves into an advisor, identifying issues in your training jobs, providing insights, and suggesting optimizations. Whether it's tweaking the batch size or altering the distributed training strategy, Debugger guides you towards optimal performance.

- **CloudWatch integration**: Stay in the loop with Debugger's integration with CloudWatch. Configure alerts for specific conditions and ensure you are always ahead of potential hiccups.

- **Downloadable reports**: Don't miss a beat—download HTML reports summarizing Debugger's insights and profiling results for thorough offline analysis.

In a nutshell, Amazon SageMaker Debugger emerges as a holistic toolkit, empowering you to monitor, profile, and debug your ML models with finesse. It's not just a tool; it's your ally in the journey to model optimization. In the next section, you will understand the usage of SageMaker AutoPilot/AutoML.

SageMaker Autopilot

ML model development has historically been a daunting task, demanding considerable expertise and time. Amazon SageMaker Autopilot emerges as a game-changer, simplifying this intricate process and transforming it into a streamlined experience.

Amazon SageMaker Autopilot presents a rich array of features to facilitate the development of ML models:

- **Automatic model building**: SageMaker Autopilot removes the complexities of constructing ML models by taking charge and automating the entire process with a simple mandate from the user: provide a tabular dataset and designate the target column for prediction.

- **Data processing and enhancement**: Autopilot seamlessly handles data preprocessing tasks, filling in missing data, offering statistical insights into dataset columns, and extracting valuable information from non-numeric columns. This guarantees that input data is finely tuned for model training.

- **Problem type detection**: Autopilot showcases intelligence by automatically detecting the problem type—whether it's classification or regression—based on the characteristics of the provided data.

- **Algorithm exploration and optimization**: Users can explore a myriad of high-performing algorithms, with Autopilot efficiently training and optimizing hundreds of models to pinpoint the one that aligns best with the user's requirements. The entire process is automated, lifting the burden off the user.

- **Real-world examples**: Picture a retail company aiming to predict customer purchasing behavior. With SageMaker Autopilot, the company inputs historical purchase data, designates the target variable (e.g., whether a customer makes a purchase or not), and Autopilot takes the reins, autonomously exploring and optimizing various ML models. This facilitates deploying a predictive model without the need for profound ML expertise. In another scenario, a financial institution assessing credit risk can leverage SageMaker Autopilot. By providing a dataset with customer information and credit history, and specifying the target variable (creditworthiness), the institution can harness Autopilot to automatically build, train, and optimize models for precise credit risk prediction.

- **Model understanding and deployment**: SageMaker Autopilot not only automates model creation but places a premium on interpretability. Users gain insights into how the generated models make predictions. The Amazon SageMaker Studio Notebook serves as a platform for accessing, refining, and recreating models, ensuring continuous model enhancement.

Amazon SageMaker Autopilot heralds a shift in the landscape of ML, making it accessible to a wider audience. By automating the heavy lifting of model development, Autopilot empowers users to focus on the strategic aspects of their business problems, liberating them from the intricacies of ML. As organizations embrace ML for decision-making, SageMaker Autopilot emerges as a revolutionary tool, unlocking the power of AI without the need for extensive data science expertise. In the next section, you will dive deeper into model monitoring.

SageMaker Model Monitor

In the ever-evolving realm of ML, ensuring the reliability and robustness of models in real-world production settings is paramount. In this section, you will delve into the profound significance, practical applications, and potent features of Amazon SageMaker Model Monitor—an instrumental component tailored to tackle the challenge of model drift in live production environments:

- **The essence of model monitoring**: As ML models venture into real-world deployment, the ongoing degradation of their effectiveness—attributed to shifts in data distributions or alterations in user behavior—poses a substantial threat known as model drift. Continuous monitoring becomes the linchpin for proactively identifying and rectifying these deviations, safeguarding the accuracy and reliability of ML predictions and, consequently, business outcomes.

- **An automated guardian**: Amazon SageMaker Model Monitor emerges as a guiding light in the ML landscape, delivering an automated solution for the continual vigilance of ML models in production. From detecting data drift to ensuring model quality, it presents a comprehensive suite to meet the challenges posed by the ever-evolving nature of real-world data.

- **Automated analysis**: Model Monitor takes the reins of model analysis, automating the inspection of deployed models based on predefined or user-provided rules at regular intervals. This relieves users from the burden of constructing custom tooling.

- **Statistical rules**: With built-in statistical rules, Model Monitor spans a spectrum of potential issues, covering outliers, completeness, and drift in data distributions. These rules empower the system to pinpoint anomalies and deviations from the anticipated model behavior.

- **CloudWatch integration**: Seamlessly integrating with Amazon CloudWatch, Model Monitor emits metrics when rule violations occur. Users can set up alarms based on these metrics, ensuring prompt notification and allowing timely intervention.

- **Data drift monitoring**: Excelling in identifying changes in data distributions, Model Monitor provides insights into how input data evolves over time. Whether it's a shift in units or a sudden influx of null values, Model Monitor remains vigilant.

- **Model quality monitoring**: Beyond data drift, the system monitors the performance of the model itself. Degradation in model accuracy triggers alerts, notifying users of potential issues that might impact the model's predictive capabilities.

Amazon SageMaker Model Monitor orchestrates a seamless end-to-end flow for deploying and monitoring models. From model deployment and data capture to baselining and continuous monitoring, the process ensures a comprehensive approach to maintaining model stability over time.

In the expansive landscape of ML, Amazon SageMaker Model Monitor stands as a guiding force, addressing the critical need for the continuous monitoring of models in production. Its automated analysis, integration with CloudWatch, and focus on both data and model quality drift make it an indispensable tool for organizations relying on ML for pivotal decision-making. As businesses increasingly depend on the stability and accuracy of ML models, SageMaker Model Monitor stands tall, offering a robust solution to the ever-evolving challenges of the ML landscape. In the next section, you will learn about making our SageMaker training process faster with Training Compiler.

SageMaker Training Compiler

If you've reached this section, you are about to delve into the world of **SageMaker Training Compiler (SMTC)**, a game-changing tool designed to supercharge the training of your ML models on SageMaker by optimizing intricate training scripts. Picture this: faster training, swifter model development, and an open door to experimentation. That's the primary goal of SMTC—improving training speed to bring agility to your model development journey. The following are the major advantages of using SMTC:

- **Scaling challenges**: Embarking on the journey of training large-scale models, especially those with billions of parameters, often feels like navigating uncharted engineering territory. SMTC, however, rises to the occasion by optimizing the entire training process, conquering the challenges that come with scaling.

- **Efficiency at its core**: SMTC takes the reins of GPU memory usage, ushering in a realm where larger batch sizes become not just a possibility but a reality. This optimization translates into accelerated training times, a boon for any data scientist seeking efficiency gains.

- **Cost savings**: Time is money, and in the realm of ML, it's no different. By accelerating training jobs, SMTC isn't just speeding up your models; it's potentially reducing your costs. How? Well, you pay based on training time, and faster training means less time on the clock.

- **Throughput improvement**: The tool has demonstrated throughput improvements, leading to faster training without sacrificing model accuracy.

A couple of examples of efficiency, cost savings, autoscaling through SMTC in the scenarios/use cases of LLMs, and batch size optimization for NLP problems are as follows:

- **Large Language Models (LLMs)**: SMTC is particularly beneficial for training LLMs, including BERT, DistilBERT, RoBERTa, and GPT-2. These models involve massive parameter sizes, making the scaling of training a non-trivial task.

- **Batch size optimization**: SMTC allows users to experiment with larger batch sizes, which is especially useful for tasks where efficiency gains can be achieved, such as in **Natural Language Processing (NLP)** or computer vision.

SageMaker Training Compiler is not just a black box; it's a meticulous craftsman at work. It takes your deep learning models from their high-level language representation and transforms them into hardware-optimized instructions. This involves graph-level optimizations, dataflow-level optimizations, and backend optimizations, culminating in an optimized model that dances gracefully with hardware resources. The result? Faster training, thanks to the magic of compilation. In the next section, you will learn about Amazon SageMaker Data Wrangler—an integral component within SageMaker Studio Classic.

SageMaker Data Wrangler

In this section, you'll unravel the significance and benefits of Data Wrangler, dissecting its role as an end-to-end solution for importing, preparing, transforming, featurizing, and analyzing data:

- **Importing data with ease**: Data Wrangler simplifies the process of importing data from various sources, such as Amazon **Simple Storage Service (S3)**, Amazon Athena, Amazon Redshift, Snowflake, and Databricks. Whether your data resides in the cloud or within specific databases, Data Wrangler seamlessly connects to the source and imports it, setting the stage for comprehensive data handling.

- **Constructing data flows**: Picture a scenario where you can effortlessly design a data flow, mapping out a sequence of ML data preparation steps. This is where Data Wrangler shines. By combining datasets from diverse sources and specifying the transformations needed, you sculpt a data prep workflow ready to integrate into your ML pipeline.

- **Transforming data with precision**: Cleanse and transform your dataset with finesse using Data Wrangler. Standard transforms, such as those for string, vector, and numeric data formatting, are at your disposal. Dive deeper into feature engineering with specialized transforms like text and date/time embedding, along with categorical encoding.

- **Gaining insights and ensuring data quality**: Data integrity is paramount, and Data Wrangler acknowledges this with its **Data Insights and Quality Report** feature. This allows you to automatically verify data quality, identify abnormalities, and ensure your dataset meets the highest standards before it becomes the backbone of your ML endeavors.

- **In-depth analysis made simple**: Delve into the intricacies of your dataset at any juncture with Data Wrangler's built-in visualization tools. From scatter plots to histograms, you can analyze features with ease. Data analysis tools like target leakage analysis and quick modeling can also be leveraged to comprehend feature correlation and make informed decisions.

- **Seamless export for further experiments**: Data preparation doesn't end with Data Wrangler—it extends to the next phases of your workflow. Export your meticulously crafted data prep workflow to various destinations. Whether it's an Amazon S3 bucket, SageMaker Model Building Pipelines for automated deployment, the SageMaker Feature Store for centralized storage, or a custom Python script for tailored workflows—Data Wrangler ensures your data is where you need it.

Amazon SageMaker Data Wrangler isn't just a tool; it's a powerhouse for simplifying and enhancing your data handling processes. The ability to seamlessly integrate with your ML workflows, the precision in transforming data, and the flexibility in exporting for further utilization make Data Wrangler a cornerstone of the SageMaker ecosystem. In the next section, you will learn about SageMaker Feature Store – an organized repository for storing, retrieving, and seamlessly sharing ML features.

SageMaker Feature Store

Imagine you are building a recommendation system. In the absence of Feature Store, you'd navigate a landscape of manual feature engineering, scattered feature storage, and constant vigilance for consistency.

Feature management in an ML pipeline is challenging due to the dispersed nature of feature engineering, involving various teams and tools. Collaboration issues arise when different teams handle different aspects of feature storage, leading to inconsistencies and versioning problems. The dynamic nature of features evolving over time complicates change tracking and ensuring reproducibility. SageMaker Feature Store addresses these challenges by providing a centralized repository for features, enabling seamless sharing, versioning, and consistent access across the ML pipeline, thus simplifying collaboration, enhancing reproducibility, and promoting data consistency.

Now, user data, including age, location, browsing history, and item data such as category and price, have a unified home with Feature Store. Training and inference become a joyride, with easy access and sharing of these features, promoting efficiency and unwavering consistency.

To navigate the terrain of SageMaker Feature Store, let's familiarize ourselves with some key terms:

- **Feature store**: At its core, a feature store is the storage and data management layer for ML features. It stands as the single source of truth, handling storage, retrieval, removal, tracking, sharing, discovery, and access control for features.

- **Online store**: This is the realm of low latency and high availability, allowing real-time lookup of records. The online store ensures quick access to the latest record via the GetRecord API.

- **Offline store**: When sub-second latency reads are not a priority, the offline store stores historical data in your Amazon S3 bucket. It's your go-to for storing and serving features for exploration, model training, and batch inference.

- **Feature group**: The cornerstone of Feature Store, a feature group contains the data and metadata crucial for ML model training or prediction. It logically groups features used to describe records.

- **Feature**: A property serving as an input for ML model training or prediction. In the Feature Store API, a feature is an attribute of a record.

- **Feature definition**: Comprising a name and data type (integral, string, or fractional), a feature definition is an integral part of a feature group.

- **Record**: A collection of values for features tied to a single record identifier. The record identifier and event time values uniquely identify a record within a feature group.

- **Record identifier name**: Each record within a feature group is defined and identified with a record identifier name. It must refer to one of the names of a feature defined in the feature group's feature definitions.

- **Event time**: The time when record events occur is marked with timestamps, which are vital for differentiating records. The online store contains the record corresponding to the latest event time, while the offline store contains all historic records.

- **Ingestion**: The process of adding new records to a feature group, usually achieved through the PutRecord API.

Let's combine the tools covered in this chapter so far to navigate through an example of fraud detection in financial transactions. *Table 9.2* shows a synthetic dataset for financial transactions:

TransactionID	Amount	Merchant	CardType	IsFraud
1	500.25	Amazon	Visa	0
2	120.50	Walmart	Mastercard	1
3	89.99	Apple	Amex	0
4	300.75	Amazon	Visa	0
5	45.00	Netflix	Mastercard	1

Table 9.2 – Example dataset for financial transactions

You will now see the applications of SageMaker Feature Store, SageMaker Training Compiler, SageMaker Debugger, and SageMaker Model Monitor on the above dataset.

1. **Feature engineering with SageMaker Feature Store**: You can store transaction (financial transactions, in this example) features intelligently and it ensures consistency across the training and inference stages. Versioning comes into play, offering a timeline of your features' evolution.

   - Define the features: `Amount`, `Merchant`, `CardType`

   - Ingest data into Feature Store: Use the SageMaker Feature Store API to ingest the dataset into Feature Store:

   ```
   # Example code for ingesting data into Feature Store
   from sagemaker.feature_store.feature_group import
   FeatureGroup
   feature_group_name = "financial-transaction-feature-
   group"
   feature_group = FeatureGroup(name=feature_group_name,
   sagemaker_session=sagemaker_session)
   feature_group.load_feature_definitions(data_frame=df)
   feature_group.create()
   feature_group.ingest(data_frame=df, max_workers=3,
   wait=True)
   ```

2. **Optimize training with SageMaker Training Compiler**: You can utilize SageMaker Training Compiler to optimize and compile training scripts:

   ```
   # Example code for defining a training job with SageMaker
   Training Compiler
   from sagemaker.compiler import compile_model

   compiled_model = compile_model(
       target_instance_family='ml.m5.large',
       target_platform_os='LINUX',
       sources=['train.py'],
       dependencies=['requirements.txt'],
       framework='pytorch',
       framework_version='1.8.0',
       role='arn:aws:iam::123456789012:role/service-role/
   AmazonSageMaker-ExecutionRole-20201231T000001',
       entry_point='train.py',
       instance_type='ml.m5.large',
   )
   ```

3. **Precision debugging with SageMaker Debugger**: You can integrate SageMaker Debugger hooks into your training script for real-time monitoring to identify training issues in real time, such as vanishing gradients or model overfitting:

```
# Example code for integrating SageMaker Debugger in the
training script
from smdebug import SaveConfig
from smdebug.pytorch import Hook
# Create an instance of your model
model = FraudDetectionModel(input_size, hidden_size,
output_size)
hook = Hook.create_from_json_file()
hook.register_hook(model)
# Your training script here...
# Train the model train_model(model, train_loader,
criterion, optimizer, num_epochs=5)
```

4. **Model deployment and inference**: You can deploy your trained model with SageMaker, tapping into the rich repository of features stored in the Feature Store. Real-time monitoring with SageMaker Model Monitor ensures the model's health in the dynamic world of inference.

5. **Continuous monitoring with SageMaker Model Monitor**: The story doesn't end with deployment. SageMaker Model Monitor becomes your sentinel, continuously guarding the deployed model. Detecting concept drift and data quality nuances, it ensures your model remains a reliable guide in the real-world production environment. Use SageMaker Model Monitor to capture baseline statistics for your deployed model:

```
# Example code for capturing baseline statistics with
SageMaker Model Monitor
from sagemaker.model_monitor import DefaultModelMonitor
from sagemaker.model_monitor.dataset_format import
DatasetFormat

monitor = DefaultModelMonitor(
    role=role,
    instance_count=1,
    instance_type='ml.m5.large',
    volume_size_in_gb=20,
    max_runtime_in_seconds=3600,
)

baseline_data_uri = 's3://path/to/baseline_data'
```

```
monitor.suggest_baseline(
    baseline_dataset=baseline_data_uri,
    dataset_format=DatasetFormat.csv(header=True),
    output_s3_uri='s3://path/to/baseline_output',
)
```

In the next section, you will learn about Amazon SageMaker Edge Manager, a service provided by AWS to facilitate the deployment and management of ML models on edge devices.

SageMaker Edge Manager

SageMaker Edge Manager is designed to address the challenges faced by ML developers when operating models on fleets of edge devices. Some of the key functions that SageMaker Edge Manager can perform are highlighted as follows:

- **Model compilation**: Utilizes Amazon SageMaker Neo to compile models for various target devices and operating environments, including Linux, Windows, Android, iOS, and macOS.

- **Model deployment**: Signs each model with an AWS key, packages it with its runtime, and includes all necessary credentials for deployment on specific devices.

- **Model server concept**: Introduces a model server concept to efficiently run multiple models on edge devices, optimizing hardware resource utilization.

- **Continuous monitoring**: Provides tools for continuous monitoring of model health, allowing developers to collect metrics, sample input/output data, and send this data securely to the cloud.

- **Model drift detection**: Allows the detection of model quality decay over time due to real-world data drift, enabling developers to take corrective action.

- **Integration with SageMaker Ground Truth**: Integrates with SageMaker Ground Truth for data labeling and retraining, ensuring that models stay accurate and effective.

Now let's understand a few real-world challenges and their solutions using SageMaker Edge Manager:

- **High resource requirements:**

  - **Challenge**: ML models, especially deep learning models, can have high resource requirements.

  - **Solution**: SageMaker Edge Manager uses SageMaker Neo to compile models, making them more efficient and allowing them to run up to 25 times faster on certain target hardware.

- **Running multiple models:**

  - **Challenge**: Many ML applications require running multiple models simultaneously.

  - **Solution**: Introduces a model server concept, enabling the efficient execution of multiple models in series or in parallel on edge devices.

- **Model quality decay in production:**

  - **Challenge**: Real-world data drifts over time, causing model quality decay.

  - **Solution**: SageMaker Edge Manager supports continuous monitoring, allowing developers to detect and address model quality decay using metrics and drift detection tools.

The following are some examples showcasing different applications of SageMaker Edge Manager:

- **Real-time predictions in autonomous vehicles**: Edge devices in autonomous vehicles need to provide real-time predictions for navigation and obstacle avoidance. SageMaker Edge Manager optimizes models for these devices, ensuring low-latency predictions.

- **Privacy-preserving personal devices**: Personal devices such as smartphones and smart cameras can keep data on the device using SageMaker Edge Manager, preserving user privacy and reducing the need for extensive data transfer to the cloud.

- **Continuous monitoring in Industrial IoT**: Industrial IoT deployments with sensors on machines can benefit from the continuous monitoring provided by SageMaker Edge Manager. This helps identify and address model quality decay in a dynamic environment.

In summary, Amazon SageMaker Edge Manager streamlines the deployment and management of ML models on edge devices, addressing resource constraints, enabling efficient model execution, and ensuring continuous monitoring for sustained model accuracy. In the next section, you will learn about a no-code solution offered by Amazon SageMaker.

SageMaker Canvas

In this section, you will learn the core of SageMaker Canvas, elucidating its features and the significance it holds for organizations keen on infusing ML into their decision-making processes.

Amazon SageMaker Canvas is a cloud-based service offered by AWS that streamlines the ML process through a visual interface for constructing, training, and deploying ML models—all without the need for coding. Nestled within the Amazon SageMaker suite, it caters to a diverse audience by democratizing ML:

- **Code-free model building**: SageMaker Canvas obliterates the traditional barriers encountered when adopting ML, enabling users to forge models without the need for code. This feature proves pivotal for business professionals seeking to harness the potency of ML for predictive analytics, despite lacking coding expertise.

Case study: A marketing professional without any ML knowledge can utilize SageMaker Canvas to predict customer churn. The intuitive interface guides them through the process, making predictive analytics accessible to a wider audience.

- **Versatile user interface**: The user-friendly interface of SageMaker Canvas accommodates users with varying levels of expertise. It empowers users to create predictions across diverse use cases, from inventory planning to sentiment analysis, rendering it a versatile tool for businesses spanning different industries.

Case study: A supply chain manager can leverage SageMaker Canvas to predict optimal inventory levels based on historical data, seasonality, and market trends, streamlining the planning process and minimizing stockouts.

- **Built-in data preparation functions**: SageMaker Canvas comes equipped with built-in data preparation functions and operators, facilitating the import and analysis of disparate cloud and on-premises data sources. This feature streamlines the exploration and visualization of relationships between features, enabling the seamless creation of new features.

Case study: A data analyst can import and analyze customer data from various sources using SageMaker Canvas. This allows them to identify key factors influencing purchasing decisions and create predictive models to enhance targeted marketing strategies.

- **Collaboration and model sharing**: SageMaker Canvas fosters collaboration by enabling users to share, review, and update ML models across different tools and teams. This collaborative aspect ensures that knowledge and insights derived from ML are disseminated effectively within the organization.

Case study: A data science team collaborates with business analysts using SageMaker Canvas to develop a fraud detection model. The model can be shared seamlessly, allowing real-time updates and improvements based on evolving data patterns.

Amazon SageMaker Canvas acts as a catalyst for transforming ML from a specialized skill to a tool accessible to a broader audience. Its features, including code-free model building, a versatile user interface, and collaborative capabilities, underscore its importance in simplifying the ML lifecycle. As organizations strive to harness the power of data-driven insights, SageMaker Canvas stands at the forefront, enabling them to innovate, make informed decisions, and thrive in an increasingly competitive landscape.

You have now reached the end of this section and the end of this chapter. Next, let's summarize what you have learned.

Summary

In this chapter, you learned about the usage of SageMaker for creating notebook instances and training instances. As you went through, you learned how to use SageMaker for hyperparameter tuning jobs. As the security of your assets in AWS is an essential part of your work, you also learned the various ways to secure SageMaker instances.

AWS products are evolving every day to help you solve IT problems. It's not easy to remember all the product names. The only way to learn is through practice. When you are solving a problem or building a product, focus on different technological areas of your product. Those areas can be scheduling jobs, logging, tracing, monitoring metrics, autoscaling, and more.

Compute time, storage, and networking are the baselines. It is recommended that you practice some examples for each of these services. Referring to the AWS documentation to resolve any doubts is also a useful option. It is always important to design your solutions in a cost-effective way and exploring cost optimizations when using these services is as important as building the solution itself. I wish you all the best!

Exam Readiness Drill – Chapter Review Questions

Apart from a solid understanding of key concepts, being able to think quickly under time pressure is a skill that will help you ace your certification exam. That is why working on these skills early on in your learning journey is key.

Chapter review questions are designed to improve your test-taking skills progressively with each chapter you learn and review your understanding of key concepts in the chapter at the same time. You'll find these at the end of each chapter.

> **How To Access These Resources**
>
> To learn how to access these resources, head over to the chapter titled *Chapter 11, Accessing the Online Practice Resources*.

To open the Chapter Review Questions for this chapter, perform the following steps:

1. Click the link – https://packt.link/MLSC01E2_CH09.

   Alternatively, you can scan the following **QR code** (*Figure 9.14*):

Figure 9.14 – QR code that opens Chapter Review Questions for logged-in users

2. Once you log in, you'll see a page similar to the one shown in *Figure 9.15*:

Figure 9.15 – Chapter Review Questions for Chapter 9

3. Once ready, start the following practice drills, re-attempting the quiz multiple times.

Exam Readiness Drill

For the first three attempts, don't worry about the time limit.

ATTEMPT 1

The first time, aim for at least **40%**. Look at the answers you got wrong and read the relevant sections in the chapter again to fix your learning gaps.

ATTEMPT 2

The second time, aim for at least **60%**. Look at the answers you got wrong and read the relevant sections in the chapter again to fix any remaining learning gaps.

ATTEMPT 3

The third time, aim for at least **75%**. Once you score 75% or more, you start working on your timing.

Tip

You may take more than **three** attempts to reach 75%. That's okay. Just review the relevant sections in the chapter till you get there.

Working On Timing

Target: Your aim is to keep the score the same while trying to answer these questions as quickly as possible. Here's an example of how your next attempts should look like:

Attempt	Score	Time Taken
Attempt 5	77%	21 mins 30 seconds
Attempt 6	78%	18 mins 34 seconds
Attempt 7	76%	14 mins 44 seconds

Table 9.3 – Sample timing practice drills on the online platform

---

Note

The time limits shown in the above table are just examples. Set your own time limits with each attempt based on the time limit of the quiz on the website.

With each new attempt, your score should stay above **75%** while your "time taken" to complete should "decrease". Repeat as many attempts as you want till you feel confident dealing with the time pressure.

10

Model Deployment

In the previous chapter, you explored various aspects of Amazon SageMaker, including different instances, data preparation in Jupyter Notebook, model training with built-in algorithms, and crafting custom code for training and inference. Now, your focus shifts to diverse model deployment choices using AWS services.

If you are navigating the landscape of model deployment on AWS, understanding the options is crucial. One standout service is Amazon SageMaker – a fully managed solution that streamlines the entire **machine learning** (**ML**) life cycle, especially when it comes to deploying models. There are several factors that influence the model deployment options. As you go ahead in this chapter you will learn different options to deploy models using SageMaker.

Factors influencing model deployment options

Here are the primary factors that play a crucial role in determining a model deployment option:

- **Scalability requirements**

  - **High traffic:** Imagine you are developing a recommendation system for a popular e-commerce platform expecting fluctuating traffic throughout the day. If the application anticipates high traffic and varying loads, services such as Amazon SageMaker with autoscaling capabilities or AWS Lambda may be preferable. This is crucial to maintain performance during peak hours.

- **Real-time versus batch inference**

  - **Real-time inference**: Consider a fraud detection system for a financial institution where immediate decisions are essential for transaction approval or denial. For such real-time predictions, services such as Amazon SageMaker and AWS Lambda are suitable. For fraud detection, these services provide low-latency responses, enabling quick decisions on the legitimacy of transactions. Real-time transactions trigger immediate predictions through SageMaker's inference endpoints in this case.

- **Batch inference:** In a healthcare setting, you may need to process a large volume of patient data periodically to update predictive models for disease diagnosis. This is a batch processing use case, and a combination of SageMaker and services such as Amazon S3 can be employed. You can efficiently handle large datasets, perform periodic model updates, and ensure that predictions align with the latest information, which is crucial for maintaining accuracy in healthcare predictions.

- **Infrastructure management complexity**

  - **Managed deployment versus custom deployment:** Suppose you are developing a computer vision application for analyzing satellite images, requiring specialized configurations and dependencies. In cases where custom configurations are necessary, opting for custom deployments using EC2 instances allows more control over the infrastructure. SageMaker's managed services are ideal for scenarios where you prioritize ease of management and do not want to delve into intricate infrastructure details.

- **Cost considerations**

  - **Pay-per-use:** Consider a weather forecasting application where the computational demand varies based on weather events. AWS Lambda's pay-per-use model is advantageous in situations where the workload fluctuates. You pay only for the compute time consumed, making it cost-effective for applications with sporadic, unpredictable usage patterns compared to alternatives with fixed costs.

SageMaker deployment options

Amazon SageMaker offers diverse deployment options to deploy ML models effectively. In this section, you will explore different ways of deploying models using SageMaker, providing technology solutions with scenarios and examples.

Real-time endpoint deployment

In this **scenario**, you have a trained image classification model, and you want to deploy it to provide real-time predictions for incoming images.

Solution

Create a SageMaker model and deploy it to a real-time endpoint.

Steps

1. Train your model using SageMaker training jobs.
2. Create a SageMaker model from the trained model artifacts.
3. Deploy the model to a real-time endpoint.

Example code snippet

```
from sagemaker import get_execution_role
from sagemaker.model import Model
from sagemaker.predictor import RealTimePredictor
role = get_execution_role()
model_artifact='s3://your-s3-bucket/path/to/model.tar.gz'
model = Model(model_data=model_artifact, role=role)
predictor = model.deploy(instance_type='ml.m4.xlarge',
endpoint_name='image-classification-endpoint')
```

Batch transform job

In this **scenario**, you have a large dataset, and you want to perform batch inference on the entire dataset using a trained model.

Solution

Use SageMaker batch transform to process the entire dataset in a batch.

Steps

1. Create a SageMaker transformer.

2. Start the batch transform job.

Example code snippet

```
from sagemaker.transformer import Transformer

transformer = Transformer(model_name='your-model-name',
                          instance_count=1,
                          instance_type='ml.m4.xlarge',
                          strategy='SingleRecord',
                          assemble_with='Line',
                          output_path='s3://your-s3-bucket/
output')

transformer.transform('s3://your-s3-bucket/input/data.csv',
content_type='text/csv')
transformer.wait()
```

Multi-model endpoint deployment

In this **scenario**, you have multiple versions of a model, and you want to deploy them on a single endpoint for A/B testing or gradual rollout.

Solution

Use SageMaker multi-model endpoints to deploy and manage multiple models on a single endpoint.

Steps

1. Create and train multiple models.

2. Create a SageMaker multi-model.

3. Deploy the multi-model to an endpoint.

Example code snippet

```
from sagemaker.multimodel import MultiModel
multi_model = MultiModel(model_data_prefix='s3://your-s3-
bucket/multi-models')
predictor = multi_model.deploy(instance_type='ml.m4.xlarge',
endpoint_name='multi-model-endpoint')
```

Endpoint autoscaling

In this **scenario**, your application experiences varying workloads, and you want to automatically adjust the number of instances based on traffic.

Solution

Enable auto-scaling for SageMaker endpoints.

Steps

1. Configure the SageMaker endpoint to use autoscaling.

2. Set up the minimum and maximum instance counts based on the expected workload.

Example code snippet

```
from sagemaker.predictor import Predictor
predictor = Predictor(endpoint_name='your-endpoint-name',
sagemaker_session=sagemaker_session)
predictor.predict('input_data')
```

Serverless APIs with AWS Lambda and SageMaker

In this **scenario**, you want to create a serverless API using AWS Lambda to interact with your SageMaker model.

Solution

Use AWS Lambda to invoke the SageMaker endpoint.

Steps

1. Create an AWS Lambda function.

2. Integrate the Lambda function with the SageMaker endpoint.

Example code snippet

```
import boto3
import json

def lambda_handler(event, context):
    # Perform preprocessing on input data
    input_data = event['input_data']
    # Call SageMaker endpoint
    # ...

    return {
        'statusCode': 200,
        'body': json.dumps('Inference successful!')
    }
```

In the realm of deploying ML models, Amazon SageMaker emerges as a robust choice. Its managed environment, scalability features, and seamless integration with other AWS services make it an efficient and reliable solution for businesses navigating diverse deployment scenarios. Whether you are anticipating high traffic or need a hassle-free deployment experience, SageMaker is your ally in the journey of model deployment excellence. In the next section, you will learn about creating pipelines with Lambda functions.

Creating alternative pipelines with Lambda Functions

Indeed, SageMaker is an awesome platform that you can use to create training and inference pipelines. However, you can always work with different services to come up with similar solutions. One of these services, which you will learn about next, is known as **Lambda functions**.

AWS Lambda is a serverless compute service where you can run a function as a service. In other words, you can concentrate your efforts on just writing your function. Then, you just need to tell AWS how to run it (that is, the environment and resource configurations), so all the necessary resources will be provisioned to run your code and then discontinued once it is completed.

Throughout *Chapter 3, AWS Services for Data Migration and Processing*, you explored how Lambda functions integrate with many different services, such as Kinesis and AWS Batch. Indeed, AWS did a very good job of integrating Lambda with 140+ services (and the list is constantly increasing). That means that when you work with a specific AWS service, you will remember that it is likely to integrate with Lambda.

It is important to bear this in mind because Lambda functions can really expand your possibilities to create scalable and integrated architectures. For example, you can trigger a Lambda function when a file is uploaded to S3 in order to preprocess your data before loading it to Redshift. Alternatively, you can create an API that triggers a Lambda function at each endpoint execution. Again, the possibilities are endless with this powerful service.

It is also useful to know that you can write your function in different programming languages, such as Node.js, Python, Go, Java, and more. Your function does not necessarily have to be triggered by another AWS service – that is, you can trigger it manually for your web or mobile application, for example.

When it comes to deployment, you can upload your function as a ZIP file or as a container image. Although this is not ideal for an automated deployment process, coding directly into the AWS Lambda console is also possible.

As with any other service, this one also has some downsides that you should be aware of:

- **Memory allocation for your function**: This ranges from 128 MB to 10,240 MB (AWS has recently increased this limit from 3 GB to 10 GB, as stated previously)

- **Function timeout**: This is a maximum of 900 seconds (15 minutes)

- **Function layer**: This is a maximum of five layers

- **Burst concurrency**: This is from 500 to 3,000, depending on the AWS Region

- **Deployment package size**: This is 250 MB unzipped, including layers

- **Container image code package size**: This is 10 GB

- **Available space in the /tmp directory**: This is 512 MB

Before opting for Lambda functions, make sure these restrictions fit your use case. By bringing Lambda functions closer to your scope of alternative pipelines for SageMaker, you can leverage one potential use of Lambda, which is to create inference pipelines for the models.

As you know, SageMaker has a very handy `.deploy()` method that will create endpoints for model inference. This is so that you can call to pass the input data to receive predictions back. Here, you can create this inference endpoint by using the API gateway and Lambda functions.

If you do not need an inference endpoint and you just want to make predictions and store results somewhere (in a batch fashion), then all you need is a Lambda function, which is able to fetch the input data, instantiate the model object, make predictions, and store the results in the appropriate location. Of course, it does this by considering all the limitations that you discussed earlier.

Alright, now that you have a good background about Lambda and some use cases, you can take a look at the most important configurations that you should be aware of for the exam.

Creating and configuring a Lambda Function

First of all, you should know that you can create a Lambda function in different ways, such as via the AWS CLI (a Lambda API reference), the AWS Lambda console, or even deployment frameworks (for example, *the serverless framework*).

Serverless frameworks are usually provider and programming language-independent. In other words, they usually allow you to choose where you want to deploy a serverless infrastructure from a varied list of cloud providers and programming languages.

> **Important note**
>
> The concept of serverless architecture is not specific to AWS. In fact, many cloud providers offer other services similar to AWS Lambda functions. That is why these serverless frameworks have been built – to help developers and engineers to deploy their services, wherever they want, including AWS. This is unlikely to come up in your exam, but it is something that you should know so that you are aware of different ways in which to solve your challenges as a data scientist or data engineer.

Since you want to pass the AWS Certified Machine Learning Specialty exam, here, you will walk through the AWS Lambda console. This is so that you become more familiar with its interface and the most important configuration options.

When you navigate to the Lambda console and request a new Lambda function, AWS will provide you with some starting options:

- **Author from scratch**: This is if you want to create your function from scratch
- **Use a blueprint**: This is if you want to create your function from sample code and a configuration preset for common use cases
- **Container image**: This is if you want to select a container image to deploy your function
- **Browse serverless app repository**: This is if you want to deploy a sample Lambda application from the AWS Serverless Application Repository

Starting from scratch, the next step is to set up your Lambda configurations. AWS splits these configurations between basic and advanced settings. In the basic configuration, you will set your function name, runtime environment, and permissions. *Figure 10.1* shows these configurations:

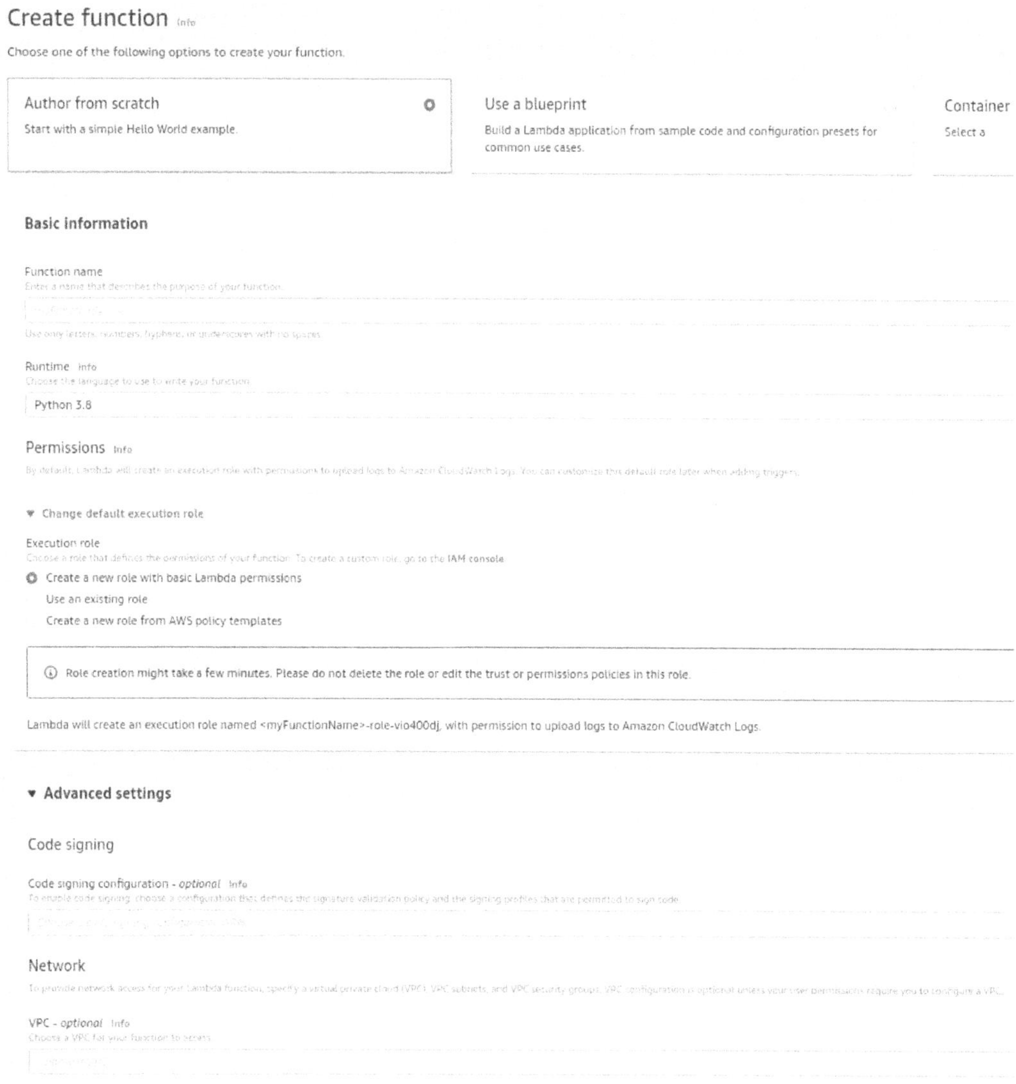

Figure 10.1 – Creating a new Lambda function from the AWS Lambda console

Here, you have a very important configuration that you should remember during your exam – the **execution role**. Your Lambda function might need permissions to access other AWS resources, such as S3, Redshift, and more. The execution role grants permissions to your Lambda function so that it can access resources as needed.

You have to remember that your VPC and security group configurations will also interfere with how your Lambda function runs. For example, if you want to create a function that needs internet access to download something, then you have to deploy this function in a VPC with internet access. The same logic applies to other resources, such as access to relational databases, Kinesis, and Redshift.

Furthermore, to properly configure a Lambda function, you have to, at least, write its code, set the execution role, and make sure the VPC and security group configurations match your needs. Next, you will take a look at other configurations.

Completing your configurations and deploying a Lambda function

Once your Lambda is created in the AWS console, you can set additional configurations before deploying the function. One of these configurations is the event trigger. As mentioned earlier, your Lambda function can be triggered from a variety of services or even manually.

> **Important note**
> A very common example of a trigger is **Amazon EventBridge**. This is an AWS service where you can schedule the execution of your function.

Depending on the event trigger you choose, your function will have access to different event metadata. For example, if your function is triggered by a PUT event on S3 (for example, someone uploads a file to a particular S3 bucket), then your function will receive the metadata associated with this event – for example, the bucket name and object key. Other types of triggers will give you different types of event metadata!

You have access to that metadata through the event parameter that belongs to the signature of the entry point of your function. Not clear enough? You will now look at how your function code should be declared, as follows:

```
def lambda_handler(event, context):
    TODO
```

Here, lambda_handler is the method that represents the entry point of your function. When it is triggered, this method will be called, and it will receive the event metadata associated with the event trigger (through the event parameter). That is how you have access to the information associated with the underlying event that has triggered your function! The event parameter is a JSON-like object.

If you want to test your function but do not want to trigger it directly from the underlying event, that is no problem; you can use **test events**. They simulate the underlying event by preparing a JSON object that will be passed to your function.

Figure 10.2 shows a very intuitive example. Suppose you have created a function that is triggered when a user uploads a file to S3, and now, you want to test your function. You can either upload a file to S3 (which forces the trigger) or create a test event.

By creating a test event, you can prepare a JSON object that simulates the **S3-put** event and then pass this object to your function:

Figure 10.2 – Creating a test event from the Lambda console

Another type of configuration that you can set is an **environment variable**, which will be available on your function. *Figure 10.3* shows how to add environment variables in a Lambda function:

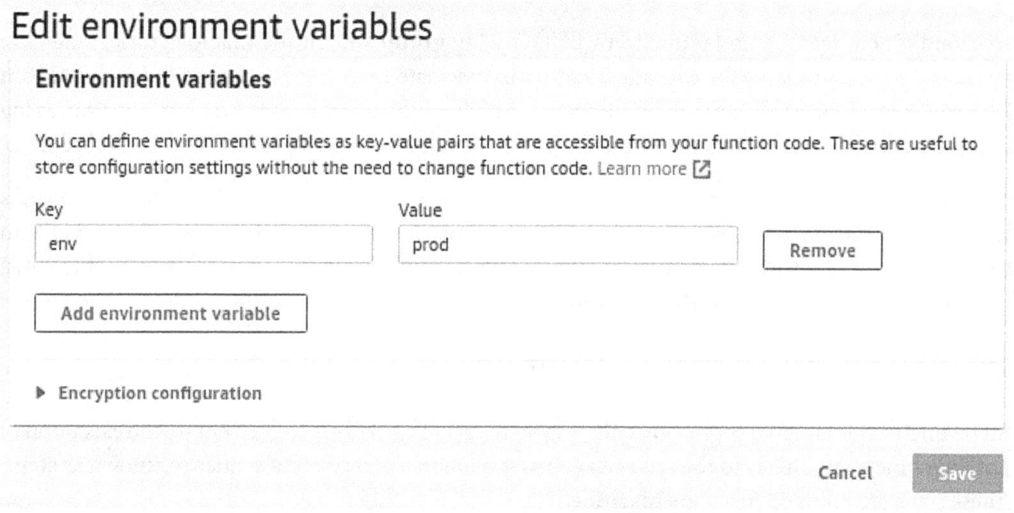

Edit environment variables

Environment variables

You can define environment variables as key-value pairs that are accessible from your function code. These are useful to store configuration settings without the need to change function code. Learn more ⬚

Key	Value	
env	prod	Remove

Add environment variable

▶ **Encryption configuration**

Cancel   Save

Figure 10.3 – Adding environment variables to a Lambda function

You can always come back to these basic settings to make adjustments as necessary. *Figure 10.4* shows what you will find in the basic settings section:

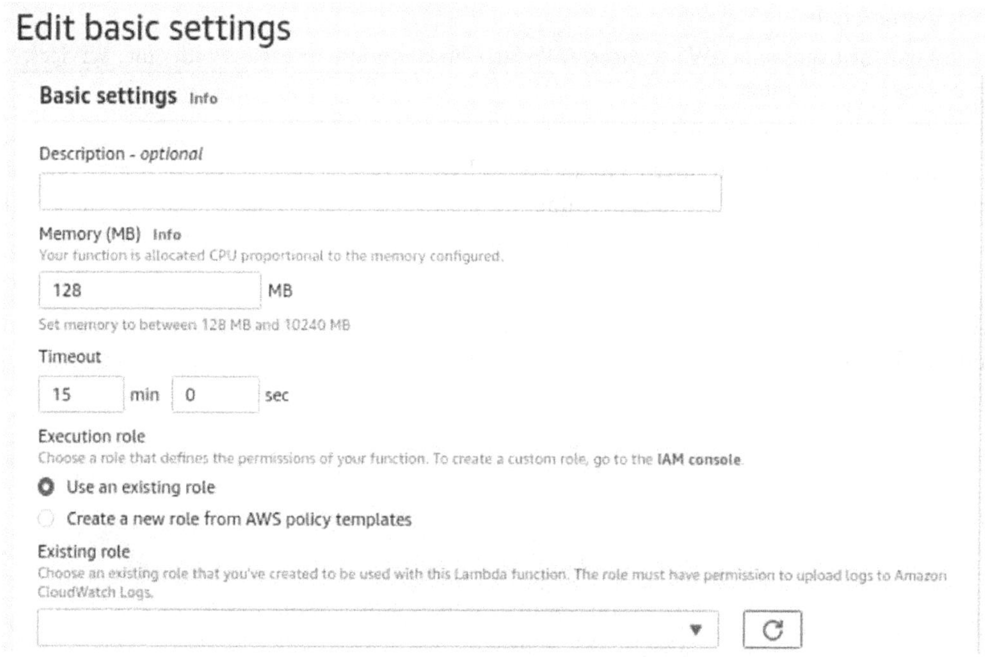

Edit basic settings

Basic settings Info

Description - *optional*

Memory (MB) Info
Your function is allocated CPU proportional to the memory configured.

128   MB

Set memory to between 128 MB and 10240 MB

Timeout

15   min   0   sec

Execution role
Choose a role that defines the permissions of your function. To create a custom role, go to the **IAM console**

🔘 Use an existing role

⚪ Create a new role from AWS policy templates

Existing role
Choose an existing role that you've created to be used with this Lambda function. The role must have permission to upload logs to Amazon CloudWatch Logs.

▼   C

Figure 10.4 – Changing the basic settings of a Lambda function

In terms of monitoring, by default, Lambda functions produce a **CloudWatch Logs** stream and standard metrics. You can access log information by navigating through your `Lambda function monitoring` section and clicking on **View logs in CloudWatch**.

In CloudWatch, each Lambda function will have a **log group** and, inside that log group, many **log streams**. Log streams store the execution logs of the associated function. In other words, a log stream is a sequence of logs that share the same source, which, in this case, is your Lambda function. A log group is a group of log streams that share the same retention, monitoring, and access control settings.

You are now reaching the end of this section, but not the end of this topic on Lambda functions. As mentioned earlier, this AWS service has a lot of use cases and integrates with many other services. In the next section, you will look at another AWS service that will help orchestrate executions of Lambda functions. This is known as **AWS Step Functions**.

Working with step functions

Step Functions is an AWS service that allows you to create workflows to orchestrate the execution of Lambda functions. This is so that you can connect them in a sort of event sequence, known as **steps**. These steps are grouped in a **state machine**.

Step Functions incorporates retry functionality so that you can configure your pipeline to proceed only after a particular step has succeeded. The way you set these retry configurations is by creating a **retry policy**.

> **Important note**
> Just like the majority of AWS services, AWS Step Functions also integrates with other services, not only AWS Lambda.

Creating a state machine is relatively simple. All you have to do is navigate to the AWS Step Functions console and then create a new state machine. On the **Create state machine** page, you can specify whether you want to create your state machine from scratch or from a template, or whether you just want to run a sample project.

AWS will help you with this state machine creation, so even if you choose to create it from scratch, you will find code snippets for a various list of tasks, such as AWS Lambda invocation, SNS topic publication, and running Athena queries.

For the sake of demonstration, you will now create a very simple, but still helpful, example of how to use Step Functions to execute a Lambda function with the `retry` option activated:

```
{
"Comment": "A very handy example of how to call a lamnbda
function with retry option",
"StartAt": "Invoke Lambda function",
"States": {
"Invoke Lambda function": {
"Type": "Task",
"Resource": "arn:aws:states:::lambda:invoke",
"Parameters": {
"FunctionName": "arn:aws:lambda:your-function-identification",
"Payload": {
"Input": {
"env": "STAGE"
}
}
},
"Retry": [
{
"ErrorEquals": ["States.ALL"],
"IntervalSeconds": 60,
"MaxAttempts": 5,
"BackoffRate": 2.0
}
],
"Next": "Example"
},
"Example": {
"Type": "Pass",
"Result": "Just to show you how to configure other steps",
"End": true
}
}
}
```

In the preceding example, you created a state machine with two steps:

- **Invoke a Lambda function**: This will start the execution of your underlying Lambda

- **Execute** *Example*: This is a simple pass task just to show you how to connect a second step in the pipeline

In the first step, you have also set up a retry policy, which will try to re-execute this task if there are any failures. You set up the interval (in seconds) to try again and to show the number of attempts. *Figure 10.5* shows the state machine:

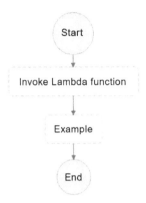

Figure 10.5 – The state machine

In the next section, you will explore various autoscaling scenarios and different ways to handle them.

Scaling applications with SageMaker deployment and AWS Autoscaling

Autoscaling is a crucial aspect of deploying ML models in production environments, ensuring that applications can handle varying workloads efficiently. Amazon SageMaker, combined with AWS Auto Scaling, provides a robust solution for automatically adjusting resources based on demand. In this section, you will explore different scenarios where autoscaling is essential and how to achieve it, using SageMaker model deployment options and AWS Auto Scaling.

Scenario 1 – Fluctuating inference workloads

In a retail application, the number of users making product recommendation requests can vary throughout the day, with peak loads during specific hours.

Autoscaling solution

Implement autoscaling for SageMaker real-time endpoints to dynamically adjust the number of instances, based on the inference request rate.

Steps

1. Configure the SageMaker endpoint to use autoscaling.

2. Set up minimum and maximum instance counts based on expected workload variations.

Example code snippet

```
from sagemaker import get_execution_role
from sagemaker.model import Model
role = get_execution_role()
model_artifact='s3://your-s3-bucket/path/to/model.tar.gz'
model = Model(model_data=model_artifact, role=role)
predictor = model.deploy(instance_type='ml.m4.xlarge',
endpoint_name='real-time-endpoint', endpoint_auto_scaling=True)
```

Scenario 2 – The batch processing of large datasets

Performing batch inference on a large dataset periodically may lead to resource constraints if not managed dynamically.

Autoscaling solution

Utilize AWS batch transform with SageMaker and configure autoscaling for efficient resource utilization during batch processing.

Steps

1. Set up an AWS batch transform job.

2. Enable autoscaling for the underlying infrastructure to handle varying batch sizes.

Example code snippet

```
from sagemaker.transformer import Transformer
transformer = Transformer(model_name='your-model-name',
                          instance_count=1,
                          instance_type='ml.m4.xlarge',
                          strategy='SingleRecord',
                          assemble_with='Line',
                          output_path='s3://your-s3-bucket/
output',
                          max_concurrent_transforms=4)  # Set
max_concurrent_transforms for autoscaling
```

Scenario 3 – A multi-model endpoint with dynamic traffic

Multiple models are deployed on a single endpoint for A/B testing, and the traffic distribution between models is dynamic.

Autoscaling solution

Leverage SageMaker multi-model endpoints with autoscaling to handle varying traffic loads across different model versions.

Steps

1. Create and deploy multiple models to a SageMaker multi-model endpoint.

2. Enable autoscaling to adjust the instance count based on traffic distribution.

Example code snippet

```
from sagemaker.multimodel import MultiModel
multi_model = MultiModel(model_data_prefix='s3://your-s3-
bucket/multi-models')
predictor = multi_model.deploy(instance_type='ml.m4.xlarge',
endpoint_name='multi-model-endpoint', endpoint_auto_
scaling=True)
```

Scenario 4 – Continuous Model Monitoring with drift detection

You monitor models for concept drift or data quality issues and automatically adjust resources if model performance degrades.

Autoscaling solution

Integrate SageMaker Model Monitor with AWS CloudWatch alarms to trigger autoscaling when drift or degradation is detected.

Steps

1. Set up CloudWatch alarms to monitor model quality metrics.

2. Configure autoscaling policies to trigger when specific alarm thresholds are breached.

Scaling applications with SageMaker model deployment options and AWS Auto Scaling provides a flexible and efficient solution for handling varying workloads and ensuring optimal resource utilization. By understanding the different scenarios requiring autoscaling and following the outlined steps, you can seamlessly integrate autoscaling into your ML deployment strategy, enhancing the scalability and reliability of your applications. In the next section, you will learn and explore different ways of securing AWS SageMaker applications.

Securing SageMaker applications

As ML applications become integral to business operations, securing AWS SageMaker applications is paramount to safeguard sensitive data, maintain regulatory compliance, and prevent unauthorized access. In this section, you will first dive into the reasons for securing SageMaker applications and then explore different strategies to achieve security:

- **Reasons to secure SageMaker applications**

  - **Data protection**: ML models trained on sensitive data, such as customer information or financial records, pose a significant security risk if not adequately protected. Securing SageMaker ensures that data confidentiality and integrity are maintained throughout the ML life cycle.

  - **Compliance requirements**: Industries such as healthcare and finance are subject to stringent data protection regulations. Securing SageMaker helps organizations comply with standards such as the **Health Insurance Portability and Accountability Act (HIPAA)** or the **General Data Protection Regulation (GDPR)**, avoiding legal ramifications and reputational damage.

  - **Preventing unauthorized access**: SageMaker instances and endpoints should only be accessible to authorized personnel. Unauthorized access can lead to data breaches or misuse of ML capabilities. Robust authentication mechanisms are crucial for preventing such security lapses.

  - **Model intellectual property protection**: ML models represent intellectual property. Securing SageMaker ensures that the models, algorithms, and methodologies developed remain confidential and are not susceptible to intellectual property theft or reverse engineering.

- **Ways to secure SageMaker applications**

  - **Virtual Private Cloud (VPC) endpoints for SageMaker**: Deploy SageMaker instances within a VPC and use VPC endpoints for secure communication. This prevents public internet access to SageMaker endpoints, reducing the attack surface. An example code snippet is given here:

```
from sagemaker import get_execution_role
from sagemaker import Session

role = get_execution_role()
sagemaker_session = Session()

vpc_config = {'SecurityGroupIds': ['sg-xxxxx'],
'Subnets': ['subnet-xxxxx']}
predictor = model.deploy(instance_type='ml.m4.xlarge',
endpoint_name='secured-endpoint', vpc_config_
override=vpc_config)
```

- **Identity and Access Management (IAM) roles and policies**: Leverage IAM roles to control access to SageMaker resources. Define granular policies to ensure users and services have the minimum required permissions. An example IAM policy is given here:

```
{
  "Version": "2012-10-17",
  "Statement": [
    {
      "Effect": "Allow",
      "Action": "sagemaker:CreateModel",
      "Resource": "arn:aws:sagemaker:region:account-
id:model/model-name"
    },
    {
      "Effect": "Deny",
      "Action": "sagemaker:CreateModel",
      "Resource": "*"
    }
  ]
}
```

- **Encryption in transit and at rest**: Enable encryption for data in transit and at rest. SageMaker supports encrypting data during model training, inference, and storage. An example code snippet is given here:

```
from sagemaker import get_execution_role
from sagemaker import Session

role = get_execution_role()
sagemaker_session = Session()


predictor = model.deploy(instance_type='ml.m4.xlarge',
endpoint_name='encrypted-endpoint', encrypt_
parameters=True)
```

- **Model monitoring with SageMaker Model Monitor**: Implement continuous monitoring using SageMaker Model Monitor to detect and remediate data drift or model quality issues. This ensures that the deployed models remain accurate and reliable over time. An example code snippet is given here:

```
from sagemaker.model_monitor import ModelQualityMonitor
from sagemaker.model_monitor import EndpointInput
from sagemaker import get_execution_role
role = get_execution_role()
monitor = ModelQualityMonitor(
```

```
        role=role,
        instance_count=1,
        instance_type='ml.m4.xlarge',
        volume_size_in_gb=20,
        max_runtime_in_seconds=1800
    )
```

Securing AWS SageMaker applications is not just a best practice; it is a critical imperative in the era of data-driven decision-making. By implementing robust security measures, such as utilizing VPC endpoints, IAM roles, encryption, and continuous monitoring, organizations can fortify their SageMaker applications against potential threats and ensure the integrity of their ML workflows. As SageMaker continues to empower businesses with ML capabilities, a proactive approach to security becomes indispensable for sustained success. You have now reached the end of this section and the end of this chapter. Next, take a look at a summary of what you have learned.

Summary

In this chapter, you dived into deploying ML models with Amazon SageMaker, exploring factors influencing deployment options. You looked at real-world scenarios and dissected them to try out hands-on solutions and code snippets for diverse use cases. You emphasized the crucial integration of SageMaker deployment with AWS Auto Scaling, dynamically adjusting resources based on workload variations. You focused on securing SageMaker applications, presenting practical strategies such as VPC endpoints, IAM roles, and encryption practices. Referring to the AWS documentation for clarifying any doubts is also the best option. It is always important to design your solutions in a cost-effective way, so exploring the cost-effective way to use these services is equally important as building the solution.

Exam Readiness Drill – Chapter Review Questions

Apart from a solid understanding of key concepts, being able to think quickly under time pressure is a skill that will help you ace your certification exam. That is why working on these skills early on in your learning journey is key.

Chapter review questions are designed to improve your test-taking skills progressively with each chapter you learn and review your understanding of key concepts in the chapter at the same time. You'll find these at the end of each chapter.

> **How To Access These Resources**
>
> To learn how to access these resources, head over to the chapter titled *Chapter 11, Accessing the Online Practice Resources*.

To open the Chapter Review Questions for this chapter, perform the following steps:

1. Click the link – `https://packt.link/MLSC01E2_CH10`.

    Alternatively, you can scan the following **QR code** (*Figure 10.6*):

Figure 10.6 – QR code that opens Chapter Review Questions for logged-in users

2. Once you log in, you'll see a page similar to the one shown in *Figure 10.7*:

Figure 10.7 – Chapter Review Questions for Chapter 10

3. Once ready, start the following practice drills, re-attempting the quiz multiple times.

Exam Readiness Drill

For the first three attempts, don't worry about the time limit.

ATTEMPT 1

The first time, aim for at least **40%**. Look at the answers you got wrong and read the relevant sections in the chapter again to fix your learning gaps.

ATTEMPT 2

The second time, aim for at least **60%**. Look at the answers you got wrong and read the relevant sections in the chapter again to fix any remaining learning gaps.

ATTEMPT 3

The third time, aim for at least **75%**. Once you score 75% or more, you start working on your timing.

> **Tip**
> You may take more than **three** attempts to reach 75%. That's okay. Just review the relevant sections in the chapter till you get there.

Working On Timing

Target: Your aim is to keep the score the same while trying to answer these questions as quickly as possible. Here's an example of how your next attempts should look like:

Attempt	Score	Time Taken
Attempt 5	77%	21 mins 30 seconds
Attempt 6	78%	18 mins 34 seconds
Attempt 7	76%	14 mins 44 seconds

Table 10.1 – Sample timing practice drills on the online platform

> **Note**
> The time limits shown in the above table are just examples. Set your own time limits with each attempt based on the time limit of the quiz on the website.

With each new attempt, your score should stay above **75%** while your "time taken" to complete should "decrease". Repeat as many attempts as you want till you feel confident dealing with the time pressure.

11

Accessing the Online Practice Resources

Your copy of *AWS Certified Machine Learning - Specialty (MLS-C01) Certification Guide, Second Edition* comes with free online practice resources. Use these to hone your exam readiness even further by attempting practice questions on the companion website. The website is user-friendly and can be accessed from mobile, desktop, and tablet devices. It also includes interactive timers for an exam-like experience.

How to Access These Resources

Here's how you can start accessing these resources depending on your source of purchase.

Purchased from Packt Store (packtpub.com)

If you've bought the book from the Packt store (`packtpub.com`) eBook or Print, head to `https://packt.link/mlsc01practice`. There, log in using the same Packt account you created or used to purchase the book.

Packt+ Subscription

If you're a *Packt+ subscriber*, you can head over to the same link (`https://packt.link/mlsc01practice`), log in with your `Packt ID`, and start using the resources. You will have access to them as long as your subscription is active.

If you face any issues accessing your free resources, contact us at `customercare@packt.com`.

Purchased from Amazon and Other Sources

If you've purchased from sources other than the ones mentioned above (like *Amazon*), you'll need to unlock the resources first by entering your unique sign-up code provided in this section. **Unlocking takes less than 10 minutes, can be done from any device, and needs to be done only once**. Follow these five easy steps to complete the process:

STEP 1

Open the link `https://packt.link/mlsc01unlock` OR scan the following **QR code** (*Figure 11.1*):

Figure 11.1 – QR code for the page that lets you unlock this book's free online content.

Either of those links will lead to the following page as shown in *Figure 11.2*:

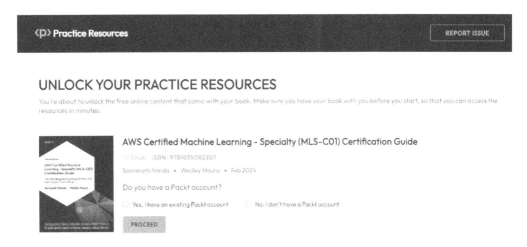

Figure 11.2 – Unlock page for the online practice resources

STEP 2

If you already have a Packt account, select the option `Yes, I have an existing Packt account`. If not, select the option `No, I don't have a Packt account`.

If you don't have a Packt account, you'll be prompted to create a new account on the next page. It's free and only takes a minute to create.

Click `Proceed` after selecting one of those options.

STEP 3

After you've created your account or logged in to an existing one, you'll be directed to the following page as shown in *Figure 11.3*.

Make a note of your unique unlock code:

`MJM8028`

Type in or copy this code into the text box labeled 'Enter Unique Code':

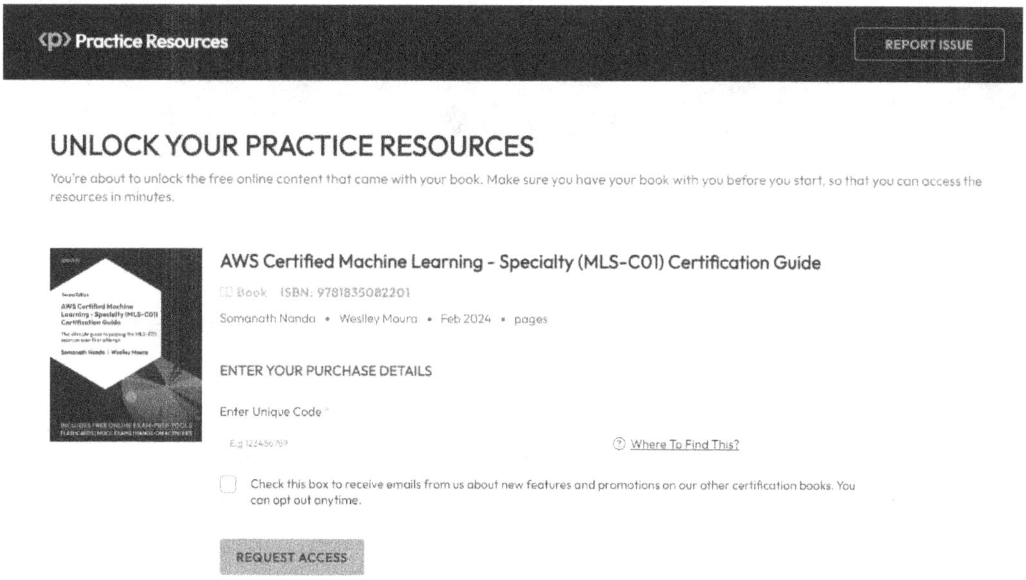

Figure 11.3 – Enter your unique sign-up code to unlock the resources

> **Troubleshooting Tip**
>
> After creating an account, if your connection drops off or you accidentally close the page, you can reopen the page shown in *Figure 11.2* and select Yes, I have an existing account. Then, sign in with the account you had created before you closed the page. You'll be redirected to the screen shown in *Figure 11.3*.

STEP 4

> **Note**
>
> You may choose to opt into emails regarding feature updates and offers on our other certification books. We don't spam, and it's easy to opt out at any time.

Click Request Access.

STEP 5

If the code you entered is correct, you'll see a button that says, OPEN PRACTICE RESOURCES, as shown in *Figure 11.4*:

Figure 11.4 – Page that shows up after a successful unlock

Click the OPEN PRACTICE RESOURCES link to start using your free online content. You'll be redirected to the Dashboard shown in *Figure 11.5*:

Figure 11.5 – Dashboard page for AZ-900 practice resources

Bookmark this link

Now that you've unlocked the resources, you can come back to them anytime by visiting https://packt.link/mlsc01practice or scanning the following QR code provided in *Figure 11.6*:

Figure 11.6 – QR code to bookmark practice resources website

Troubleshooting Tips

If you're facing issues unlocking, here are three things you can do:

- Double-check your unique code. All unique codes in our books are case-sensitive and your code needs to match exactly as it is shown in *STEP 3*.

- If that doesn't work, use the `Report Issue` button located at the top-right corner of the page.

- If you're not able to open the unlock page at all, write to `customercare@packt.com` and mention the name of the book.

Practice Resources – A Quick Tour

This book will equip you with all the knowledge necessary to clear the exam. As important as learning the key concepts is, your chances of passing the exam are much higher if you apply and practice what you learn in the book. This is where the online practice resources come in. With interactive mock exams, flashcards, and exam tips, you can practice everything you learned in the book on the go. Here's a quick walkthrough of what you get.

A Clean, Simple Cert Practice Experience

You get a clean, simple user interface that works on all modern devices, including your phone and tablet. All the features work on all devices, provided you have a working internet connection. From the `Dashboard` (*Figure 11.7*), you can access all the practice resources that come with this book with just a click. If you want to jump back to the book, you can do that from here as well:

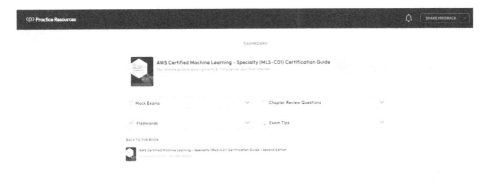

Figure 11.7 – Dashboard interface on a desktop device

Practice Questions

The **Quiz Interface** (*Figure 11.8*) is designed to help you focus on the question without any clutter.

You can navigate between multiple questions quickly and skip a question if you don't know the answer. The interface also includes a live timer that auto-submits your quiz if you run out of time.

Click End Quiz if you want to jump straight to the results page to reveal all the solutions.

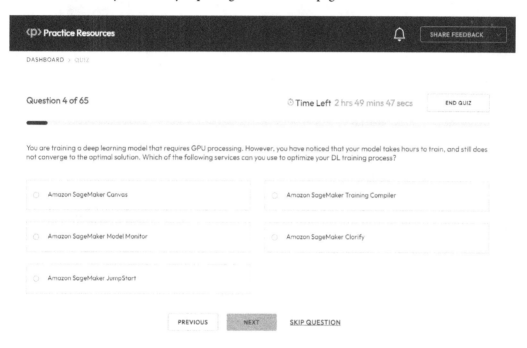

Figure 11.8 – Practice Questions Interface on a desktop device

Be it a long train ride to work with just your phone or a lazy Sunday afternoon on the couch with your tablet, the quiz interface works just as well on all your devices as long as they're connected to the internet.

Figure 11.9 shows a screenshot of how the interface looks on mobile devices:

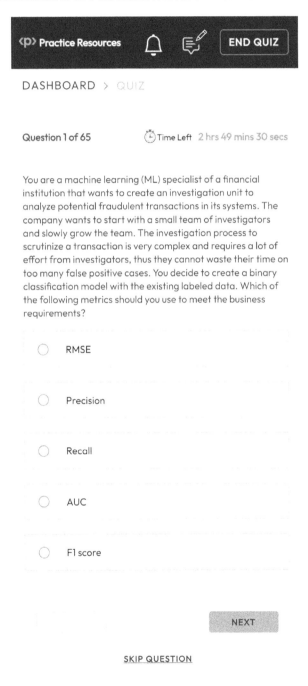

Figure 11.9 – Quiz interface on a mobile device

Flashcards

Flashcards are designed to help you memorize key concepts. Here's how to make the most of them:

- We've organized all the flashcards into stacks. Think of these like an actual stack of cards in your hand.

- You start with a full stack of cards.

- When you open a card, take a few minutes to recall the answer.

- Click anywhere on the card to reveal the answer (*Figure 11.10*).

- Flip the card back and forth multiple times and memorize the card completely.

- Once you feel you've memorized it, click the `Mark as memorized` button on the top-right corner of the card. Move on to the next card by clicking Next.

- Repeat this process as you move to other cards in the stack.

You may not be able to memorize all the cards in one go. That's why, when you open the stack the next time, you'll only see the cards you're yet to memorize.

Your goal is to get to an empty stack, having memorized each flashcards in that stack.

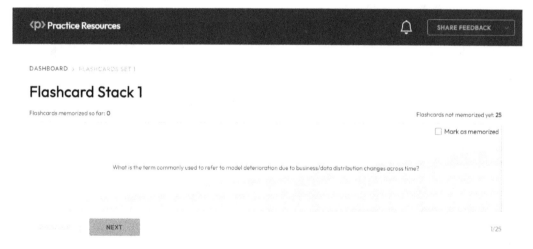

Figure 11.10 – Flashcards interface

Exam Tips

Exam Tips (see *Figure 11.11*) are designed to help you get exam-ready. From the start of your preparation journey to your exam day, these tips are organized such that you can review all of them in one go. If an exam tip comes in handy in your preparation, make sure to mark it as helpful so that other readers can benefit from your insights and experiences.

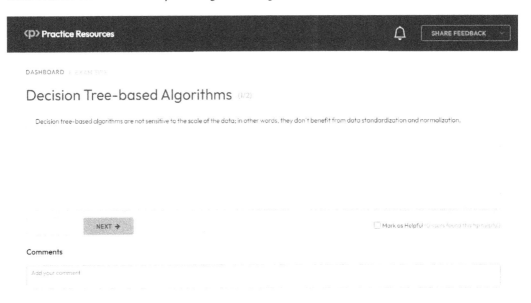

Figure 11.11 – Exam Tips Interface

Chapter Review Questions

You'll find a link to **Chapter Review Questions** at the end of each chapter, just after the *Summary* section. These are designed to help you consolidate your learning from a chapter before moving on to the next one. Each chapter will have a benchmark score. Aim to match that score or beat it before picking up the next chapter. On the *Chapter Review Questions* page, you'll find a summary of the chapter for quick reference, as shown in *Figure 11.12*:

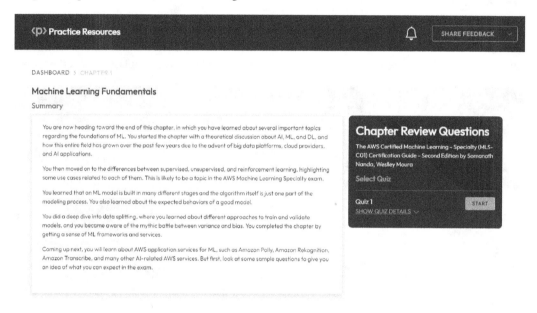

Figure 11.12 – Chapter Review Questions Page

Share Feedback

If you find any issues with the platform, the book, or any of the practice materials, you can click the Share Feedback button from any page and reach out to us. If you have any suggestions for improvement, you can share those as well.

Back to the Book

To make switching between the book and practice resources easy, we've added a link that takes you back to the book (*Figure 11.13*). Click it to open your book in Packt's online reader. Your reading position is synced so you can jump right back to where you left off when you last opened the book.

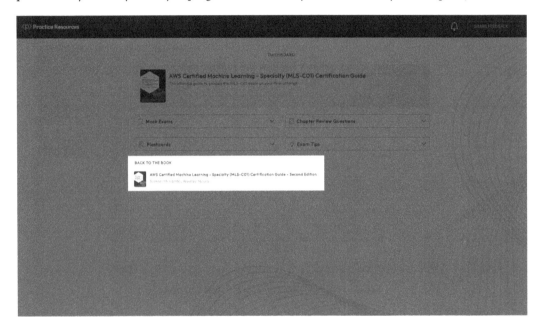

Figure 11.13 – Jump back to the book from the dashboard

> **Note**
> Certain elements of the website might change over time and thus may end up looking different from how they are represented in the screenshots of this book.

Index

www.packtpub.com

Subscribe to our online digital library for full access to over 7,000 books and videos, as well as industry leading tools to help you plan your personal development and advance your career. For more information, please visit our website.

Why subscribe?

- Spend less time learning and more time coding with practical eBooks and Videos from over 4,000 industry professionals

- Improve your learning with Skill Plans built especially for you

- Get a free eBook or video every month

- Fully searchable for easy access to vital information

- Copy and paste, print, and bookmark content

At www.packtpub.com, you can also read a collection of free technical articles, sign up for a range of free newsletters, and receive exclusive discounts and offers on Packt books and eBooks.

Other Books You May Enjoy

If you enjoyed this book, you may be interested in these other books by Packt:

Machine Learning Engineering on AWS

Joshua Arvin Lat

ISBN: 978-1-80324-759-5

- Find out how to train and deploy TensorFlow and PyTorch models on AWS
- Use containers and serverless services for ML engineering requirements
- Discover how to set up a serverless data warehouse and data lake on AWS
- Build automated end-to-end MLOps pipelines using a variety of services
- Use AWS Glue DataBrew and SageMaker Data Wrangler for data engineering
- Explore different solutions for deploying deep learning models on AWS
- Apply cost optimization techniques to ML environments and systems
- Preserve data privacy and model privacy using a variety of techniques

Data Engineering with AWS, Second Edition

Gareth Eagar

ISBN: 978-1-80461-442-6

- Seamlessly ingest streaming data with Amazon Kinesis Data Firehose
- Optimize, denormalize, and join datasets with AWS Glue Studio
- Use Amazon S3 events to trigger a Lambda process to transform a file
- Load data into a Redshift data warehouse and run queries with ease
- Visualize and explore data using Amazon QuickSight
- Extract sentiment data from a dataset using Amazon Comprehend
- Build transactional data lakes using Apache Iceberg with Amazon Athena
- Learn how a data mesh approach can be implemented on AWS

Share Your Thoughts

Now you've finished *AWS Certified Machine Learning - Specialty (MLS-C01) Certification Guide, Second Edition*, we'd love to hear your thoughts! Scan the QR code below to go straight to the Amazon review page for this book and share your feedback or leave a review on the site that you purchased it from.

https://packt.link/r/1835082203

Your review is important to us and the tech community and will help us make sure we're delivering excellent quality content.

Download a Free PDF Copy of This Book

Thanks for purchasing this book!

Do you like to read on the go but are unable to carry your print books everywhere?

Is your eBook purchase not compatible with the device of your choice?

Don't worry, now with every Packt book you get a DRM-free PDF version of that book at no cost.

Read anywhere, any place, on any device. Search, copy, and paste code from your favorite technical books directly into your application.

The perks don't stop there, you can get exclusive access to discounts, newsletters, and great free content in your inbox daily.

Follow these simple steps to get the benefits:

1. Scan the QR code or visit the link below:

https://packt.link/free-ebook/9781835082201

2. Submit your proof of purchase.
3. That's it! We'll send your free PDF and other benefits to your email directly.